TAKING MIDWAY

TAKING MIDWAY

NAVAL WARFARE, SECRET CODES, AND THE BATTLE THAT TURNED THE TIDE OF WORLD WAR II

MARTIN DUGARD

DUTTON

DUTTON

An imprint of Penguin Random House LLC
1745 Broadway, New York, NY 10019
penguinrandomhouse.com

Maps by Gene Thorp

BOOK DESIGN BY KATY RIEGEL

LIBRARY OF CONGRESS CATALOGING-IN-PUBLICATION DATA

Names: Dugard, Martin author
Title: Taking Midway : naval warfare, secret codes, and the battle that turned the tide of World War II / Martin Dugard.
Other titles: Naval warfare, secret codes, and the battle that turned the tide of World War II
Description: [New York, New York] : Dutton, [2025] |
Includes bibliographical references and index.
Identifiers: LCCN 2024046944 | ISBN 9780593473245 hardcover |
ISBN 9780593473269 ebook
Subjects: LCSH: Midway, Battle of, 1942 | World War, 1939-1945—Naval operations, American | World War, 1939-1945—Naval operations, Japanese | World War, 1939-1945—Naval operations—Submarine
Classification: LCC D774.M5 D84 2025 |
DDC 940.54/26699—dc23/eng/20250311
LC record available at https://lccn.loc.gov/2024046944

Printed in the United States of America
1st Printing

The authorized representative in the EU for product safety and compliance is Penguin Random House Ireland, Morrison Chambers, 32 Nassau Street, Dublin D02 YH68, Ireland, https://eu-contact.penguin.ie.

To Calene

TAKING MIDWAY

PROLOGUE

The Pacific claimed her lifetimes ago.

She rests upright, three miles beneath the waves, thick steel hull cased in mud. Complete darkness. Freezing water. Marine life but too deep for fish. Sailors and officers, already dead as she goes under, ride her to the bottom that horrible morning. Their ghosts keep her company. Once an aircraft carrier with the hull number CV-5, she is now classified a "war grave."

"C" is for "cruiser," because a carrier's original role was that of an advance scout, like a battle cruiser in World War I. Nobody is saying for certain why the U.S. Navy added a "V." Some claim the letter stands for the French word *voler*—"to fly." Proof is hard to come by. No one questions whether or not this is true; the service is known to possess an unpredictable fondness for romance.

A crane operator at Newport News brings her into the world eight years before a torpedo tears the hole in her side that takes her out. He lowers a steel plate hewn from the coal mines of Appalachia, then forged in a blast furnace belching the heat of the sun; he guides that foundational chunk of metal down from the blue Virginia sky carefully until it nestles against a straight line of keel blocks almost as long as two football fields.

No ceremony. No name. Yard number 359.

"Just another ship," they say as she takes shape, though the welders and fitters know it isn't true. This is a new class of vessel, designed to wage a different style of war. She is not the first of her kind. That happens on November 13, 1921, when Japan christens a ship specifically configured to launch airplanes. *Hōshō* is followed by Britain's *Hermes* one year later. Right about then, the United States adds a flat upper flight deck to a collier and makes *Langley* CV-1.

The era of conversions is over. Thirteen years later, as she is laid down on May 21, 1934, CV-5 is a purpose-built aircraft carrier.

Days of construction in Newport News become months, then a year and another, time marked by the punctual howl of the shipyard whistle. More steel. A cradle of ribs rises from those bottom pieces to make her tall and wide. Decks. Boilers. Pipes. Wires. Galleys. Mess. Wardrooms. Racks by the thousands. Showers. Heads. Finally, a superstructure island towering over a flight deck covered in two acres of split and sanded Douglas fir.

USS *Yorktown* (CV-5)   *Public domain / U.S. Navy* All Hands *magazine, March 1954, p. 27*

A name replaces the yard number, borrowed from a time when hulls were wood and wind brought power. She is USS *Yorktown*, the third United States ship in history so named.

First Lady Eleanor Roosevelt smashes a bottle of champagne across her bow on christening day. An "impressive sight" she calls the moment the towering steel vessel slides gracefully into the Atlantic.

USS *Yorktown* soon has sisters also built at Newport News. They are *Enterprise* and *Hornet*, one of whom now also rests on the bottom of the Pacific. The three revolutionary carriers fight side by side just once.

Warm first week in June. Patch of smooth blue ocean smack-dab in the middle between San Francisco and Tokyo. 1942. Until this day, battleships define naval warfare. An epic duel between *Yorktown*-class siblings and aircraft carriers of the Imperial Japanese Navy ends that school of thinking.

Yorktown's watery grave stands along exalted names like Thermopylae, Gettysburg, Waterloo. Pivotal battles in locations insignificant before the fighting makes them sacred. Picture two small islands—a giant circle of coral crisscrossed by runways and inhabited by thousands of seabirds—that take their name from that location in the very center of the Pacific:

Midway.

Japan was supreme,

and we everywhere were weak and naked.

WINSTON CHURCHILL

EPISODE ONE

———

PRINCE OF WALES

Admiral Sir Tom Phillips

TOM THUMB

Admiral Sir Tom Phillips sails into dark waters.

A man not fond of taking advice. Steel deck beneath polished white shoes. Whites. Epaulets. Five foot two. A small box on the bridge to stand on so he can see the view.

The Battle of Midway is six months away. Events leading up to this clash began decades ago, a mélange of poor treaties, technological advances, empire building, and, from the Japanese perspective, racism. One by one, dominoes fell. All that is missing as HMS *Prince of Wales* parts the waters on this scorching December night are the date and location of the fight—and one last tile to topple.

Unfortunately for the sailors and officers of *Wales*, that is her.

The past seventeen hours have shattered the Pacific balance of power. Shocking Japanese surprise attacks from one side of the ocean to the other. Thousands of good men dead. "The Japs," as the British openly refer to their enemy, need a reminder of who's boss before this thing gets out of control.

Admiral Tom Phillips will do the reminding. A full head shorter than any man on his staff, "Tom Thumb" is the newly promoted commander in chief, China Station. Fifty-three, 126 pounds, one of the youngest admirals in the Royal Navy. His warships defend China, Singapore, Malaya, Hong Kong, and the western rim of the Pacific Ocean stretching all the way south to Australia. As of one week ago, Singapore is the new home port for this "Force Z."

Wales is Phillips' flagship. No less than British Prime Minister Winston Churchill ordered her to sail for Singapore, considering the new battleship Britain's greatest deterrent weapon. Red Cross of St. George on a white background flying from its mainmast, denoting the admiral is on board. Captain John Leach, the much-loved skipper of *Wales*, shares the bridge. Leach gives the orders for his sailors and maintains discipline on his vessel, even as Phillips directs all of Z.

The order from London came thirteen hours ago:

"Commence hostilities with Japan at once."

When that directive arrives, it is Captain Leach who immediately speaks on the ship's loudspeakers, informing his sailors Britain is at war. Preparations for battle begin immediately. Today brought intense equatorial heat to Singapore and the emergency decision to get underway. Shore

Captain John Leach   *Public domain*

leaves canceled. British sailors strip to the waist, sweating out last night's beer, lining up on deck and gangways, loading ammunition for the sudden fight to come. Just after noon, senior naval officers listen for thirty minutes as Phillips lays out battle plans around *Wales'* polished conference table in his admiral's quarters. There is history to this mahogany slab. Winston Churchill sat here four months ago, sharing dinner with United States President Franklin Roosevelt. Brandy, tobacco, alliance. That was diplomacy; this is war. The admiral does not open the floor to discussion.

The Royal Air Force, whose aircraft offer Force Z protection from the skies, is not invited. Phillips believes battleships have little to fear from aerial attack. He does so at the risk of his own life and those of thousands of his men, even as intelligence reports tell of Japanese bombers and fighters stationed within range at nearby Saigon.

Stubborn Tom Thumb should know better. One of Britain's biggest naval victories was recently achieved through aerial attack. No less than *Prince of Wales* played a prominent role. His recent post in London afforded him access to the highest levels of naval intelligence.

"One day, Tom, you will be standing on your box on a bridge," Phillips has been warned about his disbelief in airpower by Admiralty peers, "and your ships will be smashed to pieces by bombers and torpedo aircraft."

Phillips gives the order to sail just before dusk. The admiral wishes to be away in darkness to conceal his plans from the enemy. Captain John Leach made time to leave *Wales* earlier this afternoon to join his naval officer son, Henry, for a swim and a gin before setting out. No goodbyes. Just *See you soon.* Now Leach stands on the bridge as his ship prepares to cast off its lines. He no longer controls her fate. That is all Tom Thumb.

"Hands fall in for leaving harbor" booms over ships' loudspeakers.

Spectators wave from shore. *Wales* glides past stately waterfront homes. Evening air still wretched with heat. There is no ventilation belowdecks and sailors endure temperatures nearing 100 Fahrenheit—50 degrees hotter in the boiler rooms. Shifts are shortened and men rotated in and out of hot engine and boiler spaces to get vital jobs done.

The endurance is just beginning.

Winston Churchill walking the deck on HMS *Prince of Wales*
Public domain / Imperial War Museum

Low green hills rise above the shoreline. Scents of frangipani, palms, and the sweet tang of tembusu trees from Orchard Road fade away as land falls behind. In their place, men on deck inhale the odors of oxidizing steel, diesel fuel, seagull shit—a battleship smelling like a battleship. The yard's dry docks, towering cranes, and oil tanks fall away. A perfume of salt air, sea-foam, and mermaids heralds open ocean.

Wales' outdated but still deadly older cousin, *Repulse*, casts her thick hemp lines and joins the prowl. Sultans of the sea, the both of them, behemoths so tall and long that it seems they stand still and the world rotates around them.

Destroyer escort appears in the dusk. *Vampire, Electra, Tenedos*, and *Express* form a protective screen.

Moods among the crew range from patriotic righteousness to superstitious fear. Euphoric journalists on board *Repulse* feel lucky to get an eyewitness look at what could be an extremely important naval battle. American reporter Cecil Brown of CBS News has informed his bosses he will be out of reach for four days as he chases a "swell story." He wears expensive new shoes and is upset there is no room for him on *Wales*.

Night falls. Sultry tropical humidity blankets the world of Force Z. Light sheets of rain. Stiff warm wind. Mercury and Jupiter rise. Neptune is up there, too, but unseen. Venus owns the sky, blazing a hole in thickening black clouds.

Now, for the sailors, comes the waiting. The not knowing. Yesterday was for drinking in dockside canteens after a hard cruise from Scotland. Tomorrow could be anything. The men haven't been told where they're going, but everyone knows a sudden departure will lead to battle.

***

THE FIRST JAPANESE surprise attack came just after midnight. Kota Bharu, a beachhead on the Malay Peninsula four hundred miles north of Singapore, fell to amphibious invasion. Startled British pilots and troops abandoned nearby airfields with barely a fight.

Forty minutes later and six thousand miles east, where the sun was just rising on December 7, Japanese torpedo bombers laid waste to the lush green island jewel known as Oahu, sinking four American battleships and damaging four more at a port named Pearl Harbor. The number of murdered United States military and civilian personnel is 2,403.

The drama shifted back to a cluster of islands near the Asian landmass hours later. Japanese forces hit the teeming cities and thick jungles of the Philippines. Invasion followed.

The strikes kept coming. From west to east: metropolitan Hong Kong; rugged, mountainous Guam; the Pan American Clipper base on the wishbone-shaped atoll known as Wake Island. Two Japanese destroyers lobbed nuisance shells at tiny Midway.

Within seven hours, across a swath of the Pacific twice as wide as the Atlantic Ocean, and four times the size of Adolf Hitler's European

battlefront stretching from London to Moscow, Japan turned its ambition
from domination of the Asian landmass to total control of the Pacific.
Australia was in reach. New Guinea. Oil-rich Borneo. Even that western-
most tip of the United States known as the Aleutian Islands.

The tactical linchpin to those scenarios was Singapore. Thirty-three
hundred miles from Tokyo by air, 5,480 over land. Japan believes all of
Asia should be—*is!*—theirs. Despite how far the British naval base at
the tip of the Malay Peninsula is from their homeland, a distance
greater than the width of the United States, they call it "sword at our
heart."

The inevitable Japanese attack came this morning at shortly after four
a.m. Singapore time. Seventeen Japanese naval bombers attacked airfields
at Tengah and Seletar. Sixty-one Chinese residents were killed and 133
more injured. Chinatown, Raffles Place, and Keppel Harbor were bombed
in the ten-minute raid.

It is one thing to bomb a target, quite another to take possession of it.
Singapore is still home to eighty-five thousand British soldiers and sailors. No military targets are hit. In Hawaii, the Pearl Harbor attack may
have been devastating, but there are one hundred commissioned warships in port. Only sixteen were damaged by Japan's stunning blow. The
navy's fuel depot was not bombed. Dry docks and other repair facilities are
unscathed. Absolutely none of America's new aircraft carriers are bothered
in the slightest, *Saratoga*, *Enterprise*, and *Lexington* safely away at sea.

So even after the raids, it can be said—*still*—that the U.S. Navy controls the eastern side of the Pacific and the Royal Navy the west.

For now.

Japanese ground troops already ashore on the Malay Peninsula mean
the fall of Singapore is a remote possibility.

Hawaii must be prepared for a second attack.

Losing either one seems unthinkable.

Logistics say otherwise.

Japan launches Imperial Japanese Army Air Service aircraft from forward bases in Vietnam and Taiwan. Imperial Navy planes take off from carriers at sea. No target in the Pacific is out of range. The nation is committed to airpower, having built 5,088 aircraft in 1941 alone. She is at the forefront of building aircraft carriers, obsessed with this new method of waging war.

The United States is ramping up aircraft production as the likelihood of war approaches. Just 3,611 planes were built in America in 1940, compared to 18,466 in 1941. Unlike Japan's focus on fighters and bombers, the majority of new American planes are transport and training aircraft.

Japan roams the Pacific on the sea and in the air, unbothered by the United States and Great Britain, allies who see this as a secondary battlefield after Nazi Germany and Europe. Japan's *Kidō Butai*—the "Mobile Force" of the *Akagi, Kaga, Sōryū, Hiryū, Shōkaku*, and *Zuikaku* and the dozens of ships in their escort—prowls in the most remote stretches of water, almost impossible to find.

Limited radar. Cloak of invisibility. The *Kidō Butai* strikes without warning, as the survivors of Pearl Harbor will long remember.

The Pacific is all too often described as "vast." Though that word is overused, no other works as well. Anything but gentle, as her given Spanish name states, she is eight thousand miles from Singapore to San Francisco. No large landmass between. Islands. Water as far as the eye can see.

For those who believe Hawaii is too big to conquer, one need only look to the Philippines, a much larger collection of islands where Japanese soldiers are already establishing a beachhead. Should Japan capture Hawaii, the U.S. Navy must flee thousands of miles back to the mainland and fight from San Francisco, Long Beach, and San Diego.

The key to taking Hawaii is capturing the small U.S. naval base on Midway. Japan will then possess an advance installation for its aircraft well within striking distance of the Hawaiian Islands. Ships can refuel; men can be housed; supplies can be cached.

Should Japan come to own that island, planes *will* launch. Wave after endless deadly wave.

***

FORCE Z POWERS into the South China Sea on the evening of December 8, 1941. Japan's potential attack on Midway is theory. An American problem. Not of the slightest concern to Admiral Tom Phillips.

More important: Surprising new intelligence intercepts warn a follow-up horde of Japanese invaders is steaming toward the Malay Peninsula. Singapore will remain safe if *Prince of Wales* stops them. Should Japan's troops land successfully, it is foolish to think they will remain in place, happy to own a beachhead. The Imperial Japanese Army will most certainly turn south and race through the moist, broad-leaved forests, bent on conquest, overwhelming the "sword at our heart."

Admiral Tom Phillips' career depends on stopping them. Failure means disgrace. He is considered the smartest man in the Admiralty, capable of confidently predicting where Britain's enemies will strike next. That was on land, in committee rooms and meetings given over to budgets and procedures and formal protocols. This is the real thing. Tom Thumb must save Singapore.

Force Z races through the night in search of the Japanese invaders.

***

SUNRISE. 0600. DECEMBER 9. Z has traveled 220 miles. One more full day at sea to reach the assumed location of the new Japanese invasion force. Rain and low clouds keep enemy reconnaissance aircraft on the ground. Just to be safe, Tom Thumb orders *Wales* to sail zigzag. Captain Leach relays the order.

At 0621, a *Vampire* lookout spots a lone aircraft low on the horizon. He watches for a full minute before the plane disappears into a cloud bank. The eagle-eyed sailor provides a course bearing but is unsure whether he spied friend or foe. Admiral Phillips, despite his having been more than a decade away from a sea command and all the technological changes that have happened since the days of World War I dreadnoughts, confidently chooses to believe Force Z has not been spotted. At 0713, *Prince of Wales*, *Repulse*, and their escorts turn left at the Anambas Islands and sail northwest toward the suspected enemy landing site.

Seventeen minutes later, at 0730, officers in *Wales'* wardroom listen to the radio as, thousands of miles away in Washington, President Franklin Roosevelt speaks to the American Congress. It seems surreal that the president once visited this very battleship. He rails about the attacks on Pearl Harbor, calling December 7 a "date which will live in infamy."

Lofty words from a man safe from harm. But even as these officers sip their morning tea on the other side of the world, Roosevelt's words spur America into action. A declaration of war is immediate, almost unanimous. A nation that has been dithering for two years about global evil is suddenly hot for blood.

The men of *Wales* listen, likely thinking about life and death. Wondering if tomorrow will be the last day of their lifetimes and whether drowning—or death by explosion or dismemberment—is painful and scary; dreading the claustrophobia of being trapped belowdecks; imagining wives without husbands and children without fathers and being replaced in their marriage beds by lesser men, maybe even some of those American soldiers about to flood into England; envisioning how the lads will respond at the local, their words the most honest obituaries. Will Christmas back home, just seventeen days from now, be a time of festivity or of mourning?

But maybe, just maybe, *Wales* will save Singapore and they'll all get medals.

Not a man tips his hand. Hopefully, that scout plane didn't see Force Z. Hopefully, Japan has no idea Force Z is coming.

Hopefully.

HUNTING

The view is unclear.

Periscope up. Officer of the watch rotates the glass slowly right and left. Rough day up there. Spume, mist, and waves. Nothing to see.

Japanese submarine *I-65* is gray and streamlined like a tiger shark. Ten years old, 320 feet long, six torpedo tubes in the bow and two more in the stern. Crew of seventy-five. Traveling twelve feet below the choppy surface at eight knots. Each swell rocks the hull.

I-65's first war patrol. Sailed from China four days ago. Her orders are to protect transport ships as they prepare to invade the Malay Peninsula; then she is to march south toward Singapore. Air inside the pressurized inner hull is humid in these equatorial waters. Constant aromas of diesel fuel, cooked fish, body odor. Monotony, routine, claustrophobia. Off-duty sailors sleep half naked in their bunks or on sacks of rice to keep cool.

The Imperial Japanese Navy denotes "I" for large submarines over a thousand tons. "Ro" is for medium submarines. "Ha" is for small submarines weighing less than five hundred tons. These come from the *Iroha* prayer, a Japanese pangram. Linguistically, the order is very much the same as "A, B, C" in English.

Standards are more formal on the bridge, where officers in uniform are calm and focused on maintaining an easterly patrol line for the invasion force. Two other Japanese submarines perform the same role closer to the Malay Peninsula.

Suddenly, a sighting.

Two vessels on the horizon. Distance and rain make it tough to differentiate friend from foe. Officer of the watch summons the submarine's captain, Lieutenant Commander Hakue Harada, for a second opinion. Flotilla commander Captain Masao Teraoka is also on board today. Both senior officers take turns looking through the periscope.

Neither man knows what he is seeing.

The mystery vessels might be Dutch. Their profiles are clearly not Japanese. These cannot possibly be the Great British battleships *Prince of Wales* and *Repulse*, both of which possess the speed and might to disrupt landings like no other naval presence in the Far East. As of this time yesterday, Japanese aerial reconnaissance reported them still docked in Singapore.

Teraoka and Harada consult a manual of enemy ships. Leadership, discernment, and education at Japan's Imperial Naval Academy have played a vital role in their careers. Right now, with the second wave of Japan's invasion force vulnerable to decimation, there is only one thing to do about the identity of these unknown warships:

Guess.

"Two *Repulse*-style enemy battleships spotted," Teraoka broadcasts to the fleet. He is so nervous, he mistakenly sends the message on a seldom-used wavelength.

I-65 surfaces and follows from a distance. Neither *Prince of Wales* nor *Repulse* is aware they have been discovered.

I-65's top speed submerged is just eight knots, but she is twice as fast on the surface. *Prince of Wales* and *Repulse* are traveling at a slow eighteen knots to accommodate the destroyers sailing nearby to screen them from Japanese submarines.

But luck is on the side of Force Z. December is northeast monsoon season. The afternoon remains hot and wet. High winds. Low clouds touch the water. Choppy sea, whitecapped swells, chaos reaching to the horizon in every direction. No symmetry to this tempest. Symmetry can be introduced to the open ocean only by man. Eagle-eyed reconnaissance aircraft pilots know this well.

Yet Japanese flights remain grounded. Captain Teraoka's wavelength mistake ensures *I-65*'s radio message has not been received.

A squall blocks the captain's periscope view at 1550, two hours before sunset. The submarine loses all contact with *Wales* and *Repulse*. The captain knows the mystery ships are no longer a naval problem. Now more than ever, the Japanese need clear skies to let the air force take over.

***

JAPAN LEANS HEAVILY on airpower.

In addition to aircraft carriers launching planes of the Imperial Japanese Navy, army air service pilots take off from bases throughout the Pacific: the Marshall Islands, Saipan, Vietnam, and Taiwan. No beach is out of reach. No islands, no atolls, no ports, no military installations, and, most relevant right now, no battleships in the Pacific are safe from Japanese airpower.

The Royal Air Force and Royal Navy are not so like-minded. Despite the stunning success of Fighter Command during the Battle of Britain in the summer of 1940, those two branches of the service remain at odds. There is a Royal Air Force presence in Singapore; those airmen are well aware they were not invited to Admiral Phillips' strategy meeting before Z sailed. The omission is not just a breach of protocol; it's rude.

Yet even if the fliers had been invited, they would have stood little chance against Japan's superior air force. This is not the RAF that fought Adolf Hitler's Luftwaffe to a standstill, skillfully utilizing cutting-edge Spitfires and Hurricanes to seek out and destroy the enemy. The pilots in those single-seaters are aerial virtuosos selected to fly fighters after an arduous winnowing-out process.

By contrast, most British pilots in the Far East are the refuse and rejects of the Royal Air Force, passed over for Spits and Hurries for lack of talent and assigned to slow Brewster Buffalos, Bristol Blenheim bombers, Short Sunderland flying boats, Short Singapore flying boats, and Vickers

Vildebeest torpedo bombers. All told there are just 215 British aircraft stationed on the Malay Peninsula.

Were.

Many no longer exist. Dozens of these outdated planes were destroyed during yesterday's surprise attacks.

So it is that Force Z now sails into Japanese-controlled waters without air cover. This is a calculated risk by Admiral Phillips. In addition to his belief that airplanes are not a threat to surface warfare vessels, Phillips labors under the misguided belief that Japanese bombers lack the range to take off from Saigon and attack his vessels in the Gulf of Siam.

Mitsubishi G3M ("Nell") and G4M ("Betty") can fly twice that distance and return safely to base.

Now, just before sunset on December 9, Admiral Phillips believes his gamble will succeed. Weather prevents aerial attack. Phillips is quite sure Z has gone undetected.

Then the rain stops. The clouds disappear. The wind grows soft. The skies turn blue. A bright orange sun shines down on the South China Sea.

In an amazing coincidence, the urgent radio warning sent hours ago by Captain Teraoka on *I-65* finally gets through to 22nd Air Flotilla headquarters in Saigon. *Chōkai*, the heavy cruiser serving as invasion headquarters for Vice Admiral Jisaburō Ozawa, also receives the message. Within moments, news that *Prince of Wales* and *Repulse* are in the vicinity races through the Japanese fleet. Finding and sinking the British warships becomes top priority.

Things happen fast: Two battleships, nine cruisers, and four destroyers are redirected from waters off Vietnam toward *Prince of Wales'* course heading. Four search aircraft catapult off the cruisers *Kinu*, *Kumano*, *Yura*, and *Suzuya* to scour the seas. The Aichi E13A floatplanes have a range of thirteen hundred miles and can fly fourteen hours without having to land. Ungainly, fitted with two massive, fixed pontoons instead of landing gear. Crew of three. These four Aichi vector toward the task force's last-known position.

Forty minutes after takeoff, with dark blue water reflecting the setting sun, three lucky Japanese Aichi E13A crews spot six zigzag parallel wakes scoring the South China Sea.

Symmetry.

Crews on board *Wales* and *Repulse* startle at the drone of aircraft engines, swiveling their heads to the sky in fear. To a man, they know these planes cannot be British. Men on deck watch helplessly as the three Japanese aircraft circle just out of gun range. "We stood on the upper deck and watched the Jap float plane in the now-fading light," one medical officer on board *Wales* writes. "I thought what a curse a vivid imagination could be and wished we could hurry up and get on with it."

A pall descends over the British sailors. They pray for night to hide them. Men prepare for battle stations, changing into long-sleeved shirts and pants to prevent bare arms and legs from getting sudden powder burns. Many wrap life preservers around their waists, ready to inflate when the order comes to abandon ship. Sailors secure their money in condoms so the cash won't get wet when they leap into the sea.

Sunset sees *Tenedos* turn around and run home to Singapore. She is low on diesel. Admiral Phillips has decided that only battleships will be used for tomorrow's assault on the invasion beaches.

A black curtain finally descends over the South China Sea. Lights are off. Every ship runs dark.

Even Tom Thumb feels trepidation. He realizes there is no point in going on, certain Japanese invasion vessels have scattered into safer waters. Phillips has no air cover, no element of surprise, and no targets at which to aim his big guns.

At 2050, Admiral Phillips orders Force Z to turn around.

"I have most regretfully cancelled the operation," Phillips signals to *Repulse*, "because, having been located by aircraft, surprise was lost, and our target would be almost certain to be gone by morning, and the enemy prepared for us."

Force Z maintains radio silence. The message is Morse code, sent via a blue signaling lamp used only at night. Tight guts unclench as crews breathe a sigh of relief.

Wales and *Repulse* are hardly safe. A second Japanese submarine, the *I-56*, picks up the scent, then fires five torpedoes at *Wales*. But *I-56* is old. One torpedo tube hatch gets stuck. The British ships are no longer in point-blank range by the time it is fixed. All five shots miss. Admiral Phillips is completely unaware *Wales* is under attack.

I-56 continues stalking from a distance. She reports the sighting to 22nd Air Flotilla headquarters.

In Saigon, the order is passed: Launch bombers at first light.

EPISODE TWO

———

FRANKLIN AND WINSTON (FOUR MONTHS EARLIER)

WINSTON CHURCHILL

The prime minister has an important American guest.

"After dinner: Meeting with Harry Hopkins," Winston Churchill pens in his daily engagement calendar. Churchill is now sixty-six years old. Thickset. Broad shoulders. Fondness for Scotch in the morning, brandy after dinner, and Pol Roger champagne at lunch—drunk from a tankard complete with a handle. A romantic, a bully, a visionary. Just the man Britain needs right now.

"Harry Hopkins came into the garden of Downing Street," Churchill writes in his memoirs, "and we sat together in the sunshine."

Harold Lloyd Hopkins is thin, gray, widowed. Fifty. Learning to live with stomach cancer. Witty, urbane, deeply intelligent. Shares Churchill's relentless work ethic. United States President Franklin Roosevelt's trust in the adviser is so great that Hopkins has his own bedroom in the White House residence.

Winston Churchill knows that when he speaks with Harry Hopkins, he is speaking to Roosevelt. FDR is paralyzed from polio, Churchill has been informed by British intelligence services, but this disability is kept secret from the American people—the president is often photographed sitting behind a desk or at the wheel of a car, but never walking or in his wheelchair. Travel is difficult. He sends Hopkins around the world in his place. From London, the adviser will fly directly to Moscow to meet with

Joseph Stalin. Germany invaded the Soviet Union a month ago. Roosevelt is promising support. Having Hopkins deliver the message makes it personal.

Churchill and Hopkins enjoy each other's company. The reason for this afternoon's meeting soon becomes clear: "Presently, he said the president would like to have a meeting with me in some lonely bay or other."

A remarkable statement. Churchill and Roosevelt have been communicating since the start of the war. Even before the prime minister was the prime minister. At the time of their first communication in 1939, Churchill was not in office. However, Roosevelt initiated their discussions because he correctly believed the veteran British legislator would one day ascend to that role. Through telephone calls and telegrams, they have come to know each other. Roosevelt enjoys direct communication with Churchill so much that he refuses to discuss the conversations with American Ambassador Joseph P. Kennedy.

Churchill and Roosevelt are navy men and politicians. If there is a central thesis to Churchill's side of the relationship, it is to somehow pull America into World War II. England cannot stand alone forever. Roosevelt helps when he can. The president likes being courted but is noncommittal.

Now he wants to meet. Something very important must be transpiring. "I need to explain things to him face to face," Hopkins says, relaying FDR's words.

Intrigued, the prime minister agrees. For the first time in this war, he will meet Roosevelt in person.

"Thus, all was soon arranged," Churchill writes. "Placentia Bay in Newfoundland was chosen. The date of August 9 was fixed. And our latest battleship, *Prince of Wales*, was placed under orders accordingly."

FRANKLIN ROOSEVELT

President Franklin Roosevelt proceeds cautiously.

Harry met with Winston in London hours ago. Hopkins called the president to confirm the discussion, even putting an excited prime minister on the line. The summit is on. Now comes the meeting that will give president and prime minister something to talk about.

The official work of running America is done in the Oval Office, which is on the ground floor in a facility adjacent to the White House known as the West Wing.

But here, on the second floor of the executive mansion, is where FDR lives his life. Roosevelt calls it the Oval *Study*. The White House is ever evolving. This room was first used by the second president, John Adams, as a drawing room. It was decorated in yellow damask in 1809 by Dolley Madison and given the nickname "Yellow Oval." The first White House Christmas tree was erected here in 1889.

Right now this lair is the world of a man limited in his movements and thus a snapshot of his entire existence. Cigarette smoke. A nautical theme. A big room filled with clutter piled on top of clutter: books, wooden sailing ship models, framed photographs. Files and papers and pretty much everything else that might interest the president stacked in uneven pyramids on the Resolute Desk. The fireplace is never lit when the wheelchair-using

Roosevelt is alone in the room, for fear he will be unable to escape should flames get out of control. Double doors lead to the bath and the bedroom where the president sleeps alone. Sometimes FDR just putters in this room with his stamp collection, other times with his black Scottish terrier, Fala. But it is here, on the second floor of the White House in the Yellow Oval, that FDR comes alive.

President Roosevelt wheels to his desk after a long afternoon in the West Wing. Acting Secretary of State Sumner Welles, Chief of Naval Operations Admiral Harold Raynsford "Betty" Stark, and the Japanese ambassador, Admiral Kichisaburō Nomura, enter through wooden double doors. The diplomat and president have been friends for two decades. Normally at this time of day, Roosevelt plays bartender. He might pour Nomura one of his horrible happy hour cocktails, following no recipe and throwing in random ingredients as he makes his version of a martini, which the recipient is expected to eagerly imbibe.

This is not that sort of meeting.

Roosevelt has tired eyes, nicotine stains, a jaunty inflection to an upper-class voice. Fifty-nine. Married to a niece of former President Theodore Roosevelt, a woman who is his own fifth cousin once removed. Franklin and Eleanor stopped sharing their marital bed more than twenty years and six children ago when she discovered his affair with her personal secretary. The president was once a vigorous man standing six foot two. Polio makes it difficult to walk unassisted, but such is his bearing that he still looks tall sitting down.

Admiral Nomura is blind in one eye, the result of a bomb thrown by a Korean independence protester nine years ago. He is sixty-three. Balding. A dark suit and tie with thick round glasses. Front teeth flat, as if filed, and stained with nicotine and plaque. The easy smile of a nice man.

The subject of this meeting is disappointment.

Nomura knows why he's here before Roosevelt speaks a word. Yesterday, Japanese troops completed their conquest of Indochina. Bordered by Thailand and China, draped like a stole along the broad shoulders of Southeast Asia and the South China Sea. Portions of this region are also known as Vietnam. Indochina (French: *Indochine*) refers to the intermingling of Indian and Chinese cultures in the nations of Cambodia, Vietnam, and Laos. The term was coined in 1811 by Scottish poet John Leyden, who lived and worked in the region. Nineteen forty-one will not be the last time America will become embroiled in the conflicts and politics of this portion of Southeast Asia.

Indochina is almost three thousand miles from Tokyo. The Imperial Japanese Army has never strayed farther from the home islands. It appears they are on the verge of going much farther.

In the course of the last year, Japan has signed an alliance with Nazi Germany to gain a global ally, signed a neutrality pact with the Soviet Union to protect her northern borders, then expanded south into Vietnam, inching closer to the rich petroleum beds of the South China Sea. Clearly, a nation posturing for war.

Anticipating this aggression for years, Roosevelt has already ordered the buildup of American naval bases in the Pacific. He ordered the fleet to relocate from the safety of American continental shores to the Hawaiian Islands, putting U.S. warships twenty-five hundred miles closer to Tokyo. The American navy has all but left the Atlantic, in a manner of speaking, placing its top battleships and aircraft carriers at Pearl Harbor. If Singapore is a "sword at our heart" to the Japanese, then Pearl is surely a saber in the back.

The Imperial Japanese Navy is currently larger than the combined American and British naval forces in the Pacific. The U.S. Congress authorized a rapid American naval buildup one year ago. Those new ships will even the balance of power by the summer of 1942.

Japan must attack the United States before then, should they plan to wrest control of the Pacific from the United States Navy. Stationing troops in Vietnam might seem to have nothing to do with Pearl Harbor, six thousand miles to the east, but in fact it is a bold step toward war.

***

JAPAN HAS BEEN fighting in one conflict or another for decades, attempting to build the Greater East Asia Co-Prosperity Sphere—another name for total control of Asia and the Pacific. European powers have colonized that continent over the centuries. Japan sees no harm in doing the same.

Portugal claims Malacca in 1511. Spain grabs a large collection of islands and names them for King Phillip II in 1521. Guam the same year. The Dutch arrive in 1641. Captain James Cook of the Royal Navy makes Australia and Hawaii known to the world during his three voyages of exploration beginning in 1769. A trade station for Britain's merchant fleet opens in Singapore in 1819. Missionaries from the United States descend upon Hawaii in 1832. Somewhere in the midst, Germany joins the party, claiming a few small random islands.

This European stranglehold is interrupted, as Japan emerges from centuries of international isolation in the middle of the nineteenth century. Western shipbuilding techniques are adopted. Students travel abroad to study at foreign naval academies. The Imperial Japanese Navy is founded in 1869, a response to perceived threats from the U.S. and Britain. Japan occupies Taiwan in 1895. By 1905, the IJN is powerful enough to defeat the Russians in war, sinking twenty-one enemy ships and capturing or disarming thirteen more. Never in modern times has an Asian nation defeated a traditional European power. Five years later, Japan annexes Korea.

After World War I, Japan's South Seas Mandate means taking control of islands coveted since the establishment of the Imperial Japanese Navy: the Marianas, the Carolines, the Marshall Islands, and Palau. Small specks of land in the middle of the vast Pacific. Seemingly unimportant. Yet Japan plays the long game. Engineers begin the process of hollowing out island mountains to turn them into fortresses. The Mandate for the German Possessions in the Pacific Ocean Lying North of the Equator, also known as the South Seas Mandate, was a 1920 League of Nations edict giving Japan possession of former islands of the German colonial empire.

The invasions continue: Manchuria in 1931, followed by a deeper penetration into China in 1937. Indochina falls in 1940, followed by Vietnam in 1941. What's next is anyone's guess.

***

PRESIDENT ROOSEVELT AND his three guests sit facing one another. Admiral Stark waits to be called upon. FDR does the talking for America. Thick drapes cover the windows behind the president, open just enough to let in fading summer sunlight. Ambassador Nomura is frank but unapologetic. A flurry of cables has gone back and forth between U.S. diplomatic officials in Washington and Tokyo about the content of today's discussions.

Secretary Welles takes copious minutes. His legacy will be the term "no comment," which he coins. In keeping with that theme of cautious verbiage, every word of this meeting is rehearsed—particularly those FDR holds back for maximum impact.

Welles believes that if Nomura attempts "to explain away the Indochina move by saying that it had been brought about by peaceful means, then such 'peaceful means' were completely contrary to the spirit of the discussions between the United States and Japanese Governments looking toward a friendly settlement in the Pacific."

Everyone in the room knows Japan cherishes three commodities for building their war machine: steel, rubber, and oil. Without these, industrialized Japan will shut down. Her home islands of Honshu and Hokkaido are known for fish, forestry, and bad coal. The occupied territories in Korea, Taiwan, and Manchuria are little better.

Unlike steel and oil, rubber grows on trees. Japan purchased that commodity from the Dutch East Indies and British Malaya prior to invading Indochina. Vietnam's rubber plantations now make that unnecessary.

For oil and steel, Japan relies on the United States. In 1939, two million tons of scrap metal were exported from the U.S. to Japan, where it was recycled to build guns and bombs. Throughout the 1930s, Japan purchased twenty-six million barrels of oil a year from the United States. They pay for much of this through commercial fishing, exporting tuna, shrimp, salmon, and whale.

The Imperial Japanese Navy currently has a six-month reserve supply of fuel. Without heavy marine diesel, those ships will remain in port. The most imperative need of Japan's war machine is for that pipeline from America to remain open.

Every man in the Oval Study knows this fact quite well.

The solution should be simple: If America wants to get its way in the Pacific, stop selling oil to Japan. It's the perfect leverage.

But the ground far beneath the Dutch East Indies and British Malaya also contains large amounts of petroleum. Japan will have no choice but to invade those European colonies and grab their refineries if Roosevelt decides to turn off the spigot. This puts Winston Churchill and Singapore in peril.

Three days ago, Admiral Stark presented FDR with a navy memorandum predicting this would happen. Stately, sixty, white-haired, glasses with thin gold frames. Not a man given to fantastical claims. A career of following orders and writing formal reports that must stand up to intense scrutiny. And through it all, he has been known as "Betty." This playful nickname was coined by history-minded United States Naval Academy classmates comparing him to Elizabeth Page Stark, wife of Revolutionary War General John Stark. The amazing fact is not that it stuck, but that such a fastidious man is extremely comfortable with the president of the United States calling him by a woman's name.

This same president also has complete faith in Stark's recent findings.

Clearly, *something* must be done.

So President Roosevelt gives Ambassador Nomura a message for his superiors in Japan.

FDR does so in his own charming way. He tells a story. Earlier this very morning—why, just before lunch, he tells the admiral—the president was visited by a group led by New York Mayor Fiorello La Guardia. There were questions about why America sells oil to Japan.

"At the present time," Roosevelt explains to Nomura, "the Ambassador undoubtedly knows there is a very considerable shortage in the oil supply of the eastern part of the United States. The average American man and woman are unable to understand why, at a time when they themselves are asked to curtail their use of gasoline oil, the United States

Government should be permitting oil supplies to continue to be exported to Japan, when Japan during these past two years has given every indication of pursuing a policy of world conquest in conjunction with the policy of world conquest and domination which Hitler is carrying on.

"The average American citizen cannot understand why his government is permitting Japan to be furnished with oil in order that such oil might be utilized by Japan in carrying on her purposes of aggression."

A breath. The Yellow Oval quiets as the president lets that settle in.

Then Roosevelt gets right to the point: "This new move by Japan in Indochina creates an exceedingly serious problem for the United States."

Ambassador Nomura very calmly tells the president that he sympathizes. He uses the words "deplores" and "personally not in agreement" with reference to the invasion.

Roosevelt keeps the room friendly, folksy even, leaning into his longtime friend's admission. "I have a proposal to make. It occurred to me just before you came in. I haven't even had time to discuss it with Ambassador Welles."

Another pause for emphasis.

"It might be too late for me to make this proposal, but I feel that no matter how late the hour might be, I still wish to seize every possible opportunity of preventing the creation of a situation between Japan and the United States."

The record does not show if FDR is smoking a cigarette through one of the long, slender black holders for which he is known. Or whether he rocks back in his thick, fabric-upholstered desk chair. Or puts two elbows down firmly on the Resolute Desk and leans forward to emphasize the next line. But this is the most dramatic moment of the meeting, velvet words draped over an iron fist. "Oil" is not mentioned by name. There's no need to do so.

Roosevelt demands that Japan pull all "military and naval forces" out of Indochina. Or else.

Admiral Nomura says he will inform his superiors. He quotes a Chinese proverb—"He who brandishes the sword eventually kills himself"—though it is unclear which nation he refers to.

The meeting concludes at five fifty-five. Forty-eight minutes on the dot. Guests file out. Ambassador Nomura soon goes back on his word, finding the U.S. proposal so catastrophic that he refuses to share it with Tokyo.

In doing so, the ambassador chooses to believe Roosevelt is bluffing.

Admiral Nomura is wrong.

***

FDR REMAINS ALONE in the Yellow Oval for another ninety minutes. No decision since taking office eight years ago carries more weight than what he is prepared to do right now. As recently as this afternoon's two p.m. Cabinet meeting, he ardently opposed extreme measures. The president reiterated those words later in the day, saying that selling oil to Japan means "keeping war out of the South Pacific, for our own good, for the good of the defense of Great Britain, and the freedom of the seas."

Then came the meeting with Nomura, where he completely reversed course, knowing embargo is the most lethal arrow in his quiver.

Japan believes the United States will never punish their aggression. This colors their tactical thinking. Americans are well-known to favor neutrality, the Monroe Doctrine still a bellwether for isolationists and pacifists.

This is just one interpretation. The Monroe Doctrine was a warning from President James Monroe to European powers that attempting to colonize the western hemisphere would be met with force. Monroe made these comments to Congress on December 2, 1823, during his Annual Message. The doctrine is often interpreted as meaning the United States will not intervene in foreign wars.

There is also the interpretation put forth by FDR's fifth cousin Teddy in his 1905 Annual Message to Congress, allowing American intervention in international politics.

Yet now, in 1941, the nation has little stomach for war. Waging war in the Pacific, in particular, is considered unthinkable by a majority of America's electorate. Roosevelt has walked this political tightrope for years, even as Hitler has conquered Europe and Japan has rampaged through Asia.

Roosevelt's response during the *Panay* incident in 1937 further emboldens Japan. Japanese airplanes bomb the USS *Panay* as it evacuates American citizens from China. Three civilians are killed, forty-three sailors and five other civilians are wounded. The U.S. and Japan are not at war, yet the *Panay* is repeatedly bombed and machine-gunned, despite the ship's prominent display of American flags. FDR accepts Japan's apologies and does not inflict punishment.

Yet FDR has also taken action, selling arms to the Chinese. Extending credit to this Asian foe of Japan's for the purchase of bombs and guns. American "Flying Tiger" P-40 fighter pilots defiantly engaging in combat missions high above China against Japanese aircraft.*

The president leaves the Yellow Oval for dinner with Eleanor at seven thirty. Most Americans do not know about FDR's wheelchair; nor do they know that his marriage to Eleanor is political, founded upon the appearance the Roosevelts are a couple. At eleven ten, FDR boards a train for his home in Hyde Park, New York, to spend the weekend there.

On Saturday, July 26, President Roosevelt amends an earlier executive order that froze German assets in the United States. The order now includes all Japanese funds and possessions. This is a cautious move, meant to make Japan uncomfortable. Monies will be released on a case-by-case basis. The sale of fuel is still allowed but regulated. Roosevelt remains cautious, hoping Japan will pull out of Indochina.

Later that afternoon, the War Department announces fabled American

---

* Among the fliers is a unique officer named Albert "Ajax" Baumler. The U.S. Army pilot has twice resigned his commission to fly in foreign conflicts. The first time was in 1936, when he flew with a Soviet squadron in the Spanish Civil War. Baumler returned to the U.S. Army in 1937, credited with shooting down five enemy aircraft in Spain. He resigned his commission again in 1941 to fly with the Flying Tigers. He was on Wake Island, en route to Burma, when Japan attacked on December 7, 1941. Baumler later served in Korea as an air traffic controller. He died in 1973 at the age of fifty-nine.

General Douglas MacArthur is taking charge of U.S. troops in the Philippines, an area within striking distance of Japanese air bases in Southeast Asia.

Two days later, Japan moves 140,000 *more* troops into Vietnam.

On July 31, a top secret message from Tokyo to Ambassador Nomura is decoded by U.S. cryptologists: "There is more reason than ever before to arm ourselves to the teeth for all-out war."

CHURCHILL AND ROOSEVELT

Marylebone station. Platform 4. Sunday.

Great Britain's top admirals and generals board a long private train, uncertain of their destination. Given just twenty-four hours' notice for what promises to be a trip of uncertain length. Secrecy paramount. Nobody dares speak aloud about where they might be going. First and only stop is Wendover, ninety minutes northwest of London. A cherubic figure smoking a cigar stands awaiting their arrival. He has been spending the weekend at Chequers, official country residence of the prime minister.

Riviera begins. Everything about this operation to bring Winston Churchill and Franklin Roosevelt to a remote meeting place is confidential—"the best kept secret I can remember in Whitehall," marvels Colonel Leslie Hollis of the War Cabinet, among the functionaries along for the mission.

Winston Churchill boards for the overnight journey to Thurso. Lunch of steak and raspberry tart washed down with champagne. The adventure has begun. The prime minister is delighted.

Churchill departs the train in the morning, boarding the destroyer *Oribi* for his journey to the naval base at Scapa Flow in the Orkney Islands. Harry Hopkins, exhausted from his whirlwind trip to Moscow, arrived two days ago. He comes bearing caviar and vodka. President Roosevelt's emissary will travel to Newfoundland with Churchill.

A motor launch transfers Churchill to the waiting *Prince of Wales*. The ship rises out of the mist. Ship's complement lines the decks at attention, awaiting the arrival of a very important guest whose name they have not been told.

This makes them only more curious. Calm seas. Low clouds. Heels together as the men stand at attention, toes pointed apart at forty-five-degree angles. No speech allowed. No facial or bodily movement.

The crew beholds a sight that makes them break the rules. They can't help themselves. "It's Winston," the company whispers in delight as the launch draws near and a certain thickset figure presents himself on deck.

Churchill bounds up the gangway, now dressed in sea coat and the matching cap that makes him look like a train conductor. Captain John Leach of *Wales* stands waiting, a tall, trim man in blue with perfect posture and a telescope tucked beneath one arm. The lanky captain bows slightly to the shorter man as the two greet each other. Churchill demands to be taken at once to the bridge. Leach leads the way, a documentary film crew following to record the prime minister's every movement. The prime minister bends down to pet Blackie, the ship's lucky cat.

Journalist Henry Canova Vollam Morton is along for the ride. "H.V." for short. Considered the "world's greatest living travel writer," he is a British institution, among the few invited to attend the opening of King Tut's tomb in 1923. The journey on board *Prince of Wales* is another feather in his cap. The author is a last-minute addition to the guest manifest, invited along to record the Newfoundland summit for posterity. Unbeknownst to the prime minister, H. V. Morton is a Nazi sympathizer, enthralled with Adolf Hitler.

"I said something about the responsibility of taking Winston Churchill across the Atlantic in wartime," Morton relates of meeting Captain Leach for the first time. "I received in reply an eloquent glance of tired blue eyes and a weary but contented smile."

Princes of Wales gets underway at four p.m.

***

SUNDAY MORNING, AUGUST 3. Blazing hot in Washington, DC. FDR takes a train to Connecticut. There, he boards the presidential yacht, USS

Potomac, which then motors off the coast north toward Cape Cod. Up to now, the media believes this a normal presidential fishing trip. *Potomac* anchors off Martha's Vineyard. The all-white vessel halts for the night. In the morning, summer vacationers and sightseers eagerly thrill to the sight of Roosevelt's yacht so close to shore, and they strain for a glimpse of the great man walking about the deck.

Yet the president is no longer on board. He left the *Potomac* hours ago and is currently two hundred miles away. Roosevelt secretly transferred to the USS *Augusta*, flagship of the Atlantic Fleet. His top admirals and generals were already on board.

Augusta immediately sets a northerly course for Newfoundland. Speed is a brisk thirty-two knots—too fast for the German U-boats known to patrol North Atlantic waters.

"U-boat" is an abbreviation of *Unterseeboot*—undersea boat. Though the U.S. is not at war in late summer and autumn 1941, U-boat attacks on

USS *Augusta* *Public domain / Naval History and Heritage Command*

American ships are so frequent, President Roosevelt will soon issue a "shoot on sight" order. U.S. Navy vessels will be allowed to fire on any German ship threatening an American vessel.

That is all to come.

As Franklin Roosevelt suspected when proposing that Winston Churchill and he break bread, the two men will soon meet in the lonely bay.

Meanwhile, back to *Prince of Wales*.

CAPTAIN LEACH

H MS *Prince of Wales* is cursed.
And in a hurry.
Thirty-three knots. Radio silence. Running dark. Hauling precious cargo through atrocious seas to a fishing village no one has ever heard of. More than a thousand Guz sailors belowdecks brace at each dip and heave of the bow.

A quick aside.

The etymology of "guz" is very much in question. It is said that once upon a time, men of the sea marveled at Plymouth citizens' fondness for Devonshire cream and Cornish pasties. They derided them as "guzzlers" for this passion. In 1911, the food service at Devonshire was upgraded, leading some to say sailors "guzzled" their food. One other explanation is that a guz is a unit of measuring textiles in Asia, similar in length to the yard. Men returning home from the sea applied this term to the local naval base as a substitute for "yard," the common name of the Devonport Dockyard. For what it's worth, the Portsmouth manning depot is nicknamed "Pompey" and Chatham is "Chats."

Back to our story.

Captain John Leach sips tea on the bridge, feet planted, patiently guiding his vessel to its destination. Rumpled uniform. Needs a shower and shave. Worried but doesn't show it.

Leach is a special sort of career navy man, not pompous or self-important, radiating "calmness, gentleness, kindness, and humor," in the words of a fellow officer.

The crew adores their "Trunky." Until last Friday, Leach had been gone five weeks for surgery and recovery. When the men heard he was returning to the ship, they crowded the decks to cheer him back on board.

The no-nonsense Leach, surprised, wept.

Forty-six, six feet tall, thirty years in the Royal Navy. Married to Evelyn, his dynamic raven-haired bride of twenty-four years. Three sons. Left-handed bowler on the cricket pitch. So athletic he's RN champion in squash and tennis. A naval gunner by training, thus hard of hearing from years of standing too close to barrels ten feet longer than a double-decker bus launching round after round.

To his face, the men of *Wales* call Leach "Skipper" and "Old Man." "Trunky," behind his back, is for the elephantine nose.

Wales is Leach's reward for years of exceptional service. The Royal Navy is the strongest in the world. Its roughly four-hundred-ship fleet consists of battleships and battle cruisers, aircraft carriers, destroyers, and sixty-six submarines. *Prince of Wales* is among the greatest of them all. A battleship, a monster, a symbol—precisely the sort of fighting vessel to change the course of what is being called "World War II."

From this journey to Newfoundland to the actions that will bring about the Battle of Midway, *Wales* will do just that.

In a most unexpected way.

She is one of the most modern fighting ships in the British fleet, laid down at Cammell Laird Shipyard in Birkenhead on New Year's Day 1937, just as CV-5 is sprouting steel ribs across the Atlantic in Newport News. Two years later, a shoulder-to-shoulder crowd of fifty thousand looks on as Mary, Princess Royal, the forty-two-year-old daughter of the deceased King George V, christens *Wales* under gray spring skies.

Prince of Wales is one of five identical ships belonging to the *King George V* class. *King George V* is launched in February 1939. Then *Prince of Wales, Duke of York, Anson,* and finally *Howe,* the last of which is launched in April 1940.

Just like the American *Yorktown*-class carriers, they look so much alike that non-sailors can't tell them apart. At 745 feet, she is almost as long as an aircraft carrier, though with vastly more firepower. Crew of 1,521. Hull painted in bold camouflage swirls of white, Home Fleet grey, and a daunting tone of blue-green so dark that it's almost midnight. Guns mounted on enormous turrets bristle at every angle from the deck, the largest with barrels fifty-two feet long, capable of launching a fourteen-hundred-pound shell twenty miles with pinpoint accuracy. She is 103 feet at the beam, 44,500 tons fully loaded. In a throwback to the age of sail, *Wales'* main deck is wooden—tight-grained teak—which retards sparks from shells and propellants that might cause a devastating explosion.

At her waterline are sixteen fat inches of armor.

"We saw a giant among giants," one of the ship's guests will later write of his first time motoring toward *Wales.* "How beautiful she looked that morning as she appeared out of the mist, full of power, strength, and pride. As we approached her . . . the battleship, which from a distance had looked so graceful and so lithe, now towered above us like a mighty hill of steel."

So for John Leach to be chosen as her captain is quite a coup.

This journey across the Atlantic is fraught with peril, with Leach personally responsible for the fate of Winston Churchill—thus the captain's tired blue eyes. Churchill is the precious cargo. Should *Wales* be sunk, the results will be horrific. Great Britain will lose a prime minister and the men most knowledgeable about waging war. FDR will be without the gaunt Hopkins. "I feel he is taking a gambler's risk, with large stakes, appalling losses," says Canadian Prime Minister Mackenzie King upon learning of Churchill's voyage. "It is a matter of vanity. There is no need for any meeting. Everything essential can be done better by cable communication."

In a bold gamble, *Wales* temporarily drops her destroyer escort to run faster. This makes her an easy target for lurking Nazi submarines. No less than Admiral Dudley Pound, Britain's First Sea Lord, makes the call, deciding risk is worth reward. He is an old sixty-three, with a brain tumor and a bum hip, but in no hurry to die. Pound's trust in *Wales*' speed is complete. She is three times faster than any U-boat.

That Nazi threat, however, is always present. Even as towering waves wash over the main deck, lookouts keep watch day and night for periscopes and long straight lines of churning white water that signal a torpedo barreling toward its target. Nazi skippers are brazen in their attacks, unafraid to launch their deadly fish in the worst of conditions. Seventy British ships sank in June. *Prince of Wales* would be a glorious kill.

Then comes the U-boat sighting.

JONAH

P*rince of Wales* escapes the German submarine.

"Have altered [course] to avoid the U-boat reported by HMS *St. Apollo*," reads the message sent to the Admiralty in London. Speed is twenty-two knots, impossible for any submarine to match.

The threat is no more. Yet Captain Leach's men remain on edge.

When, and if, a U-boat commander gazes at *Wales* through his periscope, he will see the hull, bridge, quarterdeck, main deck—and all those behemoth guns, of course. But there are many other decks within, where escape is unlikely should that torpedo slam home. Here, among crowded workspaces and dense living quarters, is where the rumor thrives.

"Jonah."

The sailors are from the Devonport manning depot in the southern English port of Plymouth. Just like centuries of Royal Navy sailors before them, they are proud men eager to sail the globe and defend empire. Duty is four hours at a time. Slumber comes side by side in hammocks swaying with the ship. Fond of shore leave and the daily rum tot. Working class. Little education.

Superstitious.

A majority of men begin the war as "hostilities only" ratings, inexperienced recruits who only joined the navy when the war broke out. All are aware that a battleship is a class society—and they are on the lower end, which makes the popularity of Captain Leach all the more remarkable.

"There was not that confidence between the officers and senior ratings—nostalgic for peacetime Navy manning, perhaps—on the one hand, and the predominant 'hostilities only' crew on the other, many who came from that stratum of society which had good cause to resent the 'gaffers' and upper class generally. I often wondered just what one of my friends from the Liverpool slums was 'fighting to defend,'" writes one sailor.

Their "Jonah" superstition borders on the irrational but has merit. Not outright panic, not entirely based in fact, just a low, uneasy buzz snaking through the men. At meals. Falling asleep. Queueing in the mess at six bells for the daily rum ration.

The rumor goes something like this: However fast or strong *Wales* might be, she is cursed. The tradition goes back millennia, based on the biblical prophet. Jonah runs from God, is thrown overboard for bringing bad luck to a ship, and is then swallowed by a whale. Anyone or anything can be a Jonah: women, clergy, redheads.

It does not escape notice that the captain's thinning hair is pale ginger.

Some warships have a way of emerging from battle unscathed. *Wales* is not among them. Thus, Jonah.

There is the German aircraft bomb that strikes her in August 1940.

The big guns that jam and will not fire in perilous moments of combat.

In May 1941, just three months ago, the crew watches the HMS *Hood* sink in minutes as German shells shear her bow. *Hood* is a popular ship and the almost total loss of her crew—just three survive out of 1,418—is a heart-wrenching blow.

That could have been *Wales*. Every man feels it. It's only a matter of time before another attack sends the ship they call home to the bottom.

Omens and divinations are a sailor's lot. Setting sail on Friday is bad luck. Bananas are horrible. A ship carrying pigs is doomed because everyone knows pigs can't swim. Whistling, too, because it implies an attempt to control the wind—and any sailor will tell you that's impossible.

It's all part of life at sea. Yet there are also good superstitions in the Royal Navy. Among them is a ship's cat—particularly one with black fur. Blackie, the lone feline on board, is as dark as the mid-Atlantic seabed.

As the crossing continues without a single torpedo fired at *Wales*, Blackie's luck appears to be holding.

Talk of a Jonah, however, does not cease.

***

CAPTAIN LEACH DOES not acknowledge the curse. From his perch on the bridge, where he so narrowly avoided death three months ago, Leach is more concerned about the weather and Nazi attack. *Wales* plows through the towering seas, alive. Her bow throws a great wave: throbbing, sensate; rising, falling, great steel hull moaning. Angry green water reaches up from the depths and curls over the rails. Wind hammers her hull. Spindrift cold as a sinner's soul pierces like hail into the face of any man stepping onto the open air of the quarterdeck.

These cold North Atlantic seas are nothing new to Leach. Particularly this stretch. When she passes south of a sea lane between Iceland and Greenland known as the Denmark Strait, Leach surely cannot help but reflect on the last time *Wales* passed through here.

Impossible to forget. Top story in newspapers around the world. Almost cost Leach his life.

Three months ago, in these icy cold waters, the skipper put this ship and these men before his vaunted career. The moment comes as *Prince of Wales* and the German *Bismarck* exchange blows like punch-drunk fighters in the Denmark Strait. Nine miles apart. Shuddering and heaving as their enormous gun barrels launch shells the size of killer whales at each other. Leach is on the compass platform when a one-ton Nazi round rips through the steel walls, passing from starboard to port, through one side, then out the other.

Supersonic percussion knocks Leach unconscious. Others on the bridge are not as lucky, almost all killed instantly. The captain wakes to a scene of blood and destruction. *Wales* has put three shells into the German but is herself badly damaged.

One of the injured is Esmond Knight, a thirty-five-year-old British actor who enlisted as a sailor. He has just lost an eye. Coincidentally, Knight will play Captain Leach in the movie *Sink the Bismarck!*

The German battleship's gunners are zeroing in, their rounds straddling *Wales*. To Captain Leach's horror, his ship's big guns jam in the heat of the fight, unable to fire back. Just a matter of time before she is sunk. Drastic measures required.

Captain John Leach has a hard decision to make. *Bismarck* is the prize of all prizes. Hitler himself attended her christening. Sinking *Bismarck* would make Trunky a national hero.

Admiral. Knighthood. Never pay for another drink in his life.

Yet for the good of the ship and the safety of his men, Captain Leach withdraws. *Wales* eventually limps back to Britain as *Bismarck* sprints through dense fog to the safety of occupied France.

The pride of Germany never makes it. Days after Leach turns for safety, *Bismarck* is located and sunk by a complement of British battleships and destroyers. Fairey Swordfish torpedo bombers launched from the aircraft carriers *Victorious* and *Ark Royal* strike *Bismarck*, silencing doubts in the naval community as to whether or not a battleship at sea is vulnerable to aircraft. *Wales* is not needed for this denouement, but Leach's decision remains controversial.

Summer in dry dock for *Prince of Wales*. Straight to the hospital for Captain Leach. A hernia suffered because of the enormous shell's shock wave required surgery. To the great surprise of all on board, an unexploded one-ton German round is found deep inside the hull during repairs and successfully removed. Throughout June and July as his body heals, the captain's reputation suffers. Leach endures cries that he be court-martialed for cowardice.

Top naval advisers come to Leach's defense, pointing out that *Wales'* gunners hit *Bismarck* three times before the captain disengaged. Sir John Tovey, commander in chief of the Home Fleet, stands firmly behind Leach's decision. Instead of a court-martial, the captain will be awarded the Distinguished Service Order. *Wales* floats out of dry dock in late July.

Leach rejoins his ship on August 1 and is immediately ordered to sea for the classified journey to Newfoundland. Evelyn is shattered by his sudden departure, having believed her husband would be home much longer. The sad truth is that Evelyn Leach will be a widow in four months.

In the meantime, the Old Man needs to get Winston Churchill to Newfoundland.

WINSTON CHURCHILL

Tonight's movie is *"Pimpernel" Smith* with Leslie Howard.*

The prime minister and his entourage of diplomats, military leaders, defense officials, personal bodyguard, and Harry Hopkins hunker down in *Wales'* wardroom to watch the anti-Nazi thriller.

Everyone dresses in formal dinner attire from the evening meal. They sit in comfortable chairs brought in for the occasion. Churchill wears the mess dress of the Royal Yacht Squadron. Waistcoat. Long rows of brass buttons. A uniform meant for a man in fighting trim, but Churchill pulls it off, if only because he is prime minister.

Prince of Wales' two bagpipers have called it a night but the bar is open. Churchill sips brandy and smokes. Ignores the ashtray. Ashes fall off his cigar onto the dark blue uniform. Churchill wipes them onto the floor for someone else to clean.

The prime minister is exhausted and excited. Crossing the Atlantic is a respite from the round-the-clock grind he has endured since taking office fifteen months ago. Radio silence means he cannot respond to war

---

* Howard, best known for his role as Ashley Wilkes in *Gone With the Wind*, will be murdered by the Nazis on June 1, 1943. A commercial aircraft in which he is flying is shot down by a German Ju88. There are theories that the plane is targeted because the Germans believe Winston Churchill is on board.

updates. Days are spent meeting with his staff around the large mahogany table in the admiral's cabin. Otherwise, the prime minister sleeps late in his pink silk pajamas, starts each morning with a large thimble of Johnnie Walker Red drenched in soda, and dons his Royal Yacht Club uniform to bound up and down the lower decks, where he meets the crew, who are thrilled to have the great man in their midst. "He's rather like a boy that's been let out of school suddenly," one British officer notes. "He says it's the only holiday he's had since the war."

More than once, Churchill has been nicknamed the "British Empire" by English citizens for his physical and symbolic heft. The prime minister has held office since May 10, 1940, the precise date on which Nazi Germany invaded France, Belgium, and the Netherlands. Britain's allies fell within weeks, giving Germany almost total control of Europe.

The prime minister's main focus has been on fending off German invasion—and convincing the Americans to help him any way they can. The Battle of Britain in summer 1940 sees the Royal Air Force block the Luftwaffe's attempt to control the English skies. Had the RAF lost, there would have been no aerial defense against a Nazi landing force.*

The Royal Air Force does not lose.

On September 7, 1940, Germany began a nine-month bombing campaign of British cities. Britons call it the "Blitz," short for *blitzkrieg*. The relentless attacks come to an end in May 1941, but England is still exposed. One after another, her European allies have fallen. With nowhere else to turn, Churchill must convince America to strengthen their friendship.

Thus, his eagerness to be part of Operation Riviera, to finally talk to Roosevelt man-to-man. Fighting Nazi Germany in Europe will be the primary topic of conversation. But Churchill and Roosevelt will not ignore Japan's wanton aggression.

"The menace from the Far East was very much on our minds," Churchill will write. "For several months, the British and American governments had been acting towards Japan in close accord. At the end of

---

* The Battle of Britain is recounted in the author's *Taking London*.

July, Japan had completed their military occupation of Indochina. By this naked act of aggression, their forces were poised to strike at the British in Malaya, at the Americans in the Philippines, and at the Dutch in the East Indies."

In retrospect, many will wonder how they did not see this path reveal itself. Each step toward war will seem so clear, the false hope for peace could have been nothing but naivete. Japan's decades of military buildup, expansionist policies, and growing refusal to take directives from Washington and London make war preordained—though only in the rearview mirror.

Yet the "many" are not anonymous scholars. Nor armchair strategists. They are the men reclining in plush chairs in the darkened, smoky *Prince of Wales* wardroom. These are a prime minister, diplomats, admirals, and generals crossing the Atlantic to insert the words "that all nations of the world, for realistic as well as spiritual reasons, must come to the abandonment of the use of force" into the document known as the Atlantic Charter, which will emerge from Operation Riviera. This agreement will bond Great Britain and the United States for decades to come.

The joint declaration also mentions its lofty goals:

"Such a peace should enable all men to traverse the high seas and oceans without hindrance."

Japan has a much different plan.

***

"PIMPERNEL" SMITH ENDS with the hero escaping Nazi capture. Outside the wardroom, the Atlantic is a maelstrom. Midnight. Time for bed. *Wales* rises and falls as the men walk carefully down steel passageways. Churchill, a night owl, is not used to retiring so early. He settles in with a copy of *Captain Hornblower, R.N.*, an omnibus of some of C. S. Forester's novels about a daring naval officer on a secret mission. These delight the prime minister, with his fondness for intrigue. Participating in his own covert operation heightens the romance.

Hornblower's villain is Napoleon Bonaparte. Churchill's is Adolf Hitler—and, by extension, Hitler's allies. Those include Japan. Since September 27, 1940, the Tripartite Pact has unified Germany and Italy with the Japanese.

Churchill knows little about the newest member of Hitler's alliance. "I do not pretend to have studied Japan, ancient or modern," the prime minister admits. "Except that presented me by newspapers and a few books."

Britain and Japan were once chums. English seafarers have visited her islands since the seventeenth century. A friendship treaty in 1854. Japan becomes a global force as it emerges from the shogunate Tokugawa period and westernizes in the Meiji period, then signs a new alliance with Britain in 1902. The Japanese honor this pact in World War I, sending warships to escort British convoys in the Mediterranean and also attacking the German colony of Tsingtao on the Chinese coast. It is here the Japanese launch the first-ever naval air raid from a ship at sea, the seaplane carrier *Wakamiya*. Four aircraft of French design bomb enemy targets, leading to the German surrender.

Seaplane carriers and aircraft carriers operate differently. A seaplane carrier lowers pontoon-equipped aircraft into the water by use of a crane. These planes use the ocean for takeoff and landing. An aircraft carrier has a special flight deck for launching and retrieving planes. HMS *Prince of Wales*, for instance, has four Supermarine Walrus seaplanes (designed by R. J. Mitchell, best known for designing the Spitfire of Battle of Britain fame) but no flight deck, making her a seaplane carrier in addition to a battleship—though hardly an aircraft carrier.

Europe demobilizes when World War I ends. Not Japan. Britons desperately long for "the war to end all wars" to be just that. Yet theirs is a colonial nation, dependent upon its empire for whatever resources and wealth the mother country lacks. These possessions must be protected, despite disarmament. So in 1921 Britain decides to construct a new naval base in tactically vital Singapore. This is an island and a city at the tip of a spear-shaped spit of land five hundred miles long known as the Malay Peninsula, stretching north through jungles filled with pythons and tigers into the ancient kingdom of Siam, recently renamed Thailand.

Singapore's position at the Strait of Malacca blocks the direct route to the Pacific from Europe, Africa, and India.

Building the facility anywhere else is silly. Hong Kong is indefensible and Sydney thousands of miles south. "Singapore should be made into a place where the British fleet can concentrate for the defense of the Empire, of our trade interests in the East, our interests in India, our interests in Australia, our interests in New Zealand, our interests in the small possessions there and for that purpose it is absolutely necessary to undertake works at Singapore," British diplomat Arthur Balfour states.

That's not the only event taking place in 1921.

At a conference between the world's naval powers in Washington, DC, Japan is ordered to restrict the size of its fleet to sixty percent of America's and Britain's sea strength. Great Britain also uses this opportunity to end the 1902 friendship pact. Japan chafes at what they view as racist undertones yet signs the Washington Naval Treaty. The Big Five naval powers in attendance at the Washington Naval Conference are the United States, the United Kingdom, France, Japan, and Italy. Germany's *Reichsmarine* is not in attendance, its size severely limited by provisions of the Versailles Treaty after World War I.

Then Japan finds a loophole.

New battleships are forbidden, *but* there are no restrictions on aircraft carriers. Japan takes advantage of that oversight, launching *Hōshō* in November 1921. Soon after, they add flight decks to the battle cruisers *Akagi* and *Kaga*. Both will fight at Midway.

The Washington Naval Treaty—finally signed in 1922—also forbids the construction or expansion of naval bases in the Pacific.

In yet another 1921 occurrence, also in America, General Billy Mitchell tests a personal theory that aircraft can sink a warship on the open ocean. He experiments by sending a squadron of bombers to drop thousand-pound bombs on two empty ships. One of these is the *Ostfriesland*, once the pride of the German High Seas Fleet, ceded as war reparations at the end of World War I. She has four different metal skins on her decks, leading many to believe she is unsinkable.

Mitchell succeeds. Navy traditionalists are enraged. They claim the bombing does not count because it did not take place in combat conditions. Mitchell sees his success as a warning about the threat aircraft pose to ships at sea in wars to come. The navy sees the sinking as a stunt and a threat to their outmoded thinking—which they don't think outmoded in the slightest. Mitchell's critics try and fail to court-martial him for not remaining silent about his triumph.

Among Mitchell's acolytes is a young lieutenant commander named Chester Nimitz, currently stationed at the Naval War College in Rhode Island. There, war game after war game is so thoroughly focused on Japan that Nimitz will claim that nothing happening later in the Pacific surprises him. Because of Mitchell, Nimitz realizes that aircraft carriers are not defensive vessels meant to protect battleships, but an amazing offensive weapon. He even devises a new method of turning carriers into the wind that will change carrier warfare.

Japan is watching but remains skeptical. "Not everyone believed that air attack was the best method of effectively sinking a large battleship. In fact, such men were in a minority," admits the Japanese Official History.

Ironically, it is Great Britain who nudges Japan toward greater reliance on carriers. In *another* 1921 occurrence, Britain sends a delegation of advisers to assist in the building of aircraft carriers, hoping to secure lucrative contracts for British manufacturers. This Sempill Mission is an enormous success—for Japan.

Scottish nobleman and former Royal Air Force pilot William Forbes-Sempill advises the Japanese on the proper development of new aircraft and design problems associated with *Hōshō*. He trains their young pilots in many essential skills, including torpedoing a ship. Sempill becomes so enamored of Japan that long after his mission is over, he secretly shares British military secrets with Tokyo. This fact will become known to MI5, Britain's security service, but Sempill's father is an aide-de-camp to King George V and a member of the House of Lords. No action is taken.

A rift grows as Britain becomes more suspicious about Japan's intentions. The Japanese chafe at the base in Singapore, their indignation growing into rage during the fifteen long years the British take to construct it. In 1934, Japan leaves the Washington Naval Treaty. No longer restricted, the Japanese navy grows larger.

By 1936, as the navy yard is completed, the divide between the two nations is enormous. Lieutenant Commander Tota Ishimaru of the Imperial Japanese Navy even writes a book boldly titled *Japan Must Fight Britain*. Eleven thousand translated copies are sold in England. "The author discusses the inevitable war between the two powers . . . a comparison from which Britain emerges as definitely the weaker. . . . He claims that the Singapore base is an insult to Japan," his publisher writes in its description of the book. "War is inevitable, and the result will be that the British Empire will be broken up forever." *Prince of Wales* and *King George V* are laid down shortly after *Japan Must Fight Britain*'s publication.

Throughout the 1930s, Winston Churchill is a very public voice for armament. He predicts to the British that there will be another great war, a notion so absurd to peace-loving England that he is publicly mocked. Winston's warnings about another global conflict are thought to be the mutterings of a warmonger. The rise of Adolf Hitler and Japan's invasion of China prove him all too correct.

Britain passes a Treachery Act on May 23, 1940. Due to his high-level personal connections, William Forbes-Sempill is allowed to keep his job at the Admiralty rather than endure a stay in His Majesty's Prison at Wandsworth, followed by hanging from the neck until dead—which happens to a spy named George Johnson Armstrong on July 9, 1941.

In August 1941, as Prime Minister Churchill speeds toward Newfoundland aboard *Prince of Wales*, it does not matter whether or not Japanese aircraft can sink a British battleship.

There are none to sink.

There is not a single British capital vessel in the Far East—"capital" being the nomenclature for a battleship or aircraft carrier. None. "We have today no forces in the Far East that could deal with the situation should it develop," Churchill has admitted to Franklin Roosevelt.

Belatedly, Admiralty plans to remedy this lack of an "Eastern Fleet" are slowly taking shape.

Which will spell trouble for *Prince of Wales*.

***

NINE A.M. SATURDAY, August 9, 1941. Winston Churchill stands on deck, hands on the railing. *Wales* glides into Placentia Bay. Gray morning. Patches of fog. Cold enough to wear a thick coat. White noise of waves crashing on a distant beach. American military aircraft drone overhead just in case. Unbeknownst to Winston Churchill, Riviera is no longer a secret. William Forbes-Sempill is still in the business of selling secrets to Japan. He is already communicating with the Japanese about the sudden disappearance of the prime minister and his top brass from London.

The press has also taken note of President Roosevelt's disappearance from Washington. The Americans have been here two days. Churchill salutes a slow parade of U.S. warships. USS *Tuscaloosa*—a cruiser—and the destroyers *McDougal, Madison, Moffett, Sampson*, and *Winslow* escort USS *Augusta* into the deep, protected inlet. Their hulls are virgin gray, never fired upon in battle. Likewise, fresh-faced American sailors lack the war-weary demeanor of their British counterparts.

On the quarterdeck behind Churchill, the Royal Marines band strikes up "The Star-Spangled Banner." The Americans respond with "God Save the King," both anthems wafting across the calm Canadian waters in a show of solidarity.

Churchill grins. There he is. Finally, the prime minister sees FDR in person for the first time since their London meeting in 1918.

"Upon her deck, surrounded by naval and military officers," H. V. Morton writes of the USS *Augusta* and its own precious cargo, "was the tall figure of the President of the United States."

AUGUSTA

USS *Augusta* is a most special ship.

President Franklin Roosevelt is another in a long line of esteemed passengers to travel on board what the U.S. Navy labels "Cruiser, Armored-31." She is as long as two football fields and a slim sixty-six feet at the beam. She can go ten thousand nautical miles on a tank of diesel, allowing her to sail from New York to Tokyo without refueling, if need be. She has many big guns capable of inflicting enormous emotional and physical damage and can race across the sea at a swift thirty-two knots. The trade-off for this speed is that *Augusta* has very little armor, her deck plate being just two inches thick. Her belt armor—the protective layer on the side of the hull extending from the main deck down below the waterline that protects her from torpedoes—is a little more than three. Sherman tanks, by comparison, have seven inches of steel in places.

Churchill and *Wales* approach. President Roosevelt stands beneath an awning next to his son. Gray suit. Homburg hat. Elliott Roosevelt, an army air corps officer stationed in nearby Gander, stands at attention in all-cotton pinks and greens. The president's son is thirty. Their affection for one another is genuine; Franklin specifically requested that Elliott join him for this conference. But standing side by side is also practical: President Roosevelt wears thick steel braces on his legs beneath baggy suit pants. He cannot stand without them. Being upright is easier with someone to lean on.

Franklin Roosevelt Jr., Winston Churchill, Franklin Roosevelt,
and Elliot Roosevelt aboard the USS *Augusta* off Newfoundland

Public domain

Elliott Roosevelt will not make another appearance in our story. FDR's third-born child will rise to the rank of general before the war is over; afterward, he will become embroiled in a financial scandal with reclusive billionaire Howard Hughes. He will marry five times and live until age eighty in the calm awareness that he is his mother's favorite child. Elliott will return the favor by writing a series of murder mystery novels featuring the First Lady as an ingenious detective.

Ensign Franklin Roosevelt Jr. is finished with this tale without even making an appearance. Young Franklin is also on board *Augusta* at his father's request. The naval officer will accompany Winston Churchill on the return voyage aboard *Prince of Wales*, a journey that plays a small but pivotal role in this narrative. The ensign is twenty-six and married to a du Pont heiress, the first of his own five wives. He will serve in Congress, hold a Cabinet post in the Kennedy Administration, and die of lung cancer seventy-four years to the day after he was born.

Admiral of the Fleet Sir Dudley Pound will make one more brief, yet also pivotal appearance in this tale. Just a mention, though quite powerful. He will not survive the war. Pound's bad hip will grow worse, making it impossible for him to sleep at night, then causing him to doze off during important daytime meetings. He will suffer a stroke after his wife dies in 1943, then resign his command when his brain tumor grows. Pound dies on October 21, 1943, a date known throughout England as Trafalgar Day. His funeral service will take place at Westminster Abbey; then the admiral will be cremated and his ashes placed in a small casket. Steel bands forged on board the HMS *Glasgow* will bond his remains to a second casket containing the ashes of his wife; then the caskets will be dropped into the Solent from the decks of *Glasgow* on October 27 as the ship's company stand in formation and bow their heads.

Since boarding *Wales* in Scapa Flow, Harry Hopkins has been taking Winston Churchill's money in late-night backgammon games. We won't be seeing any more of the mysterious world traveler. Hopkins and his adventures are worth a book all by themselves. He will marry a third time in 1942. The wedding will take place in the Yellow Oval. It takes more than a year, but his new bride convinces Hopkins to move out of the White House, despite FDR's objections. The adviser dies in 1946 of complications from stomach cancer treatment. Harry Hopkins is fifty-five. His body is cremated.

President Roosevelt will soon replace Prime Minister Churchill as the world leader most pivotal to this saga, just as *Prince of Wales* will make way for *Yorktown*, *Enterprise*, and *Hornet* to tell their own tales at Midway.

For the purposes of our story, this means the turn of a page. To Great Britain, it is the end of an empire.

FDR and the *Yorktown*-class carriers will all get their share of words before "The End" is typed. USS *Augusta* will not. She leaves us after one more chapter. So it seems appropriate to take a moment to talk about this amazing ship that plays a role in so many outstanding events during the thirty-one years between the time she is laid down in Newport News and the sad morning in 1959 when she is sold for scrap to a Florida businessman—a demise that seems almost tawdry for this naval Zelig.

Augusta is a heavy cruiser, the last of the *Northampton*-class warships built in the 1920s. Captain Pug Henry commands one in Herman Wouk's *War and Remembrance*. There have been six U.S. ships christened *Augusta*, some for the city in Georgia and others for the capital of Maine. CA-31, fourth in the lineage, is named for the former.

Augusta has been through the Panama Canal more times than her sailors can remember, though the navy is always keeping count. Her reach is global, a vessel that has journeyed many times across the great oceans. She has spent years in the Pacific, even sailing into Japanese ports as tension between the United States and Japan rises. Captain Chester Nimitz is in command during the 1933 Far East deployment. We will hear more from him soon.

General George S. Patton will cross the Atlantic to invade North Africa aboard *Augusta* in 1942. He keeps in shape for battle by running in place and performing calisthenics in his sea cabin.

She will fight in the D-Day landings in 1944, carrying U.S. First Army Commander General Omar Bradley and his staff to observe the Normandy invasion, then firing fifty-one artillery rounds on Omaha Beach beginning at six eighteen a.m. The first Allied soldiers splash ashore moments later.

King George VI pays a visit to *Augusta* in 1945 when she is anchored in Plymouth, England. The sovereign meets with President Harry Truman in the same quarters enjoyed in Newfoundland by Franklin Roosevelt. Truman is on his way home from the Potsdam Conference in Germany. While crossing the Atlantic, the president will film a message to America: A nuclear bomb has been dropped on Japan.

For all that—presidents and kings and prime ministers and famous officers who enjoy a journey aboard USS *Augusta*—it is easy for one very important individual to be overlooked. Few remember he even stepped on board.

The young officer is a cryptologist who enters the U.S. Navy at the age of seventeen, zooming up through the ranks to earn his commission before turning twenty. Good at crossword puzzles. Notices patterns. Prescient enough to become fluent in Japanese long before the winds of war. The young officer is thirty-three years old as he spends a month on board *Augusta* in 1933, teaching the art of codebreaking during an exercise known as Fleet Problem XIV. This theoretical scenario wonders what would happen if Japanese aircraft carriers ever attacked the United States.

His name is Joe Rochefort. He plays an important part in the Midway story.

Some would say the *most* important.

That is to come.

FRANKLIN ROOSEVELT

Three days since USS *Augusta* and HMS *Prince of Wales* dropped anchor in Newfoundland.

Monday morning. *Prince of Wales* bobs lazily on calm waters, awash in bright sunlight. Winston Churchill is burly but surprisingly athletic. He has no trouble balancing as he steps down a ladder to board the motor launch. Morning meeting aboard *Augusta*. Resplendent in blue uniform. The bay a flurry of constant motion. Small boats shuttle diplomats and advisers from one gray ship to the other. Junior officers and secretaries scurry to meetings, arms laden with files and confidential papers as they travel ship to ship, navigating narrow gangplanks.

Yesterday was stirring, a church service on board *Wales*. All hands in attendance. Churchill chose the hymns. Thousands of voices lifted in song carrying across the bay. Captain Leach sits with President Roosevelt and Prime Minister Churchill, FDR most curious about *Wales'* fight with *Bismarck*. Several American officers remain behind to enjoy the captain's hospitality—no alcohol is allowed on American vessels but is served on British ships.

Now Monday. Operation Riviera is no longer about stealthy adventure on the high seas. Long meetings, longer dinners, and endless negotiations now define this "Atlantic Conference." The men at the highest level call it diplomacy. Those doing the filing and typing, for whom a dinner jacket is never required, say bureaucracy.

Like Churchill on *Wales*, Franklin Roosevelt occupies *Augusta*'s cavernous admiral's quarters. FDR forces his wheelchair closer to the suite's dining room table. Churchill takes a seat. Roosevelt wears a gray suit but no tie. Joining president and prime minister in this morning's meeting are the gaunt American adviser Harry Hopkins, patrician U.S. Undersecretary of State Sumner Welles, and British career diplomat Sir Alexander Cadogan. A breeze fragrant with pine and salt air blows in through the portholes.

Welles takes the minutes, as usual, later to draw up a memorandum recording the prelunch meeting. British spy William Forbes-Sempill, still employed at his high-ranking post at the Admiralty in London, is poised to steal a copy of the transcript and pass it along to his Asian masters. Within days, the Japanese will know every word spoken in this ship's cabin.

And also be delighted to learn their nation is the primary topic of today's conversation.

After preliminary discussions about events in Portugal and the Canary Islands, the topic turns to potential war in Asia. Harry Hopkins has already made it clear to Churchill that the United States will not enter any conflict, even if Japan strikes British and Dutch holdings in the Pacific. The prime minister prefers not to believe this is true.

"I would like to discuss the situation in the Far East," begins Churchill. He has spent considerable time on the Atlantic crossing crafting a document stating that the United States will take military action if British or Dutch territories are attacked. As a show of support, Britain and the Netherlands have also frozen Japanese assets.

"He had with him a copy of a draft memorandum, of which he had already given the President a copy and which suggested that the United States, British and Dutch Governments simultaneously warn Japan that further military expansion by Japan in the South Pacific would lead to the taking of counter measures," writes Welles.

Roosevelt disagrees. He seeks peace at all costs. America is slowly coming around to the idea of war, with opinion polls showing fifty-one percent of Americans now believe armed conflict is the only way to stop Japan. But that war should not come unless America is attacked. Roosevelt will not be lured into an agreement tethering the United States with two weak colonial powers. There are now signs Japan is poised to move from Indochina into neighboring Thailand, putting them one step closer to attacking British Malaya.

The president pushes a batch of documents across the table. Dated August 6, less than a week ago. Ambassador Nomura's decision not to share Roosevelt's July 24 proposal with Tokyo turned out badly for the former admiral. The Japanese government is blindsided when the president freezes their assets. The press in Japan is increasingly hostile to the United States. Now Nomura is attempting to fix that mistake.

In a profoundly arrogant set of demands, Japan promises to halt further advances in Asia, but only when the United States rescinds economic sanctions. They request the United States remove its military from the Philippines, Guam, and Wake Island. It is also desired that the United States prod the Netherlands into providing Japan with oil. Finally, the Japanese wish the United States to broker peace in China, but they make no promises of removing their military from that nation.

"There is a reasonable chance," a hopeful Churchill responds, "that a war in the Pacific might be averted."

The words are a joke. Everyone around the table agrees. Japan is intent on getting its way. The mood grows awkward as that reality sinks in.

Roosevelt tells the room he will meet with Ambassador Nomura upon returning to Washington. He states the words calmly. There will be no backing down. Economic sanctions are paramount.

As for the prime minister's request for an alliance, the president reassures Churchill that England is not alone anywhere in the world.

"The United States will wage war but not declare it," states Roosevelt.

***

YET EVEN AS hope for peace is discussed in Newfoundland, unforeseen events in Washington are already pushing Japan closer to war.

In an unusual coincidence, the two uppermost members of Roosevelt's State Department have joined him in leaving the capital. This makes possible one of history's great misunderstandings, the literal equivalent of putting out a fire with gasoline.

Sumner Welles is traveling with the president on board *Augusta*. Welles knows precisely what FDR intended when he signed the executive order freezing Japanese assets.

Welles' interdepartmental rival, longtime Secretary of State Cordell Hull, suffers from an affliction of the lungs known as sarcoidosis. Hull, a man of violent temper, has been FDR's secretary of state for eight years. He also knows the president's mind about relations with Japan. However, the sixty-nine-year-old Tennessee native is vacationing at the Greenbrier in White Sulphur Springs, West Virginia, where the waters are known to have healing qualities.

This leaves Dean Acheson, assistant secretary of state for economic affairs, to run the shop. The forty-eight-year-old attorney has been on the job only since February. Brash, with a cartoon villain's dark upturned mustache and thick untrimmed eyebrows, Acheson is known to Winston Churchill as the bureaucrat responsible for implementing the Lend-Lease Act. This transfer of American goods to Britain and the Soviet Union has been instrumental in rearming both nations. Now Acheson comes up with his own unique translation of FDR's recent executive action: Freeze means freeze.

Acheson refuses to release so much as a dollar to Japan. Not a single drop of oil can be purchased. Acheson is confident Roosevelt will not reverse the policy on his return, knowing it will make the president look weak.

In fact, even in Newfoundland, FDR already approves of Acheson's decision. The president keeps in touch with the White House via ship's radio. He's a micromanager, with a finger in every pot. The president knows full well what Secretary Acheson is up to. He just doesn't want to look like the villain.

There will be no backing down.

Despite the faint hopes for peace being mouthed on board *Augusta*, Acheson's decision puts Japan in a corner. As Winston Churchill will write: "Japan was deprived at a stroke of their oil supplies."

War is all but ensured. *"Facilus descensus Averno est,"* moans Ambassador Joseph Clark Grew in Tokyo when he gets the news, foreseeing what is to come: *The descent into hell is easy.*

Grew is a career diplomat. Tenth year in Tokyo. So well-known for his skills that *Life* magazine published a lengthy feature story about him last year. The sixty-one-year-old attended Groton and Harvard with FDR. Powerfully built and six feet tall, he wears his salt-and-pepper hair combed straight back and his mustache always neatly trimmed. In his forty-year career, Grew has served in Cairo, Mexico City, St. Petersburg, Vienna, Berlin, and Turkey. But Japan has been his most famous and daunting posting. The ambassador's determination to maintain peace defines his every working day.

In the experienced estimation of Joseph Grew, Secretary Acheson's hard-line stance is a horrendous setback, the very opposite of diplomacy.

Acheson has no fear his actions will result in war. Believes the acting secretary of state: "No rational Japanese could believe that an attack on us could result in anything but disaster for his country."

***

OPERATION RIVIERA ENDS Tuesday, August 12. Roosevelt and Churchill sail home in the same muscular warships on which they arrived. The two leaders have cemented a friendship but solved few problems. The Japan situation is at an impasse. The Atlantic Charter, issued on August 14, is the conference's highest achievement, setting forth eight lofty goals about what the world will look like *after* the war, as if the battles were already fought and won. But the document is never formally published, a wish but not a manifesto.*

---

* Churchill outlines the document in his memoirs. To paraphrase, these are the eight tenets of the Atlantic Charter: 1) Neither nation will seek to add territory through the war; 2) territorial changes must be agreed upon by its citizens; 3) all people have the right to choose their form of government; 4) free trade; 5) economic advancement for all;

President Roosevelt arrives back in the White House on August 17. A Sunday but FDR schedules a full day of meetings. Among these is a late-afternoon meeting in the Oval Study with a rejuvenated Secretary of State Cordell Hull. This takes place from four fifteen to five thirty. The two are joined at four thirty-seven by Japanese Ambassador Nomura, who remains until five fifteen.

FDR does the talking. Secretary Hull records the exchange. "The Ambassador of Japan called to see the President at the latter's request. Following some few exchanges of preliminary remarks, the President then became serious and proceeded to refer to the strained relations between our two countries."

Hull continues: "[Roosevelt] concluded by saying that our attitude of opposition to Japan's course has been made well known, and that the next move is now up to Japan. The President inquired of the Ambassador if he had anything in mind to say in connection with the situation.

"Thereupon the Ambassador drew out of his pocket an instruction which he said was from his Government, in which the Japanese Government set forth some generalities and asserted very earnestly that it desired to see peaceful relations preserved between our two countries."

---

6) peace; 7) freedom to travel without hindrance; 8) abandonment of the use of force by all nations.

CHURCHILL

The adventure continues in most glorious fashion for Winston Churchill. For the rest of his life, all twenty-three and a half years, he will give thanks to Captain John Leach for the moment about to occur.

Prince of Wales throws up a ferocious bow wave as she runs fast through the North Atlantic. Just off Iceland, Captain Leach catches up with a convoy numbering seventy-two merchant ships carrying supplies to beleaguered England. The pack travels together for protection from U-boats. The prime minister stands on the bridge to take in the spectacle. He commands the view with Leach as *Wales* cuts right into the heart of the massive group, not slowing down to remain with them, but overtaking the lot until she is completely surrounded.

A delighted Winston Churchill moves out into the open air, where he can easily be seen. Cold North Atlantic wind buffets his chubby pink face. Thick blue uniform coat. Train conductor hat. Cigar clenched between his teeth as he holds up his famous two-fingered "V for victory" salute. Ship's horns blow in eager recognition. Sailors on every ship are astounded at seeing not just that monumental HMS *Prince of Wales* so far out in the open ocean, but also the British Empire himself in all his glory.

"I ran out and saw an amazing sight," writes H. V. Morton. "We were racing through the middle of the convoy. There were tramps, tankers, liners, and whalers, salty old tubs, and cargo boats of every age, type, and size on each side of us, the nearest only two hundred yards away, the crews clustered on decks and fo'c's'les, waving their caps and cheering like mad into the wind."*

Wales has been through so much in her short months at sea. Much worse to come. But these moments on the bone-cold gray-green waters where the ship once dueled with *Bismarck* are her company's first chance to celebrate. Jonah is temporarily forgotten as sailors come up on deck to take in the spectacle. This is no longer a convoy; it's an armada presided over by their nation's beaming prime minister.

Captain Leach skillfully threads *Wales* to the front. Nothing but open seas between here and Scapa Flow. Completely unafraid of U-boat attack. But the captain does not reduce speed to remain with those many merchantmen. Nor does he speed into the distance.

Instead, to the absolute joy of Prime Minister Winston Churchill, who is now behaving like a man who's never had so much fun in his life, Captain Leach gives the order to turn *Wales* back around in a long circle so that they might do it all over again.

The prime minister is delighted. Standing on the bridge of the omnipotent *Wales*, he believes nothing in the world is a better expression of British might in these troubled times than this unsinkable battleship.

What better weapon to send to Singapore?

"As your naval people have already been informed," the prime minister writes to President Roosevelt, "we are sending that big ship you inspected into the Indian Ocean as part of a squadron we are forming there. This ought to serve as a deterrent to Japan.

"There is nothing like having something that can catch and kill anything."

---

* In nautical terms, the forecastle (abbreviated: fo'c's'le) is the portion of the upper deck nearest the bow.

***

WITH THOSE WORDS, we leave Winston Churchill, the fate of Singapore, *Prince of Wales*, that lovely man named Captain John Leach, and Admiral Tom Thumb. For now. We'll be back.

First, let's talk about a most unusual island—one in twenty-five thousand, as they say.

EPISODE THREE

———

THE MIDWAY SAGA

BIRD POOP

1802

One in twenty-five thousand.

That's Midway.

But not *just* one in twenty-five thousand. A most special one in twenty-five thousand.

That's how many islands dot the Pacific. No body of water has more. One for every 2,552 of the ocean's 63.8 million square miles. Some are lush and tropical, a mai tai at sunset and family vacations that always feel a week too short. Others barren and windswept, baked in summer and racked by violent winter storms. Then there are the downright hostile, offering no food, shelter, or fresh water to a shipwrecked sailor, just a lonely place to die.

Few have a history as strange and dark as Midway Atoll. An atoll is a ring-shaped coral reef encircling a lagoon and island. All atolls have an island but not all islands are atolls. There are approximately 425 atolls in the world, almost all in the Pacific Ocean.

None of the others have been the object of such unconventional desire. Starting with bird poop on an island far, far away.

November 1802. Prussian-born botanist Alexander von Humboldt travels through South America as part of a five-year exploration. It is a year of discovery, enlightenment, and change. England is the new home to the Rosetta Stone. German composer Ludwig van Beethoven publishes

Piano Sonata No. 14, better known as the "Moonlight Sonata." Napoleon Bonaparte continues his rise to ultimate power in France. President Thomas Jefferson is soon to double the nation's size through the Louisiana Purchase from Napoleon and France. America's United States Military Academy opens its doors.

Because our story is a work of naval history, it must be noted that the United States Naval Academy does not open until October 10, 1845.

In Japan, a feudal samurai culture remains in power, as it has for centuries. The current Tokugawa shogunate military government enacts a harsh code of medieval discipline to maintain power. Beheading, crucifixion, and boiling alive are common punishments. An ancient form of suicide by self-disembowelment known as seppuku is becoming a cultural institution. Fishermen from this island nation rarely venture beyond sight of land as they cast their nets.

Humboldt has a naivete about the world's complexities, with his life focused so completely on science that little else matters to him. Thirty-three, polymath, extremely chatty. He sleeps just four hours a night. Hopes to witness Mercury traveling across the face of the sun from Callao, Peru. Humboldt sets up his three-foot telescope in the Real Felipe Fortress built thirty years earlier to protect this bustling port from pirates. The transit of Mercury does not take place for a few days. The apple-cheeked Humboldt has time to kill. He undertakes a lazy walk along the docks.

The creak of wooden-hulled ships bobbing gently. Tall masts. Sun-bleached sails. Warm equatorial winds. Smell of salt air and boiling tar. Sailors and languages from around the world.

All familiar smells and sounds to this traveler.

An unusual new odor wafts his way. Humboldt's nose twitches. The stench is horrible. Ammonia-ish. Sulfur-ish. Concentrated and powerful. The curious botanist is not repelled in the slightest. He eagerly investigates.

Friedrich Wilhelm Heinrich Alexander von Humboldt does not appear to be a rugged adventurer. Pale skin. Foppish. His sainted mother died six years ago, leaving Humboldt the very large sum of money that now makes it possible for him to travel the world without a schedule, indulging in a passion for plants and animals that offers no financial recompense at all. A man of impeccable manners and grooming. Believes all nature is interconnected. This includes human emotions and points of view. It is an ideology that will make Humboldt popular with European Romantics, who believe nature can be experienced only through a person's inner feelings.

The description may make Humboldt sound soft or even spoiled. He is both. Yet few men have suffered as horribly and intentionally for science.

Near-fatal electric eel shocks in the Venezuelan jungle. Legs infected by chigger bites. Gums bleeding from altitude sickness and gloveless hands shredded on sharp rocks while attempting to climb a peak known as Chimborazo, a volcano and the highest summit in South America. Humboldt believes it to be the highest mountain on earth. Humboldt's porters refuse to go any higher when the expedition reaches fifteen thousand feet. He pushes on, turning back a thousand feet from the summit, his forward path blocked by an impassable chasm, or the botanist might have made it to the top. It is thought Humboldt reached an altitude approaching twenty thousand feet, a record at the time. No man in recorded history has trekked closer to the sun—a fact in which he takes great pride.

Now Humboldt is in fragrant Callao, just west of Lima. Balmy Pacific winds, soothing autumn air. He finds the source of the toxic smell, a vessel where a yellow substance is being unloaded.

Humboldt speaks in Spanish to the locals, who tell him this acrid cargo is none other than bird droppings from the Chincha Islands, just thirteen miles off the coast of Peru. The Quechua people learned over time to paddle the strait, mine this commodity, and spread it on their crops. They call it *wanu*. The Spanish say "guano," the same name they use for the excrement of bats. The bats' diet of fruit and bugs instead of fish produces guano that has a nutrient level far lower than that of the seabirds'; as a result, it does not make for good fertilizer. Local farmers actually claim there is no better fertilizer than *wanu*. These are no ordinary bird droppings, the botanist is assured.

Humboldt asks if he might chip off a sample for himself.

And so, for a fee, he does.

The three Chincha Islands are extremely small, less than a mile long and a half mile wide. Surrounded by a current that will intrigue Humboldt so much that he lowers his scientific instruments into the ocean to make a study. The water is cold, has low salinity, flows north. Rich in plankton and vast sardine-like schools of fish. The blue-footed boobies, yellow-billed cormorants, and white-striped pelicans living on the Chinchas gorge themselves in these unique waters. Because there are no predators on the islands, the seabirds cover the barren ground like an endless carpet of multicolored feathers. Days are spent fishing, eating, reproducing, and relieving themselves, an act that appears to occur quite frequently.

The droppings long ago grew into mounds, rising over the decades and then centuries to become actual mountains of guano—piles of nitrogen, phosphorus, and potassium soaring two hundred feet into the blue Pacific sky. Excrement pillars so high these peaks are a natural part of the landscape soaring above the otherwise flat terrain. There is little rain to wash away the rich nitrogen that turns barren soil into rich farmland.

Humboldt begins his voyage home in 1804, stopping in America to spend time with fellow botanist Thomas Jefferson. The young German then sails to Europe, where he unloads crates of pinned butterflies, preserved lizards, and pressed leaves. But Humboldt never forgets Callao and his odious yellow sample from that ammonia-smelling ship's hold.

These are no ordinary bird droppings, he has been assured.

Analysis by a Prussian chemist proves the Peruvians correct.

It is a cruel fact of farming that harvesting a crop robs soil of the nutrients required to grow another. Nitrogen in particular. Thus, the need for a method of replenishment. Possessing this element at a high level never seen before, bird poop from the Chinchas, it is immediately clear, is a miracle solution—a "miracle grow," if you will.

Word gets around. Travels across Europe. Then to the United States. Conservative, isolationist Japan, a land run by shogun warlords and dotted with rice paddies, could not care less.

Demand grows. Chinese laborers are imported to "mine" guano in the Chinchas, chipping away at the enormous peaks with pickaxes and shovels, working seventeen hours a day in slavelike conditions. Many die, the fine dust fatal over time as respiratory infections set in.

The Peruvian government signs an exclusive deal with European merchants to sell the bird dung. Gibbs and Sons, a London company, is on the receiving end of a humorous insult about their amazing source of wealth: "The house of Gibbs made their dibs selling the turds of foreign birds." Farmers in England, France, Germany, and the United States become dependent upon Peru and its potent fertilizer. It's worth noting that Gibbs and Sons turned their guano empire into one of the most prestigious merchant banks in London.

American farmers beseech their politicians for *more* nitrogen-rich seabird poop. Cotton growers in the South long to increase productivity after years of crop after crop stripping the soil. Tobacco farmers in Virginia and the Carolinas petition their congressmen. Chincha bird droppings also make for amazing gunpowder, only increasing their cachet—and the demand for them.

"Guano mania" sweeps the United States. Throughout the 1840s and 1850s, tens of thousands of tons are imported each and every year. Prices skyrocket. American ships returning from the California gold fields stop in Callao to fill their empty holds with *wanu*.

In a first in the history of the American experience, President Millard Fillmore's 1850 Annual Message to Congress speaks openly about the excrement of boobies and pelicans: "Peruvian guano has become so desirable an article to the agricultural interest of the United States that it is the duty of the government to employ all the means properly in its power for the purpose of causing that article to be imported into the country at a reasonable price."*

Inevitably, American farmers realize there must be islands closer to home saturated with bird droppings. In 1854, a small group of these men invade Aves, in the Caribbean. "Bird Island" is a small rock in the vast sea, just a quarter mile long and fifty yards wide. Its only inhabitants are red-footed boobies, brown boobies, and gular-throated frigate birds living in forty-foot-tall mangrove trees. The verdant island is so replete with avian waste that passengers on boats anchored two hundred yards offshore smell the aroma as if they are ankle-deep in happy, warm piles of bird shit.

There is a problem of international proportions: The Dutch have already claimed Aves as their own. They take offense. A warship shoos away the offenders. The Americans are undeterred. Upon returning home, they petition Congress for protection. On August 18, 1856, Congress passes the Guano Islands Act. This landmark legislation allows United States citizens to take possession of unclaimed islands containing guano deposits. To avoid the appearance of colonialism and future liability, the word "appertaining" is used to describe this transaction. These islands are not considered new U.S. possessions or territories, but as temporarily belonging to the United States.

Borrowed.

Should supply of bird poop on the new island discovery run out, an abandonment clause lets the U.S. walk away, taking no responsibility for

---

* Fillmore was the thirteenth president of the United States. The 1850 Annual Message was delivered on December 2. This fulfills the Constitutional demand that a president "give to the Congress Information of the State of the Union." It was known formally as the Annual Message from 1790 to 1946. George Washington and John Adams delivered theirs in person, but Thomas Jefferson sent his in writing. A clerk then read the message to Congress. This tradition continued until Woodrow Wilson delivered his message in person in 1913. Informally, it was called the "state of the Union" message/address from 1942 to 1946. Harry Truman would make it official in 1947, renaming the Annual Message as the State of the Union Address.

whatever war or atrocity might come next. More than seventy islands in the Caribbean and the Pacific are hastily grabbed by bird-poop hunters.

Three years after passage of the Guano Islands Act, the man who started this madness dies in Berlin. May 6, 1859. Alexander von Humboldt is eighty-nine years old. A stroke and then decline. The rich waters off the Chincha Islands, where those many seabirds ate their fill, flow today in what is known as the Humboldt Current, which seems a little unfair, since it was discovered 250 years earlier by Jesuit missionary and naturalist José de Acosta.

Yet the current is just one of more than 1,600 geographical features, places, species, and institutions in the world named after the German explorer because of that lone expedition. More species are named after Humboldt than any other human being. He does not set foot outside Europe again. Humboldt never knows of a place called Midway, because that name is decades away from being applied to the atoll in the middle of nowhere.

Yet no man is more responsible for its discovery.

CAPTAIN BROOKS

1859

Midway is not done with Alexander von Humboldt even in death.

In Berlin, the botanist is honored by a stately funeral procession through the city's broad streets, his hearse pulled by six horses. At almost the same instant on the other side of the globe, a small wooden ship known as the *Gambia* sets forth from Hawaii on a three-month voyage of exploration. Some might call this coincidence. Others, fate. No matter. The universe ensures that as the destiny of one man ends, that of another begins.

The new man's name: N. C. Brooks. His mission: find guano.

May 1859. In Japan, a move from isolationism has begun. Responding to the arrival of American ships under Commodore Matthew Perry six years earlier, then a second incursion by the U.S. fleet in 1854, the Japanese begin to build their own blue-water sailing frigates, tall-masted vessels that replace the traditional low-sterned junks that so easily founder on heavy seas. The Japanese begin casting Western-style bronze cannon, replacing the wooden guns of the samurai. The nation even takes delivery of its first screw-driven steam warship, the *Kanrin Maru*, purchased from the Netherlands.

In Hawaii, the crew of the three-masted *Gambia* unfurls her sails, then aims west and north. The captain is N. C. Brooks. No photographs survive. We know he is a young man. First name and middle initial lost to the historical record. Picture an ambitious sea captain with a daring streak and fondness for the sensational, for he is about to sail into the unknown and return telling tales that some will long later consider quite tall. But treat him with the sympathy you might show a rambunctious friend who has suffered a great loss. His wife and daughter perish six years later when the steamship SS *Brother Jonathan* is lost at sea. Brooks is waiting for them in port when he gets the news. The captain will immediately sail to the watery grave in a fruitless rescue operation. The only sign of the lost ship will be a bucket rack bobbing on the water's surface.

That is all to come. For the moment young N. C. Brooks is lighthearted and eager, off to find the guano that will make his fortune. For good measure, the bark *Gambia* will hunt sharks and seals. Hawaiian natives are fond of the shark teeth and livers. The skin of seals contains fat that tastes like the sea; the Hawaiians prefer it to the more odorous fish oil. Brooks will boast of returning with 240 barrels of seal oil and 1,500 skins. Historical skeptics will call him a liar.

The last monk seal is thought to have been killed in 1824.

This is not so.

A quick historical detour: The Hawaiian monk seal is not extinct. Efforts to restore the species are ongoing. Midway Atoll is home to a small but thriving population. Brooks' claim to have killed so many is thought by some experts to be a fabrication, while others think he may have exterminated every single monk seal on Midway to reach the total. Brooks' personal journals, which might prove the veracity of his claims, are lost in the San Francisco fire of 1906.

Back to *Gambia* and the pivotal voyage of 1859.

Twelve hundred miles northwest of Honolulu, Brooks sails into a blue-green lagoon encircled by a coral reef. The color of the water is so vivid that it reflects off the low white clouds. Islands inside are barren and windblown. Fish and turtles in abundance are easily visible in the clear depths. Scaevola bushes carpet the sand, providing vegetation.

Thousands of nesting white albatross with black feet and wings waiting for their chicks to gain the strength to fly out to sea and hunt. Mysteriously, an abandoned raft shows signs of a previous inhabitant, but no human beings can be seen on the flat square mile of sand. An excited Captain Brooks drops anchor.

If the *Gambia* had arrived in November, the island would have been covered from one end to the other by even more of the enormous seabirds. Even in spring, the million-bird population seems too big to destroy, but in fact it is most fragile, for the birds are utterly without guile. A female builds a small nest in the sand, where exactly one egg is hatched each year, in exactly the same spot, in a habit known as "nest site fidelity." In October, a million birds return from the sea to lay their eggs. By November, the island is covered with breeding pairs. Otherwise, these broad-winged birds spend ninety percent of their lives at sea. The Laysan albatross travel an estimated fifty thousand miles a year through the air, over open ocean. Some birds can live to more than seventy years old if left undisturbed.

Wisdom, a Laysan albatross banded in 1956, was sighted at her nest site in March 2024. These birds do not lay eggs until they're at least five years old, which makes Wisdom at least seventy-three. This also makes Wisdom the world's oldest banded wild bird. She has hatched thirty-five eggs in her lifetime. Since 1936, some 250,000 albatross have been banded on Midway. It is estimated Wisdom has flown 3.5 million miles in her lifetime, the equivalent of seven round trips to the moon. Akeakamai, her longtime mate, ceased returning from the sea in 2021.

So it is, with that long lifespan, that a single Laysan albatross could have borne witness to the arrival of Captain Brooks in 1859 and almost lived long enough to endure the Battle of Midway in 1942.

Brooks beelines for bird nests. The albatross are the most dominant species. Yellow-headed gannets, scarlet-pouched frigate birds, black-capped terns, and red-billed bosun birds are also common. To his great relief, there is no shortage of guano, which officially allows the excited captain to claim the new discovery as "Brooks Island and Shoal." He posts a notice to that effect on a pole, to which he affixes the American flag.

Brooks staked his claim to a phenomenon millions of years in the making.

Centuries upon centuries upon centuries earlier, twelve thousand feet below the ocean surface, an enormous flow of hot molten lava spills from a seam in the earth's crust. Enough fire and brimstone to cover a swath of the ocean floor miles in every direction, then solidify and build on top of itself to form a pile of lava so many miles high, it actually pokes above the turquoise Pacific waves to form a high mountainous island. In time, the weight of all that solidified lava crushes back down into the earth. The mass sinks into the same crust from which it was born. The volcanic island is now all but underwater.

The Pacific continues the leveling. Constant high wind erodes the shore. One island becomes three as waves relentlessly pound and ultimately split the land.

Free-swimming coral larvae attach themselves to submerged rocks. They grow and expand into a reef. This living organism grows so large it forms a circle around the three islands. An atoll is born, one of the highest-latitude coral reef systems in the world. In time, it will grow wider than a football field. Spinner dolphins, sharks, green turtles, seals, algae, corals, worms, snails, and blue parrot fish fill the clear turquoise waters within. In time, Midway's lagoon will earn the designation "predator-dominated," though in ways scientists will not foresee.

The passage of time, the pounding swells, and the ebb and flow of tides grind coral, shells, rocks, and hard exoskeletons of dead marine organisms into the powder-fine substance known as sand. Wave after wave, the ocean vomits this grit up onto the dry volcanic islands. It dries. An extremely bright white layer covers every inch like a blinding reflection. Captain Brooks will name the three islands Sand, Eastern, and Spit when he finally arrives. But all that sand shifted by the constant wind fills the channel in between the islands, and sometimes turns those three islands

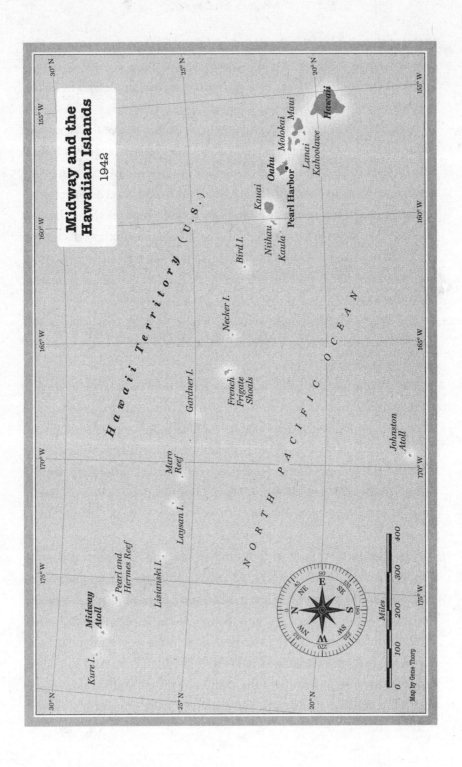

Midway and the Hawaiian Islands
1942

30° N

25° N

20° N

Hawaii Territory (U.S.)

NORTH PACIFIC OCEAN

Kure I.

Midway Atoll

Pearl and Hermes Reef

Lisianski I.

Laysan I.

Maro Reef

Gardner I.

French Frigate Shoals

Necker I.

Bird I.

Niihau

Kaula

Kauai

Oahu

Pearl Harbor

Molokai

Lanai

Maui

Kahoolawe

Hawaii

Johnston Atoll

Miles

0   100   200   300   400

Map by Gene Thorp

into two. Eastern is just over a mile long and the recipient of just enough sand to reach twelve feet above sea level. Spit Island is the smallest, an appendage off Eastern measuring just a few acres. Two-mile-long Sand Island truly lives up to its name, rising thirty-nine feet high.

This atoll forms the northeasternmost tip of a long spear that will become known as the Hawaiian Islands. The world well knows the verdant cluster farthest east: Hawaii, Maui, Lanai, Oahu, Kauai, and even barren little Niihau. These are the islands most often called "Paradise."

Yet more than three hundred miles west begin the islands that few realize are part of Hawaii's pearl necklace. Necker, French Frigate Shoals, Laysan, Lisianski, Pearl and Hermes Reef, Midway, and Kure are mostly forgotten, largely unpopulated, and unknown. No one calls them anything but "isolated." Yet the geographical relationship is real enough from a tactical point of view. Far as it might be from Oahu, Midway is even called the "Sentry for Hawaii" by Japanese war planners in 1942.

Long after their formation, centuries before N. C. Brooks, this long chain of islands still waits to be found. Birds land first. Some estimate fifteen million years ago. Finally, people, somewhere between AD 1000 and 1290, when the first Polynesian settlers arrive from the Marquesas Islands in double-hulled canoes known as *va'a*. These explorers traveled two thousand miles over open ocean, bringing plants and animals to the new home they hoped to find. They deposit these on Oahu and the other lush islands in the east. Ever restless to explore the seas, the Polynesians set off again in search of new islands. A month later, they find the ring of coral six miles wide and those islands in the middle. The Polynesians name this place *Kuaihelani*—"back bones of the heavens." Hardly impressed, the explorers duly chart this far-flung home of sand and albatrosses but deem it not worth inhabiting and return to Paradise, there to build a mighty civilization.

Gambia arrives half a millennia later, sailing through the opening in the reef. Captain Brooks takes time to map the small atoll, then sails off in search of more islands and bird poop and sharks in his small wooden bark.

Brooks leaves the same way as he arrived, carefully, over submerged coral that might shred his hull. The young captain thinks so little of his guano island that he never returns.

As if the discovery had never happened, the world forgets about Brooks Island and Shoal. Captain Brooks also calls it Middlebrook, but that name is lost on the trade winds.

For a while.

COAL

1867

Even before Captain N. C. Brooks sails into the lagoon at his eponymous island and shoal, *Gambia* is a relic. Wooden ships are being replaced by iron steamships driven by propellers, powered by coal shoveled into boilers by men with strong backs, their filthy hands and faces and sweat-soaked bare torsos covered in black dust.

The new vessels are faster and built with sturdier lines, but coal . . . Well, that's a most limiting factor. Whether lignite, bituminous, subbituminous, or anthracite, sooner or later the prehistoric energy source burns until it is gone.*

Crossing the Pacific under sail requires nothing more than the never-ending supply of wind for locomotion. Steamships need that powerful black rock like junkies will one day jones over that very different rock known as crack cocaine.

Coal is born in a swamp. Plants die and submerge. Heat, pressure, time—lots of time, more time than you can imagine, unless you can wrap your head around hundreds of millions of years—compress them into boggy peat, then solid coal. As Captain Brooks claims the island in his name, most American coal comes from West Virginia and Pennsylvania. Kentucky has coal mines. The arrival of the Union Pacific Railroad in

---

* Another name is metallurgical or "coking" coal, used in steel making.

1867 makes it possible to ship coal from new seams in Wyoming to San Francisco. From there, steamships loaded with tons of the powerful fuel set forth to cross the Pacific.

A steamship cannot wander aimlessly across the seas like *Gambia*, pushed hither and yon, sun-bleached sails billowing, with an explorer like N. C. Brooks chasing a dream. Though it does not often happen, these vessels, whether paddle wheeled or propeller driven, are without power once their finite supply of coal is used. They carry sails, just in case, but that only shows the weakness of steam. Thus, a transpacific crossing requires a chain of fueling stations. A steamship captain does not chase dreams or go with the flow. His voyage across the ocean means he can do nothing other than connect the dots from one supply depot to another. If there can be a moment in time when the age of discovery on the seas comes to an end once and for all, it is that instant the age of steam replaces the age of sail.

In 1867, having come across N. C. Brooks' detailed charts, the Pacific Mail Steamship Company sets out to see if the captain's forgotten atoll actually exists. The company's existence is reliant upon the coal it purchases and stores around the world to power its vessels. This location seems to make for a perfect coal dump.

In Japan, the capital is about to move from Kyoto to Edo—soon to be renamed Tokyo—as the shogun era ends and a new imperial regime directs the country. This Meiji period, named for the new emperor, is devoted to modernizing and westernizing after centuries of medieval rule. Japan is tired of being pushed around by the Western world.

In America, expansionist Secretary of State William Seward purchases Alaska from Russia for $7.2 million.*

And on Middlebrook Island, the schooner *Milton Badger* anchors in the small Brooks Island lagoon. Two small frame houses of California

---

* In modern currency, it's $129 million. Secretary of State William Seward, who led the 1867 purchase of Alaska from Russia in what became known as Seward's Folly, was the driving force behind the Guano Islands Act eleven years earlier while still a U.S. senator.

redwood are built for future PMSC employees. Six hundred tons of coal are dumped on the sand for future use.

One month later, the USS *Lackawanna* arrives and formally claims the island in the name of the United States. She is armed with two 11-inch (280mm) Dahlgren smoothbores, two 9-inch (230mm) Dahlgren smoothbores, one 150-pounder Parrott rifled gun, and one 50-pounder gun. These are worth mentioning because this slight armature is not the normal armory of a conquering force.

Nevertheless, Captain Brooks' previous claim is ignored—as is the eponymous name for his one and only discovery.

The United States annexes the atoll in 1867, whereupon some nameless bureaucrat with little imagination gives it a new designation: Unincorporated Territory of Midway Island. There is no record of why it was necessary to replace "Middlebrook" with "Midway," but the name sticks to this day.

Brooks will make a comeback, but for now he is banished from the geographical record. The harbor is named for former Secretary of the Navy Gideon Welles and the channel entrance for Secretary of State Seward. In 1869, Congress approves $50,000 for dredging operations.

A triumph for the Pacific Mail Steamship Company. They lobbied for this appropriation to establish Midway as a coaling station.

The side-wheel sloop of war USS *Saginaw*—a wooden vessel powered by sails and steam—soon arrives to blast a hole in the reef so that ships might enter the turquoise lagoon more easily. Six months later, Lieutenant Commander Montgomery Sicard of the *Saginaw* calls the work complete. She sails for San Francisco on October 28, 1870.

In fact, the dredging is *not* complete. The job is mismanaged as men fall to heat, sun, humidity, and Midway's treacherous currents. Or perhaps the Congressional allocation is just not enough. But after those six months, Captain Sicard has blown his budget. The channel is incapable of admitting large ships. Only small boats, in small weather, can get through.

However questionable his decision to leave might be, Captain Montgomery Sicard is a humanitarian. He knows this area's reputation for men and ships lost at sea. Rather than sail immediately east for California, he aims in the complete opposite direction for Kure, fifty miles northwest of Midway. Sicard is searching for stranded castaways. Thirty-four, a Civil War veteran, a former instructor at the U.S. Naval Academy, wedded to a descendant of a general who signed the Declaration of Independence.*

Sicard cautiously approaches the six-mile-wide reef under sail. The hour is past midnight. Moon just beginning to set. Winds howl, threatening to have their way with *Saginaw*'s sails.

In the growing darkness, Sicard's crew hear the thunder and hiss of waves crashing on the reef. They see little. *Saginaw* is closer to Kure than expected. At three fifteen a.m., just after the captain orders sails taken in, an unseen coral reef punches a hole in his hull. Sicard orders all hands to rescue as many provisions as possible before the ship breaks apart. No man is lost. All ninety-three crewmen make it to land by morning, there to await rescue. The complement has one dry match among them. They start a fire and watch it vigilantly to keep the flame alive. There is little food. The island shows scant sign of fresh water.†

Three weeks later, a twenty-two-foot ship's boat is fitted with a sail. Captain Sicard asks for volunteers to climb on board and seek rescue. Executive Officer John G. Talbot and four other men raise their hands, then courageously set out for Hawaii. Thirty-one days into the voyage and in sight of land, four men, weakened from sun and dehydration, drown when their boat capsizes in breakers off Kauai. Only Coxswain William Halford survives.

News travels quickly. Hawaiian King Kamehameha V is informed of the rescue. Within hours of the drownings, the U.S. consulate sends the

---

* The British confiscated the estate of General William Floyd of New York shortly after the general signed the Declaration. They used it as a cavalry outpost for seven years during the Revolutionary War. The home still stands and is open to the public.

† The wreckage of USS *Saginaw* was located by divers in 2003. Subsequent surveys resulted in the discovery of several artifacts, including several cannon and the ship's bell, which has been restored and is currently on display at Mokupāpapa Discovery Center in Hilo, Hawaii.

sailing coaster *Kona Packet* to the rescue. The king sends the steamship *Kilauea*. Both are dispatched to Kure. On January 4 and 5, 1871, almost ten weeks after being shipwrecked, Captain Sicard and *Saginaw*'s crew begin the journey home. Ironically, *Kilauea* is a steamship. She refuels at Midway during the return, dusting off sand deposited by years of wind and storm, then shoveling that left-behind 1867 coal into her boilers.

Meanwhile, the guano market is disappearing, if not altogether gone. The mountains of bird poop off Peru are just a memory. Chemists are making a fortune selling rock phosphate as a synthetic fertilizer that works just as well.

Midway is abandoned and forgotten yet again.

GENERAL SIEGEL

1886

General Siegel blunders into the lagoon in 1886. She is a thirty-nine-ton holdover from the days of sail, a two-masted schooner on a shark-fishing expedition struggling to find a port to weather a hard North Pacific blow. Midway's protected lagoon seems just the place. Few of the men get along. The troubled vessel sails through the opening and drops anchor just inside the reef.

The voyage goes from bad to horrible. "A tremendous sea burst through the passage until everything was white with spume and spindrift. The poor old schooner pitched, rolled, surged back and forth, and strained at her anchors, while seas swept her decks and made clean breaches over her," writes the *Siegel*'s first officer. "We hoped, of course, for the best; we were fated to have the worst. As the storm became more violent and the waves higher, both chains parted, and the *Siegel* drove upon the beach."

The sailors are shocked to come across the island's lone surviving shingled redwood house. They take refuge inside and live off albatross eggs and fish. The journey has been one skirmish after another. The small structure is just as crowded as a ship's hold—perhaps even more so. Petty grudges flared into arguments. The hierarchy of the sea breaks down. "In our idleness we couldn't keep from bickering. Our quarrels ended seriously and strangely. One of the crew, an old man, Peter Larkin, went fishing with dynamite," one survivor will remember.

"I suppose he forgot himself as he watched the movements of a shoal of fish or maybe the fuse was poor.

"Peter Larkin lost a hand," the survivor will add. He is a Dane, Adolph Jorgensen. "It was torn to shreds. Not pretty, that stump."

Larkin dies from his stupidity, the first man to be buried on Midway.

As one endless day of waiting piles on another, Jorgensen shows signs of losing his mental faculties.

"His age, I estimated, was twenty-seven; he was a giant of a man, more than six feet one inch in height; fair-haired and blue-eyed" is the way one shipmate will describe the tortured Jorgensen. "His shoulders were slightly stooped, no doubt from swinging a broadax in the shipyards of Hamburg, where he had been employed for some time. He was of a powerful build, muscular and rawboned, without an ounce of fat."

And resourceful.

Remembers Jorgensen himself: "We fitted out a boat for a voyage to the Marshall Islands, fifteen hundred miles distant. It had drifted on shore, probably from a wreck—the name *Dunnotter Castle* [sic] was on the stern. It was a strong clincher-built, double-ended boat, only slightly damaged."*

Jorgensen is a carpenter by trade. "I repaired the boat and strengthened it thoroughly to withstand heavy weather. In fact, I made it strong enough to sail around the world."

Fellow crew members work to repair a second small craft abandoned by a previous expedition. Edvert Olsen remembers a "Japanese sampan which had been left on the island by Captain Paul Bohm, when there fishing with the schooner 'Kaulilua.'"

---

* The small boat had drifted to Midway from Kure, fifty miles northwest. *Dunnottar Castle* wrecked on that reef on July 15, 1886, not far from sunken USS *Saginaw*. A small party used a ship's boat to sail for Hawaii in search of help. In the meantime, the *Dunnottar Castle*'s remaining twenty-one-man crew was rescued by a vessel heading to Chile. As they departed, three ship's dogs were left behind on Kure but later rescued. Coincidentally, the wreckage was discovered in 2006 by divers combing the reef for signs of *Saginaw*. "Clincher-built" is a method of shipbuilding that involves overlapping hull planks.

The sampan is fitted with ballast to keep her from capsizing. Short lengths of mast from *General Siegel* are affixed to her sides as outriders.

Olsen, a member of *Siegel*'s crew, will publish a magazine article in Honolulu in 1918 about what happens next. "While we were repairing the sampan, Captain Asberdine, who was a Russian Finn, Jorgensen the mate, and a sailor named Brown went over to Sand island in the 'Dunottar [*sic*] Castle's' boat, the captain being desirous of exploring the island before he left. The captain took with him a shotgun and ammunition and Jorgensen a Winchester rifle. In the afternoon Jorgensen came back to us alone."

No explanation is offered.

The bottom line is that men are dead. Terrified, the rest of the crew make plans to sink the boat from the *Dunnottar Castle* and sail away, leaving the Danish carpenter behind. The night before departure, "Jorgensen came to the door with his rifle in his hand. He was naked," Olsen writes. "While he spoke, he pointed the rifle at my breast ready to fire. I did not answer but grabbed the gun by the barrel and held the muzzle away from my body."

Jorgensen is desperate to get off the island. "My shipmates said that I could not go in the boat. I was too dangerous! This was staggering. I begged not to be left behind; I prayed to them;—they would not listen. I even offered to let them tie me hand and foot and keep me bound during the voyage," he will explain himself.

They refuse.

Setting off the next morning, six members of the crew set a course for the Marshall Islands. Jorgensen is left behind. Fourteen hundred miles in an open boat. Little fresh water. No shade. No privacy or personal space as they endure giant Pacific swells. Falling overboard could be fatal for swimmers and nonswimmers alike.

***

JORGENSEN REFURBISHES THE redwood house with bits of driftwood and pieces of *General Siegel*. Builds a veranda. Befriends a large rat that stowed away in the hold and swam to shore. To prepare for the cold winter,

Jorgensen walks the mile to the coal pile left behind by the *Saginaw* sixteen years ago, then drags chunks back to his castle.

The murderous carpenter waits. The seabirds return in November. He plunders nests and stores thousands of eggs for winter. His days are marked by the constant lapping of waves on the sand and the never-ending chatter of albatross. The bird noise is endless, yet comforting. Jorgensen will not be the last resident of Midway finding solace in seabirds.

Finally, a ship. After six months of waiting, Jorgensen leaps to his feet, whips off his shirt, and waves it madly to get the vessel's attention. Luckily, a lookout on the *Wandering Minstrel*, as she is known, spies him. The boat sails into the lagoon. Her troubled crew numbers anywhere from twenty-nine to thirty-seven. Records differ. She is on a four-month shark-hunting voyage to Hong Kong.

"While we were closing in on Midway and skirting the reef we saw a man on shore waving a rag (it proved to be his shirt) frantically, desperately, he desisted only when we hoisted our ensign in response. That was the first of a series of strange events," writes John Cameron of the *Minstrel*. The crusty veteran of the sea serves as the ship's first officer.

"I went ashore to call on and take food to the Robinson Crusoe of Midway, who had so desperately signaled to us. We found him in a small wooden building, the sole inhabitant of the island. To my astonishment he greeted me by name.

"'How do you do, Captain Cameron? My name is Jergensen [*sic*]. I met you in Honolulu.'

"I had no recollection of him," Cameron will write in his memoirs. "'How did you come here?'

"'On the schooner *General Siegel*,'" replies Jorgensen. "'We were bound from Honolulu on a sharking cruise. The vessel was wrecked, and my shipmates cleared out, leaving me behind.'"

Cameron is immediately impatient with the talkative Dane. "I begged him," the first officer will write in his published account, "to belay his jaw tackle until work was over for the day and I could listen in peace."

Jorgensen ignores the thirty-eight-year-old Scot, eagerly sharing the story of his solitary existence. "The breasts of frigate birds are very good, a fair substitute for beefsteak, tender when cooked; for a change, delicious grilled. I easily caught the fowl and also fish, which I had in great variety," Jorgensen explains to Cameron.

"They were tasty boiled, fried, roasted, or steamed. Nor did I lack eggs. A soup to smack your lips over can be made from small birds, which I snared, with well-beaten eggs added when the liquid was slightly cooled. Fish soup I made after the same recipe. As for the eggs alone—sometimes I boiled them, or fried or roasted them; or again made them into a pancake on a frying pan improvised from an old shovel. Tea and coffee consisted of beaten eggs in hot water."

When it comes time for *Wandering Minstrel* to sail away, a rescued Jorgensen signs on as crew. But a terrifying storm batters *Minstrel* the moment she sails outside the reef.

"A rain squall of cyclonic fury burst upon us. Heavy black clouds, close overhead, twisted and hurtled down to leeward, turning the dim day into sullen dusk," John Cameron will write.

"The bark bumped and shivered from stem to stern, while her masts and yards whipped like cane in all directions. Wave after wave, roaring from the sea, drove us ever closer to the reef, and after each heave the *Minstrel* pounded hard. She was doomed, yet we could do nothing to save her; we could hardly lift a finger to save ourselves until the hull, by fixing itself solidly on the rocks, should give us a lee for launching the boats."

Adds Cameron: "Day was settling into night when I bade the old *Minstrel* farewell."

All hands make it back to land. Then, like with so many shipwrecked visitors to Midway before and afterward, they wait. The shipwrecked sailors pillage nests, eating so many eggs that they swear they will never eat another when they are rescued. The most direct route from Yokohama to San Francisco is just fifty miles south but no ships sail close to Midway.

"Day pursued day, and month followed month in monotonous procession—and still no rescue," laments Cameron. He finds a lone bottle of whiskey washed ashore from the *Minstrel*. Cameron rations each mouthful, refusing to share—especially not with the ship's captain, whom every day he despises more and more for being a weak man.

Jorgensen takes charge. Decides to build another boat using *Minstrel*'s remnants. Winter is past and the birds are back at sea. The sun is hot enough that the shipwrecked men shelter under an awning by day, averting their gaze from the bright reflective sand.

The new vessel, all fourteen tons of waterlogged wood, takes days to shove from the sandy building site down into the surf. Rolled atop logs. Men shoving on one end, others straining at ropes on the other. Finally, they arrive at the shoreline.

Then, just like that, Jorgensen's boat is no more. A typhoon drags her off the beach, dashes her on the reef, and destroys her overnight. One minute she's there. The next minute she's gone. There is nothing to do. She doesn't even have a name.

The memoirs about this hard-luck voyage will be many, but none will explain how shattered each sailor feels after this potentially fatal setback. Six sailors depart in a small boat at the end of summer. They are never seen again. Jorgensen and Cameron build their own boat, departing on October 13 for the Marshall Islands. They arrive safely after a forty-three-day journey. Whereupon, the murderous Jorgensen disappears, never mentioned in the public record again.

Finally, a passing schooner, the *Norma*, rescues *Wandering Minstrel*'s remaining crew on St. Patrick's Day 1889, almost a year after their shipwreck. Sixteen of the original company make it back to Honolulu three weeks later.

By now the story of Midway is that of abandonment, shipwreck, and a strange reliance on that redwood house and those thousands of Laysan albatross. In 1892, Robert Louis Stevenson, author of *Treasure Island*, features the atoll in his new novel *The Wrecker*. "There is always the Defoe element in Mr. Stevenson. Mankind likes the story of adventure, shipwrecks, and the hunt for treasure," reads the *New York Times* review about the story that takes place on "Middlebrook Island, some forsaken coral reef in the Pacific."

Somewhere over the years, the redwood house built by that long-ago steamship company is no longer mentioned by those who visit the atoll. Its fate remains a mystery but three decades of weather, sun, and rot must have taken a toll.

Midway is again deserted.

Forsaken or not, Midway claims another victim. The *Julia E. Whalen* is bringing building materials to Midway but founders on the reef in 1903. The ship is lost but all hands are spared.

FEATHERS

1899

Japan takes an interest.

After decades of American whalers and barks and steamships seeking coal and sharks and seal fat, it is only natural that the island halfway between San Francisco and Tokyo finally receives vessels from the other side of the international date line. Awash in a newfound understanding of the open ocean and their nation's growing role in international commerce, the Japanese become only slightly less determined to take control of Midway at the turn of the century than they will in 1942.

Japan's fishermen and sailors have been content to remain in her coastal waters for centuries. Thousands of small fishing villages line the nation's 18,480 miles of coastline. No location in the entire country is more than ninety-three miles from an ocean. It is appropriate, with advances in her ships and the industrialization of her fishing industry, that Japan now begins sending vessels around the world.

However, not all Japanese sailors are devoted to casting their nets.

These particular rogues are interested in feathers.

The twentieth century looms. Ornamental hats are all the rage in Europe and North America. Women tilt their heads ever so casually to reveal chapeaus festooned with feathers plucked from birds of paradise. The plumage from this New Guinea bird is in exorbitant demand. Millinery traders cannot find enough. So, as they must, hat makers experiment with other—they hope cheaper and more plentiful—exotic species.

Nowhere better to look than the uninhabited atolls of the North Pacific, where birds are abundant, their feathers soft, their fear of humans nonexistent—and their island locations so remote that even those claimed by nations growing in international prestige like the United States are unpatrolled and ripe for exploitation.

Islands closer to the Japanese homeland have already been stripped of their bird populations by rapacious hunters seeking meat and eggs. So feather men venture farther from home. Just before the turn of the century, it begins with the *Ada*, whose crew travels to North Pacific atolls hunting sharks and is amazed by the turtle population and the startling sights of hundreds of thousands of birds wheeling in the sky by day and perched contentedly atop their nests with their lone eggs as night falls.

A subsequent expedition recommends that the Japanese government annex several of the Northwestern Hawaiian Islands. The U.S. has staked its claim, so this does not occur, but illicit birding operations grow unchecked. One tactic to avoid criminal prosecution is for poachers to be dropped off, pretend to be shipwrecked, murder thousands of birds, then magically spy a preplanned rescue ship once bound bales of albatross are ready for transport.

Midway becomes a destination for such skullduggery. Ships from Japan arrive during the November-to-January breeding season when albatross have just returned to their nests. Poachers hunt in the morning or evening, because the seabirds fly away to find food during the day. Each hunter carries a large bucket that can hold seventy-five dead birds.

The docile albatross are grabbed as they sit atop their eggs. A bamboo stick knocks them on their heads. Necks twisted and snapped. Soft breast feathers plucked. Wings hacked off. Then the limp body is dropped into the bucket. Eggs stolen. Hatched chicks left to run around in search of a mother to feed them. Poachers do not kill these young birds, not at first, preferring to wait until the youngsters have lost all their body fat and die. Easier to remove feathers from a skinny carcass.

Sometimes, adult albatross are still alive when their wings, which can span six feet, are severed. These are left to run around until they bleed out or starve—the wingless creatures having no way of flying off to feed at sea. The poachers debone wings, sprinkle them with salt, then leave the dark meat in the sun to dry. Cured and shipped to Japan. Feathers dried and packed into bales for shipment.

Fifty thousand hapless seabirds are killed on Midway each year. This does not count the loss of unhatched eggs or the deaths of chicks. The bird population plummets over time, a loss made worse by whaling ships anchoring inside the atoll to resupply their stores and the occasional shipwrecked sailor feasting on the unexpected bounty.

Japan's poachers not only continue their plunder of Midway as the twentieth century begins; they increase the harvest. This exploitation is done in secret, on an island far from the major shipping lanes. Even the most patriotic American skipper would never veer fifty miles off course to pick a fight with the hardened men who so casually slaughter thousands upon thousands of birds. It's not about fear but about being practical.

The massacre might have continued until every last albatross disappeared. That almost occurs on Marcus Island farther out in the Pacific, much closer to Japan. Hundreds of thousands of nesting seabirds are slaughtered until only seventeen remain.

This horrible outcome does not happen on Midway.

For the first time in its long and primitive history, the atoll is about to receive technology.

Just in time to save the seabirds.

TELEGRAPH

1903

Telegraphy is the new technology.

President William McKinley's 1899 Annual Message to Congress contains an unusual clause about a transpacific message service. It has been a year since the United States annexed Hawaii, fearing that Japan might slowly take control of those independent islands.

The president's concerns are not unfounded. Japanese immigrants are flooding across the ocean to work on Hawaiian sugar plantations. More than 61,000 now populate the islands, more than any other foreign ethnicity.

McKinley's underwater link will solidify the connection between the U.S. mainland and the new island possessions—and beyond, all the way to the Philippines. The line between San Francisco and American outposts in the Philippines and Guam would go through Hawaii and Midway via thousands of miles of underwater conduits. "Such communication should be established in such a way as to be wholly under the control of the United States, whether in time of peace or of war," states the Ohioan in a special message to Congress in February 1899.

Japan takes offense but says nothing.

The estimated cost of the 6,900-mile telegraph line is an astronomical $12 million—almost a half billion in modern currency. Construction on the transpacific begins in 1902. "Cable ships" unspool the first section, draping it across the seabed from Ocean Beach in California to Honolulu. Problems arise as the next segment from Hawaii to Midway is about to begin: Japanese poachers and squatters don't want to leave Midway. It's January, the height of the bird-murdering season.

It does not take long for word to reach the White House. The cable monopoly is too important. New president Theodore Roosevelt takes immediate action. On January 20, 1903, he signs Executive Order 199-A placing Midway under the "jurisdiction and control of the Department of the Navy."

Teddy Roosevelt is a big believer in the navy. He thinks nothing matters more to national strength than a powerful U.S. fleet. TR also believes that Japan is America's true Pacific enemy.

Yet the navy ignores Midway.

So the poachers keep coming. Two full years after President Roosevelt's decree, a visitor from Honolulu records the appalling carnage. "Everywhere great heaps, waist high, of dead albatross were found. Thousands upon thousands of both species had been killed with clubs, the wings and breast feathers stripped off to be used as hat trimmings, or for other purposes, and the carcasses thrown in heaps to rot."

Japan has no intention of leaving Midway. Their proprietary interest in the island extends beyond birds. The strategic importance of the island is becoming more noticeable as Japan becomes more linked to the global economy. New modes of communication like underwater telegraph and travel by fast ship shrink the globe. Ignoring President Roosevelt's decree about U.S. Navy possession of Midway, Japanese steamship company Toyo Kisen Kaisha makes plans to build a signal station and send telegraph operators to live on the island full-time. Commercial Pacific considers Midway "unfit for human habitation" and has no plans to station employees on the island. Thus, in the absence of U.S. Navy personnel or employees of the cable company, this private Japanese corporation is happy to take control of the new transpacific telegraph line. Former President McKinley's stated belief that the United States should have total power over the cable is ignored.

Three weeks later, the plot to highjack cable lines is revealed in *The Pacific Commercial Advertiser*. Whether Midway is uninhabitable or not, Commercial Pacific lands thirty employees there on April 20, 1903. Imagine being one of those unlucky dozens, impulsively summoned by their employer to put their lives on hold and sail immediately to this Pacific St. Helena. These are handymen paid to live in tents and build. No women. They bring steel and reinforced concrete for constructing offices, a mess hall, quarters for the staff, and a laundry. Midway's newfound importance is realized in yet another minor international confrontation with Japan.

The Japanese refuse to leave.

President Roosevelt has no choice but to send in the United States Marines.

On May 2, 1904, as construction continues and Japanese poachers look on, twenty-one marines splash ashore, leaving distinctly American boot prints on the sandy beaches. Their commander is Second Lieutenant Clarence S. Owens. The young officer's orders are to secure Midway as a U.S. possession. He is to protect cable employees and the albatross. *All* Japanese poachers and squatters face eviction or arrest.

Wire grass from San Francisco's waterfront dunes is planted to keep the Midway sand in place—"bind" is the word one United States Marine Corps report uses to describe the process. Ironwood trees from the Hawaiian Islands and eucalyptus from Australia provide a break from the powerful winds that rip across Midway so hard that men talk of tying ropes around their torsos to keep their clothes from flying off. Everything but palm trees; ironically, they do not thrive on the island. The permanent steel-and-concrete buildings are soon surrounded by vines and flowers, cedars, papayas, and pines. No longer the only nonhuman species, the albatross now share the land with pigs, ducks, chickens, cows, geese, and turkeys brought to the island to provide food for employees. Two burros brought in for construction become twenty. The soil and plants bring non-native insects like termites and earthworms. For the first time in their history, the albatross face nonhuman animal predators as Norway rats and mice are accidentally brought to the island aboard supply ships.

The marines now and then slap biting mosquitoes, another new arrival.

On July 4, 1903, with the transpacific cable successfully completed, President Teddy Roosevelt sends a message around the world from his home in Oyster Bay, New York. "Congratulations and success to the Pacific cable, which the genius of your lamented father and your own enterprise made possible. Theodore Roosevelt." The message takes twelve minutes to travel the globe.

The words of "Teddy"—he hates the nickname—rocket straight through Midway on their journey. The atoll is no longer a lonely outpost but a vital tactical cog in America's growing global status and reach.

Two years later, in the 1904 Annual Message to Congress, Roosevelt expands the Monroe Doctrine. His new interpretation allows American intervention in international politics.

Japan does not back down. Their 1905 victory in the Russo-Japanese War proves they have emerged from medieval ways and become a powerful player on the global stage. This transformation has taken less than forty years. Tension rises between America and Japan. Anti-Japanese discrimination and race riots in California lead to anti-American editorials in Japanese newspapers. President Roosevelt enters into a "Gentlemen's Agreement" with Japan, restricting further immigration from Japan to the United States. In a show of force, the president orders the U.S. Navy to send its battleships on a trip around the world. This "Great White Fleet," so called for the bright white paint job on each ship, stops in Japan. Of all the twenty stops the navy vessels make in their circumnavigation, the stop in Yokohama is the most important. Roosevelt is wary of Japan's growing influence in Asia, believing it stands in the way of American ambition.

Fearing violence, navy officials briefly consider confining crews to their ships while in port. The Great White Fleet is instead welcomed by schoolchildren singing a phonetically memorized version of "The Star-Spangled Banner."

Sailors get their leave.

The U.S. and Japan sign the Root-Takahira Agreement on November 30, 1908. This agreement—not a treaty—demands that each nation keep its hands off the other's Pacific possessions.

For the United States, this means the Philippines, Guam, Hawaii, Wake Island—and Midway.

Theodore Roosevelt leaves office in 1909. His successor, William Howard Taft, seeks to expand trade in the Far East but shows little interest in the islands in between. Emboldened poachers return to Midway in force. "The raiders," *Mid-Pacific Magazine* will report, "landed on the island in May, 1909, and by the fall of that year had slaughtered upwards of 300,000 birds. Not content with securing the feathers, the hunters had adopted singularly cruel methods. One practice was to throw the birds, after they were caught, into an old cistern, and there let them slowly starve to death."

The poaching finally ends in 1910. Twenty-three bird hunters are arrested, taken to Honolulu, and sentenced to jail.

Even though the poaching is no longer a major problem, tension between the two nations grows. The U.S. Supreme Court rules in 1922 that Japanese immigrants are forbidden from becoming U.S. citizens. The court rules in 1923 that Japanese Americans cannot own land. One year after that, Congress imposes the Johnson-Reed Immigration Act excluding all Asians from migrating to the United States.

Meanwhile, Japanese boats continue to prowl the Pacific, always expanding their reach. By the 1930s, Japan's fishing fleet is double the size of that of any other nation on earth. There are so many boats, and so many able-bodied hands smelling of bait and fuel working those bloody decks, that it is only natural for the Imperial Japanese Navy to absorb the watercraft and all those experienced deckhands into the growing push toward war.

HEMINGWAY

1935

"Pan American and I are old friends," writes Ernest Hemingway years later in a nostalgic magazine advertisement. The novelist smiles at the camera, rugged face sunburned, salt-and-pepper beard neatly trimmed as he reminisces about the lone time he flew to China and back. "There was the Pacific when you took a day to Midway— another to Wake—one more to Guam—one to Manila—then Hong Kong."

Hemingway thinks back fondly to his journey aboard a revolutionary aircraft known as the *China Clipper*. This seaplane service makes Midway famous. Of all its glamorous and wealthy passengers, Hemingway and his outspoken journalist wife, Martha Gellhorn, are two of the most well-known to the average American. She is on her way to China to do a story for *Collier's* magazine. The bestselling writer is along for the ride.

Hollywood director John Ford, another hard-drinking, popular American icon, entered the U.S. Naval Reserve in 1934, anticipating war even as Japan still honored the Washington Naval Treaty. Hemingway has no such patriotic ambition. He served in World War I. Should another great conflict occur, the author would prefer to treat it like this Clipper journey, a great adventure, only on a much larger scale.

Remember the terms of the 1921 Washington Naval Conference? Battleships all the fashion; loopholes big enough to build aircraft carriers?

There's more: no construction of naval bases. Article XIX of the subsequent Washington Naval Treaty specifically prohibits Britain, Japan, and America from building new fortifications or improving existing facilities in the Pacific. The Washington Naval Treaty is why Britain rushes to construct its new naval base in Singapore before the document is finalized. Had England waited, the new fortress would likely never have been built.

This should not have affected Midway. The first aircraft takes flight from the atoll on October 10, 1920. A Sunday. More than a year before diplomats and men in uniform sit down at a long conference table, the Washington Naval Conference transpires, and all parties agree on terms.

A navy Curtiss N-9 seaplane that has been disassembled and loaded aboard the small patrol vessel *Eagle 40* is brought to the lagoon. The aircraft is then reassembled and takes off from the calm waters inside the reef to conduct an aerial photographic mission. The purpose of those pictures, the scenery so gorgeous they might as well be travel postcards, is to see whether or not the island has potential as a base for transpacific flights.

Everyone agrees Midway is a fine location for a naval air base. Yet the U.S. Navy dithers. No runways are built before the Washington Naval Treaty is signed. For lack of immediate action, Midway falls into the category of Pacific naval bases that cannot be improved or fortified.

Soon it becomes 1935. Midway never rose to become the nineteenth-century coal mecca the Pacific Mail Steamship Company imagined, but that no longer matters. Steamships are relics, no more relevant to modern travel than N. C. Brooks' sail-powered *Gambia*.

Flight is all the rage. Pan American Airlines proves this with its mail service, transporting letters and packages to destinations around the globe in hours, not months. Advances in aviation technology make passenger travel a commercial reality, so the airline is planning to expand its services from carrying mail to carrying people as well. Monstrous all-metal, four-engine flying boats carrying four thousand pounds of fuel, a hundred thousand pieces of mail, and forty-six passengers. Luxury cabins. Fine dining. A stiff cocktail at the snap of the fingertips.

China Clipper, Philippine Clipper, and *Hawaii Clipper* make up the small fleet.

Yet just like steamships enslaved to coal, airplanes require a landmass where they can land and pump aviation gas into their bellies. Pan American Airlines has done very well with its Atlantic routes to the Caribbean and South America, but increasing hostilities in Europe make those relatively short journeys problematic. Flying the Pacific is a far greater distance but potentially just as lucrative. As Pan Am prepares to launch a San Francisco to China air route, it proposes to break the trip up into several legs of more than a thousand miles each: San Francisco to Honolulu to Midway to Wake Island to Guam to Manila to Hong Kong. Seventy hours in the air. An astronomical $950 per passenger—$21,000 in modern currency—to travel across the Pacific at 130 miles per hour. The cost of a single trip equals the annual average wage of an American workingman.

Genius. But Midway has zero amenities that would satisfy a blue-collar laborer, let alone Pan Am's luxury clientele. The island is home to twenty-three employees, the cable company they work for, and all those functional buildings thrown up overnight three decades ago.

And those thousands of birds still engrossed in hatching their chicks. Nothing else.

Wealthy passengers paying all that money to fly the Pacific can hardly be expected to step from the luxury of the *China Clipper* onto a remote Pacific atoll, there to spend a night on the sand like nesting albatross.

All that changes with two sudden, ambitious construction projects that alter the face of Midway once again.

March 27, 1935. The freighter *North Haven* sails from San Francisco laden with two thousand tons of construction materials and a crew to do the building. Arrives at Midway in a driving rain on April 15. Surveyors quickly mark off the "quadrangle" where the construction will take place. Temporary tent quarters are built. A power plant. Strings of lights. Windmills, water storage, fuel tanks. A pier. Floating dock.

Showing their fondness for breeding in the same site every year, the albatross build their nests atop this new topography, even on roads, as their dunes are leveled.

There are still no runways.

Technically, Midway doesn't need a hard surface to accommodate Pan Am flights. The Martin M-130 lands on water. Flying boats require at least a thousand yards of smooth water for landing and takeoff. Clear blue channels forming the new "runways" are carefully checked for underwater debris like coral and old shipwrecks as Midway turns into a seaport.

Forty-five days later, the job is done.

But Midway still needs its hotel.

On June 6, 1935, the first Pan Am Clipper from Honolulu lands. She carries a load of mail. No passengers.

Six months later, a fully laden *North Haven* again sets sail from San Francisco. Reports *The New York Times* on January 15, 1936: "Two complete, prefabricated hotels of forty-five rooms each were among the 6,000-ton cargo of the Pan American chartered supply ship *North Haven*, it was disclosed yesterday, when she sailed from San Francisco on Monday night for the island bases of the airline across the Pacific Ocean. The two hotels will be erected at Midway Island and Wake Island."

Adds the *Times*: "The prefabricated hotels of frame construction are complete in all details, including furnishings. Designed for the special conditions on tropical islands, they consist of two wings built with a central, circular lobby. They have wide verandas. Each room has a shower bath with hot water. Full furniture for the social rooms and bedrooms, down to coat hangers and ash trays, is in the vessel's cargo, as well as cashier's cages, desks, draperies, inter-room telephones and scores of other items."

In addition, *North Haven* is laden with 250,000 gallons of gasoline, six months' supply of food, and powerful lighting equipment.

The Pan American Airways Inn is born. Finally, the airline is ready to fly passengers—and Midway is ready to accept them. They will land from Honolulu shortly after two p.m., be transported to their luxurious rooms, then freshen up before enjoying a fine-dining experience. A traditional dinner, served by Chamorro waiters imported from Guam, consists of anchovy canapés, chicken broth, prime roast beef au jus, mashed potatoes, spinach, green apple pie, and black coffee. Then a night of slumber. In the morning comes a six a.m. departure for Wake Island, next stop on the transpacific odyssey. A short day, just over 1,200 miles.

The route seems impossibly plush to an America just emerging from the Depression. "Clippermania" sweeps the nation, an outrageous vacation in a series of tropical paradises culminating in the mysteries of the Orient. For citizens beginning to dream again after years of want, fascination with all things Clipper defines the brief era between hardships of the Depression and hardships of war.

Clippermania includes a motion picture and a popular song about the aerial route, complete with matching dance moves. Postage stamps, tie racks, playing cards, toy Clippers. One passenger boat in Biloxi, Mississippi, is christened *Pan American Clipper* on the date of its launch in 1937.

So it is, Midway becomes a resort. Not as populated as Hawaii, but all the more exotic for its isolation. Fishing, swimming, and a night of tropical rest.

Yet tension between the United States and Japan surfaces once again. As early as 1936, books written during Clippermania allude to growing unrest in the Pacific. Japan leaves the Washington Naval Treaty. The Asian nation can now do whatever it wants with its navy, just as Adolf Hitler is doing with his own *Kriegsmarine* in Europe.

Also unfettered from the treaty, America can now do the same.

The facade that the U.S. is not developing or improving naval bases in the Pacific is no longer needed. Pan Am's transpacific route allows the U.S. Navy to select the islands that will one day become home to forward outposts and to build the hard concrete runways that will be necessary for war in the Pacific.

The Washington Naval Treaty was supposed to prevent another world war. Those accords are now gone with the wind. In their place, the U.S. Navy's Hepburn Report prepares strategic outposts like Midway for war.

The report derives its name from Rear Admiral Arthur Hepburn. His review of American defensive capabilities leads to an enormous expansion of the U.S. military installations in the late 1930s. This investigation states that "from a strategic point of view, an air base at Midway Island is second in importance only to Pearl Harbor."

Let the building begin.

The goal is a "naval air and submarine base with facilities for two patrol-plane squadrons; two divisions of submarines; and pier, channel and turning basin within the lagoon for large auxiliaries."

The navy sets aside $13,040,000 to cover the cost—$300 million in modern money.

In August 1938, 120 engineers and the big dredge *Hell Gate* arrive to excavate a new entrance channel through the southern part of the reef. A full harbor to follow: anchorage, turning basin big enough for a battleship to pirouette into port, and a 3,100-foot breakwater tall enough to shelter ships from the wind.

What Pan Am has begun the United States Navy will finish.

The new entrance is named "Brooks Channel."

Midway's discoverer finally gets his due.

AMELIA EARHART AND
HAWAII CLIPPER

1937

As if war isn't already on the horizon, two unsolved mysteries heighten tensions.

The first occurs soon after the first *Pacific Clipper* lands on Midway in November 1935.

Famous American female pilot Amelia Earhart is planning an around-the-world flight. She hopes to be the first woman to accomplish this feat. Earhart is in her late thirties, a fearless, no-nonsense aviator with an easy grin and a fondness for long pants. Her husband is wealthy. She has connections. Publisher George Putnam contacts Eleanor Roosevelt with an unusual request. The First Lady takes this to her husband for approval. Putnam is asking permission for his wife, Amelia, to perform midair refueling over Midway Island. A tanker plane will rendezvous with her aircraft, then extend a boom into her gas tanks to fill them without need for landing. Her navigator is Fred Noonan, a man who carries a famous pedigree for serving the same function on that virgin Pan Am journey across the Pacific.

Permission granted. Not even the president of the United States dares say no to the great and beloved Amelia Earhart.

But Earhart alters her route. She decides not to fly over Midway after all. The midair refueling idea is great but touching down on terra firma is much better for rest and aircraft maintenance.

Earhart and navigator Noonan depart Miami, Florida, on June 1, 1937. By June 29, they land in New Guinea, more than 22,000 miles into their eastward adventure. On July 2, 1937, during a long overwater stretch of the Pacific, Earhart and Noonan vanish.

"Old Bessie, the fire horse," as the pilot nicknames her Lockheed Vega 5B, has not been seen since. Rumors surface that she was forced to land somewhere in the Pacific, then captured and killed by Japanese soldiers. Some believe the rumor. Others, such as President Roosevelt, brush it aside. Yet the fact that such fantastical theories exist, and that the army of Japan is mentioned by name, shows the growing discord—Americans are beginning to see the Japanese as a threat.

Earhart did not believe Midway was the best route. If the island had actual runways on land, the pilot might have chosen to follow her initial plan, pausing there to refuel rather than chancing the midair option— and thus she might have died in her bed after a long and happy life rather than seeing it cut short by tragic fate.

The second incident occurs eight months later. July 28, 1938. *Hawaii Clipper* takes off from Guam at eleven thirty-nine in the morning, bound for the Philippines. She carries 2,550 gallons of gasoline, enough to provide a cruising endurance of seventeen hours and thirty minutes at just below eight thousand feet altitude. There should be no worries about the airship's structural integrity, because it has logged 4,751 hours in back-and-forth journeys across the Pacific.

The flight crew has years of experience, with Captain Leo Terletzky owning 9,200 hours of flight time, 1,614 of those in the Martin M-130 flying boat. The first, second, third, and fourth officers all have hundreds of hours of experience in transpacific flight. Even African American flight steward Ivan Parker has 1,200 hours in the *Hawaii Clipper*. He is a man of color in an all-white Pan Am world.

Six American passengers, none of them famous, all of them men, one each hailing from New Jersey, California, Oregon, and New York, and two from Washington, DC.

A few hours into the flight, Captain Terletzky sends to the Philippines "a routine radio position report," in the words of the Federal Aviation Administration's investigation. He gives his location as 582 miles east-southeast of Manila. His transmission is acknowledged. The captain is told to stand by for a weather briefing.

No response. *Hawaii Clipper* is never heard from again.

All crew and passengers lost without a trace. The U.S. Army transport ship *Meigs* sails to the location in hope of a rescue mission. Instead, an oil slick stains the ocean surface and no wreckage is found. The search is called off after a week. Tests of the fuel discovery show there is no connection with *Hawaii Clipper*'s special aviation gasoline and the substance floating atop the water.

Other than their very loose connection with Midway, the only thing the Earhart and *Hawaii Clipper* crashes have in common is who receives the blame:

Japan.

Even the American public, which knows little about the Pacific and even less about Asia, is willing to believe that the same Imperial Japanese Army that invaded China, raped thousands of women after capturing Nanking, and machine-gunned the USS *Panay* is so aggressive that it would capture and shoot innocent pilots, crews, and passengers.

It is well-known that Japanese aircraft shadow Pan Am flights in menacing fashion as they near Asia. Since the beginning of transpacific service in 1935, the Imperial Japanese Navy has made threatening public statements about these passenger aircraft.

In this way, without any proof of hostility, the Japanese are now an enemy in American minds.

This threat is actually more real than the public imagines.

In Japan, the U.S. ambassador to Tokyo sends a coded telegram to President Franklin Roosevelt in January 1941. "My Peruvian colleague,"

Joseph Grew confides in FDR, "told a member of my staff that he had heard from many sources—including a Japanese source—that the Japanese military forces planned, in the event of trouble with the United States, to attempt a surprise mass attack on Pearl Harbor using all of their military facilities. He added that although the project seemed fantastic, the fact that he had heard it from many sources prompted him to pass on the information."

Ernest Hemingway's lone voyage on the *China Clipper* prepares to splash down in Midway lagoon three weeks after Ambassador Grew's coded transmission—February 17, 1941.

For Clipper passengers like Hemingway, the island is still a resort.

That is changing.

Regulations no longer permit passengers to roam beyond the hotel grounds.

As his *China Clipper* banks to land in the blue-green waters of the lagoon, Hemingway sees for himself the new land runways and aircraft hangars on Eastern Island. U.S. Marines march in formation, easily visible in their lightweight tropical khaki uniforms.

Even amid all the luxury, which the writer will remember so fondly for the rest of his life, war is coming to Midway Island.

As the Hepburn Report states, the fortification of Midway is "necessary of accomplishment at the earliest practicable date."

COUNTDOWN TO WAR

1941

N. C. Brooks would no longer recognize his barren, windswept discovery.

Eighty-two short years after the skipper came hunting guano, the waterfront dunes now have a hotel, barracks, and a pier. U.S. Marines drilling in precise formation. The 3rd Defense Battalion disembarks in February, after sailing from Honolulu aboard the light cruisers *Savannah*, *Philadelphia*, *Brooklyn*, and *Nashville*. These ships are new, part of the United States' massive naval buildup. America is not at war but the vessels travel to Midway with lights darkened, protected by a defensive screen of destroyers. The skeleton crew of 28 officers and 565 enlisted men disembark. They do so in secrecy, as if attack is imminent, even as tourists land in the bay and trot off to the Pan Am Hotel for an evening of luxury.

Not a full garrison. The military doesn't believe there are facilities for another few hundred marines. The men of the 3rd immediately begin constructing defenses. Sand Island and Eastern Island are appraised. Concrete bunkers are poured. Artillery emplacements are scrutinized for optimal location. Fields of fire cease being a hypothetical concept.

"Considerable effort was expended in filling and manhandling sandbags from the beach areas to the gun positions; this was necessary to preserve the limited camouflage furnished by the scaevola. Much sweat and ingenuity was [*sic*] required to install the 5-inch guns on top of the 20-foot sand dune fringing Sand Island," Lieutenant Colonel Stuart Charlesworth will write in a letter that will make its way into the official U.S. Marine report about the defensive preparations.

> It was impossible to stand on one high point of the dune and rec-
> ognize changes in elevation and direction of contours on Sand Is-
> land with its covering of dense scaevola brush. To attempt to locate
> known points while walking through the scaevola was also impos-
> sible due to the height and density of foliage. The final solution in
> locating positions for magazine installations to be constructed in
> accordance with future planning was to send out a two-man team
> of officers on a TD-9 tractor to press down trails along the inside of
> the fringing dunes and to various points in the center of the island.
> This was accomplished by one officer standing up on the back of the
> tractor in a position from which he could look above the scaveola
> and give general directions to the driver. It proved to be hot work in
> the direct sun without benefit of breeze, and many spills were taken
> from the pitching "cat."

This is the daily grind. Morale drops as rays from the sweltering summer sun burn uncovered flesh. Nothing to fill the off-duty hours, "no USO shows to attend, nor beautiful Red Cross girls to serve coffee and doughnuts," Lieutenant Colonel Erma A. Wright will remember. "Actually, there were only two imported morale-builders—movies and the arrival of the Pan-American clipper twice weekly."

On August 1, Naval Air Station Midway is formally opened. Commander Cyril T. Simard, a veteran naval pilot and former air officer on the carrier USS *Langley* (CV-1), is designated the atoll's commanding officer. Admiral Chester Nimitz, head of the navy's Bureau of Navigation in Washington, personally makes the selection.

On September 11, the 6th Defense Battalion arrives to relieve the 3rd.

Lieutenant Colonel Harold Shannon is the new commander. Rotation back to Honolulu every six months is considered vital. Remaining on Midway too long is detrimental to the restive young, single marines.

On November 5, in Tokyo, Japanese Emperor Hirohito secretly approves plans for an attack on the American naval base at Pearl Harbor.

The strike force has already been training intensively for weeks at Saiki, on Kyushu's east coast. They number six carriers. *Akagi* flies the flag of Vice Admiral Chūichi Nagumo, who commands the First Air Fleet. *Kaga* is her twin. The small and quick *Hiryū* and *Sōryū*. The new 29,800-ton *Shōkaku* and *Zuikaku*.

We'll save more in-depth descriptions of these carriers for the Battle of Midway. It is enough to know they travel as a wolf pack, six carriers and their destroyer screen bound for Honolulu. The pilots don't know where they're headed right now, but it's hard not to venture a solid guess.

***

As the Japanese strike force awaits the order to sail, the Midway marines receive unusual news from Pan Am: An unexpected guest will be arriving on November 10. He is a high-ranking Japanese official traveling via the *China Clipper* despite his nation's loathing of those enormous luxury planes. Washington is his ultimate destination.

The visitor's name is Saburō Kurusu or, in the Japanese way of placing the family name first, Kurusu Saburō. Fifty-five. Career diplomat. Less than five feet tall with a quick smile. Father of three. Married to an American woman. Speaks fluent English. Kurusu left Tokyo on just twenty hours' notice for this "very important and difficult mission," as he will tell reporters.

Tension between the United States and Japan is at an all-time high. Pan Am pilots carry coded instructions on what to do if war breaks out as they are flying the Pacific. British Prime Minister Winston Churchill is publicly stating his nation will fight alongside the United States "within the hour" if war is declared. Kurusu laughs at this certainty, telling the press that "he might as well have said he will take breakfast tomorrow morning."

Kurusu is on his way to Washington as a last-minute "peace" envoy. No Japanese diplomat more prestigious. While serving as ambassador to Nazi Germany, Kurusu signed the Tripartite Pact last year, tethering Japan's fortunes to those of Adolf Hitler.

Ironically, given the decades of Japanese–American tension in the North Pacific, Kurusu is arguably the most distinguished visitor Midway has ever received.

Kurusu is in a hurry. But the *China Clipper* is having engine problems. The ambassador might end up staying more than a night.

The United States Marine Corps takes full advantage. Anything to break the daily grind.

"We had notice of his arrival date and the ostensible nature of his mission," one officer will remember. "Elaborate plans involving precise timing were drawn up so that when Mr. Kurusu disembarked from the Pan American bowser barge . . . onto Midway, the first thing to meet his eyes would be an endless line of Marines in light marching order filing past. In addition, all available aviation strength, consisting of a squadron of PBY's, was drawn up on the seaplane apron in full view of the dock."*

The PBY Catalina is a patrol-bomber, rescue, and reconnaissance plane that can set down on land or water. The U.S. Navy ordered the design and development of these long-range aircraft during the 1930s, anticipating war in the Pacific.

"The plans worked out perfectly."

Ambassador Kurusu steps from the clear blue waters of the lagoon

---

* The PBY ("P" for patrol; "B" for bomber; "Y" code for Consolidated Aircraft, the plane's manufacturer) is an advance in seaplane development from the days of Pan Am Clippers. Early models were sold to the British, who continued the practice of naming seaplanes for coastal towns. After the plane was christened "Catalina," the name stuck and was also used by the U.S. Army Air Corps and U.S. Navy. Used most often for reconnaissance, transportation, and open-water rescue, the bird with the unusual parasol wing had a crew of seven to nine and a range of three thousand miles.

onto the pier, where marines wearing tropical khaki and vintage World War I steel doughboy helmets drill with brown-stocked M1903 .30-caliber rifles on their right shoulders.*

A color guard leads the way, displaying the Stars and Stripes and the red flag with the globe and anchor of the USMC.

The officer continues.

It just happened that Fox . . . Battery was right in front of the Pan Air hotel, being separated only by a coral road, and was due to fire a calibration shoot followed by some extensive trial fire and burst-adjustment problems for training. . . . The colonel saw no reason for not going ahead with the firing; on the contrary we embellished it somewhat. So for the duration of his enforced three-day stopover, Mr. Kurusu listened to the slamming of the 3-inch AA guns outside his window from early morning until sunset. The practice was culminated with the firing by all guns of 15 rounds adjustment at full firing rate on a burst target, which made quite an impressive noise for our guest, as well as giving our gun crews some badly needed loading practice. He was not permitted to leave the hotel, in accordance with established procedure for civilian Pan Air guests . . . , so any impressions he may have gotten of Midway were necessarily those of the "march-past," the planes, and the firing.

Ambassador Kurusu plays the game. He tells the *San Francisco Examiner* that he had a "good two days [*sic*] rest" upon reaching Hawaii, adding that "I behaved myself" when asked if he ventured into restricted areas.

On November 15, the diplomat finally reaches Washington.

Where the games quickly come to an end.

---

* The marine corps also utilized the M1 and the M1941 Johnson as standard rifles during World War II.

THE MESSAGE

December 1941

Long-floundering, high-tightrope, world-altering negotiations break down on the brink of war.

An expert of the highest caliber is required to make things right before the shit goes sideways.

Welcome to Washington via Midway, Saburō Kurusu.

Ambassador Kichisaburō Nomura, who has been negotiating with the Americans for over a year, works alongside Kurusu. Officials in Tokyo believe the admiral is in over his head but allow him to save face. Kurusu leads a new attempt to convince the United States to unfreeze Japanese assets and ignore the presence of troops in China and Southeast Asia. Neither man has been informed of the Imperial Navy's planned attack on Pearl Harbor. Their instructions are to settle disputes with the United States by the end of November 1941, nothing more.

On November 26, Secretary of State Cordell Hull presents Ambassador Nomura with a document stating ten inviolable points. These have not changed in more than a year: leave China, leave Indochina, stop further aggression.

Japan must adhere to these stipulations or risk war.

No one in Washington knows that the Japanese carrier strike force set sail from the remote gray Kuril Islands today. Destination: a spot

230 miles north of Honolulu. *Akagi, Kaga, Sōryū, Hiryū, Zuikaku,* and *Shōkaku* sail under total radio silence. The six aircraft carriers are loaded with a total of 420 planes and thousands of fuel containers for the long journey. They will perform a procedure known as ship-to-ship refueling rather than stop in port. The United States Navy also has technology for underway refueling, implemented a quarter century ago by a young officer named Chester Nimitz, whom we have met several times before—and will again.

The route of the *Kidō Butai* takes them far over the northern horizon from Midway. Vice Admiral Chūichi Nagumo's Pearl Harbor Striking Force also includes battleships, cruisers, destroyers, tankers, and submarines. "Midget" underwater vessels will scout around Hawaii. Should their proposed attack on Pearl Harbor become a reality, the two-man, two-torpedo subs will sail inside the breakwater and fire upon American ships as bombs and torpedoes are dropped from the sky.

In Tokyo, a gleeful Admiral Matome Ugaki is emboldened by the coming surprise attack. He is chief of staff for Japan's Combined Fleet.

Admiral Chūichi Nagumo
The U.S. National Archives / Picryl

America's tepid response to Ambassador Kurusu's diplomacy infuriates him. "Don't you know that a dagger will be thrust into your throat in four days?" the admiral writes in his journal.

***

JAPAN'S RESPONSE TO Secretary Hull's ten-point message comes Saturday, December 6. It is intended for delivery the following afternoon—and it will be. But unbeknownst to Japan, the verbiage will not be a surprise. The U.S. Army's Signal Intelligence Service intercepts the message from Tokyo to Ambassador Nomura long before he delivers it in person. The missive is in thirteen parts.

Once decoded, today's lengthy diatribe from Tokyo details a long list of American transgressions in Asia.

It appears there is also a fourteenth point yet to arrive.

Japan's diplomatic code and the Imperial Japanese Navy's are distinct from each other. U.S. Army and Navy cryptographers first break the Japanese diplomatic cipher in August 1940. This cipher is named for the so-called Purple machine built to decrypt diplomatic messages as they arrived in Washington. America has been reading top secret missives between Tokyo and Japan's envoys in Washington ever since. However, the Imperial Japanese Navy's codes remain unbroken.

The top secret intelligence gathered from decrypted messages is called "Magic." To keep their snooping unknown and stop Japan from switching to new codes, access to Magic documents is highly limited.

***

JUST AFTER THE first part of the message is decrypted, Ensign Takeo Yoshikawa of the Imperial Japanese Navy stands duty in the Japanese consulate in Honolulu. Twenty-nine but looks twenty. Former pilot. Spy.

For the past eight months, Yoshikawa has learned all there is to know about the U.S. Navy and Pearl Harbor—the name of every ship and plane, hull numbers, training missions. He drinks in American bars to overhear navy gossip, travels to the highest point in Honolulu after dark to observe the well-lit navy base at night, even dresses as a Filipino laborer to get a closer look at the electric fences and other fortifications. Takeo Yoshikawa works alone, a man with no thoughts of marriage or a busy social life. Without a doubt, the Japanese intelligence officer is the world's greatest authority on Pearl Harbor. He has already informed his superiors in Tokyo that Sunday is when the most ships are in port—and the best day for an attack.

"It was a clear tropical night and the taro fronds stirred gently in the breeze outside my window. As I laid down my pencil to glance outside, I could see the coral rock of the consulate drive glimmering faintly in the moonlight down by the gateposts on the palm-lined avenue. And not very far away, I knew, the avenue would be lighted much more strongly by the reflected glare of the spotlights and the overhead arc lights that would be illuminating the Pearl Harbor Navy Yard on this busy night—the first weekend since the Fourth of July that all nine battleships were in port," he later writes of this evening.

Yoshikawa is thrilled by the scenario. "Thirty-nine U.S. warships were assembled there—only the carriers and a small escort force under Halsey were at sea that night. I knew all this with certainty since my whole being had been dedicated to a concentrated study of the U.S. Pacific Fleet for the last seven years, and since I alone had been in charge of espionage for the Imperial Japanese Navy at Pearl Harbor for the last eight months."

The ensign flashes a message to Tokyo:

No barrage balloons sighted. Battleships are without crinolines.
No indications of air or sea alert wired to nearby islands.
Enterprise and *Lexington* have sailed from Pearl Harbor.

Yoshikawa knows his superiors will be disappointed by the last section but sends it anyway.

The missive is relayed from Tokyo to the carrier *Akagi*, sailing toward Oahu. Twenty past one on Sunday, December 7. Vice Admiral Chūichi Nagumo is anxious, fearing the mission will fail. The admiral tells peers he wishes he had never accepted the assignment. The moon lights the sea four hundred miles north of the Hawaiian Islands. Admiral Nagumo steps to the plotting table and confirms the location of his six powerful carriers.

***

WASHINGTON, DC. THE Magic codebreakers receive the crucial four-teenth part of the Japanese message. An addendum states when and where the remarks are to be handed to American leadership.

Ambassador Nomura is to deliver these words to Secretary of State Cordell Hull "at 1:00 P.M. on the 7th, your time."

Washington time.

***

SUNDAY, DECEMBER 7. Army Chief of Staff General George Marshall goes for an early-morning horseback ride. He arrives at his office in the War Department just past noon. Aides hand him a copy of the encrypted message. Marshall is alarmed that the time for delivery of the message is so specific—and soon. Checking his watch, the general realizes that moment is less than an hour away.

Marshall phones President Roosevelt. The general then drafts a message to military officials in Hawaii and the Philippines: "Japanese are presenting at one pm eastern standard time today what amounts to an ultimatum," the general writes. "Just what significance the hour set may have we do not know but be on the alert accordingly. Inform naval authorities of this communication."

General Marshall's message is quickly encrypted and sent by radio to commands in San Francisco, the Philippines, Panama, and Hawaii. But there is no Purple machine in Honolulu, so U.S. codebreakers at Pearl Harbor are not able to decode this message. Had they been in possession of such a device, the advance warning might have changed all that happens next.

And there is yet another setback for Honolulu: The message fails due to atmospheric disturbances. Marshall's most urgent call to arms is immediately resent by the next fastest mode of delivery, commercial telegram.

Which turns out to be not very quick at all.

***

AMBASSADOR KURUSU DOES as he is told. Even before General Marshall's urgent telegram is sent to Hawaii, he obeys the one p.m. mandate and delivers the fourteenth and final part of Japan's message:

"The Japanese Government regrets to have to notify hereby the American government that in view of the attitude of the American Government it cannot but consider that it is impossible to reach an agreement through further negotiations."

For the rest of his life, Ambassador Kurusu will claim no previous knowledge of what happens next.

Four dozen Nakajima B5N "Kate" aircraft carrying armor-piercing bombs and another forty loaded with N91 torpedoes have already launched from carriers 230 miles off Oahu's North Shore. They look down on nothing but the sea for almost two hours, then make landfall over the ironwood trees and coastal scrub of the island's northernmost tip, Kahuku Point. Thousands of eyewitnesses rouse from slumber and look up curiously at the armada thundering overhead. These observers say nothing, warn no one. For they cannot. This is a nesting colony of Laysan albatross, as common to Oahu as Midway. The birds are sitting atop their eggs in the pine straw and sand. The attackers press inland, flying over a series of low green mountains, their arrival still a secret.

The pilots maintain ten thousand feet over the red soil of pineapple plantations, then assemble in diving positions as they crest another range of mountains dividing the island, reach the other side of Oahu, and gaze for the first time upon that lush target known as Pearl Harbor. Fighter aircraft fly escort, staying at fifteen thousand feet to await the American response.

There is none.

***

GENERAL MARSHALL'S MESSAGE reaches the Honolulu RCA telegraph office sixteen minutes after being sent. The time is seven thirty-three a.m. in Hawaii. Addressed to Lieutenant General Walter C. Short, Hawaiian Department commander at Fort Shafter. Every morning is busy in its own way in Washington, but Sunday in Hawaii is the most relaxed time of the week. "Radiogram 1549" does not receive preferential treatment, slipped into the Kalihi District sorting box just like any other cable.

Motorcycle messenger and Honolulu resident Tadao Fuchikami sleeps an extra half hour. A Hawaiian civilian of Japanese descent, he arrives at work on King Street shortly after eight a.m. The sky buzzes with aircraft but that is normal. Military exercises are so common, they are no longer heard.

"Messenger Boy #9" fills his delivery bag, noting Radiogram 1549 for General Scott, whose location is five miles away. Fuchikami places his deliveries in order, scheduling several civilian stops before Fort Shafter. He wears a blue uniform with a Radio Corporation of America patch on the chest. Black hair combed straight back. Twenty-four years old.

Fuchikami steps outside to begin his route. Pearl Harbor is eleven miles west from downtown King Street. From the sounds of it, the navy is also practicing live fire drills. More distant sounds of airplanes flying low overhead. Loud explosions. The warm and fragrant Hawaiian air seems at odds with columns of thick smoke rising from the waterfront. Three distinct black pillars choke the blue skyline. Newly awakened citizens spill into the street, some commenting that the drills seem very real for a Sunday morning and others claiming America is under attack. The *Honolulu Advertiser*'s lone switchboard operator is inundated with calls requesting information—so many that the paper prints an edition telling people to stop calling.

If war is happening, Messenger Boy #9 could choose to abandon his route and save his skin. But Fuchikami's father died last year. The messenger and his two older brothers work to support their mother. So when asked if he still wants to set out on his deliveries, #9's response is that he needs the money.

Opening the throttle on his 1938 Indian Scout Twin motorcycle, the courier powers down streets filling with people running from the sounds of battle. News of an enemy attack is soon interrupted by low-flying aircraft in attack formation.

Tadao Fuchikami works the foot clutch and gear shift lever. He is detained twice at military roadblocks for his obvious Japanese appearance but not taken into custody. All roads are blocked to traffic as the messenger arrives at Fort Shafter Street and the entrance to the base. Fuchikami navigates side streets to get around.

The RCA messenger halts at the main gate. Fuchikami is recognized and admitted. Two men escort him to the signal office, but no one is working. "The Signal Corp receiving clerk was not at his desk," Fuchikami will later state. Like other personnel on duty this morning, the enlisted man can be found on the balcony of the headquarters building, staring in disbelief at the smoke and chaos across town in Pearl Harbor.

Throughout his odyssey, Tadao Fuchikami knows his message is important but doesn't know what it says. It will be ten more years until he learns that he carried a telegram that predicted all-out war.*

Fuchikami finally delivers Radiogram 1549 to Corporal Stevens, who signs for the telegram. The time is somewhere between nine thirty and ten fifteen, but the preoccupied desk clerk does not time-stamp the telegram for another hour. This will become the object of an investigation about why the telegram is not delivered in time. No matter: Several more hours pass before General Marshall's urgent appeal is decoded.

Hawaii is in tatters, every single airfield strafed and bombed, Pearl Harbor a tangled mess of listing and decimated ships. The ocean is on fire. Sunken vessels have become steel coffins. Battleship Row is chaos, confusion, odd angles, sailors gulping oil as they swim for safety. Sixty-eight civilians and 2,335 American service members are dead. Another 1,178 are wounded. Eighteen ships and 188 aircraft are damaged or lost.

The United States' Pacific possessions are either under attack or invaded. Except Midway and Wake.

Though not for long.

---

* Tadao Fuchikami will serve as a technical adviser on the 1970 movie about Pearl Harbor, *Tora! Tora! Tora!* He dies on February 7, 2006, at the age of eighty-nine. He is buried at Nuuanu Memorial Park in Honolulu.

CAPTAIN HAMILTON

December 8, 1941

D awn. Twenty-five hundred miles west of Honolulu, where the date is still December 7. The morning begins well for Captain John Hamilton. His flight has been held up twenty-four hours due to a mechanical delay, but now the veteran Pan Am pilot takes off from Wake Island. Hamilton is eager to be away. Even after hanging up his uniform jacket so he can fly in shirtsleeves, the pilot endures stifling cockpit heat as he climbs to altitude.

Midway is in the other direction and not in his plans.

That will soon change.

Seven a.m. A course westward to Guam. The moon-faced pilot in his late thirties wears a dark necktie with a white shirt. His peaked white Pan Am cap hangs from a hook near his seat. Hamilton is the best of the best, possessing Pan Am's ultimate flying designation, that of master of ocean flying boats. His skills have earned him the right to pilot this famous Martin M-130, the pride of Pan Am's fleet since she was delivered six years ago. She has transpacific speed records, has logged tens of thousands of miles, and has even been featured in *National Geographic* magazine. The words "Pan American World Airways" are painted in bold block letters on the gleaming metal fuselage. "NC14715" in black on the tail.

Just after ascending to cruising height, Captain Hamilton receives a secret code by radio telling him America is at war. Pearl Harbor has been attacked. *Philippine Clipper* must return to Wake immediately. The captain will fly patrol around the island with a fighter escort, searching for incoming Japanese aircraft. Hamilton turns back, sets down inside the lagoon, and waits. Takeoff for his reconnaissance mission is set for one p.m. Hamilton orders his plane to be refueled. Then he and his crew sweat inside NC14715 through the long morning under a tropical sun, open windows providing the only ventilation. Hamilton's flight officers are brothers John and Ted Hrutky.

Wake Island was claimed decades ago by the United States for the same strategic reasons as Midway.*

The small, wishbone-shaped spit of sand and coral is part of the Marshall Islands, which Japan claims as its own. The Wake lagoon is too shallow and covered in coral to accommodate warships. There is no potable water. There are two small islands in the atoll: Wilkes and Peale. A 4,500-foot runway has already been built on Peale by crushing coral into the earth. Eleven hundred construction workers tasked with building a new naval air base, almost five hundred marines and sailors, and forty-five Guamanian employees of Pan American call the atoll home.

In Honolulu, U.S. Navy officials are aware that building runways on Wake only makes the outpost more attractive to Japanese invasion. Admiral Husband Kimmel, commander of the Pacific Fleet, is sending six obsolete 5-inch naval guns once utilized on cruisers and battleships, twelve 3-inch antiaircraft guns, six searchlights, eighteen .50-caliber antiaircraft machine guns, and thirty .30-caliber machine guns to defend the atoll.

In addition, the USS *Enterprise* is loaning the island twelve F4F-3

---

* The United States claimed Wake in 1898 and it became a U.S. Navy protectorate in 1934. British sea captain William Wake first visited in 1796, but it is another British captain, Samuel Wake, who named the atoll after himself. The two men were not related. The islands are named for American naturalist Titian Peale and U.S. naval officer Charles Wilkes. Both visited Wake as part of the U.S. Exploring Expedition of 1841.

USS *Enterprise* (CV-6)
Public domain / U.S. Navy National Museum of Naval Aviation

Wildcats. The pilots are thrilled for a chance to get off the ship. They arrived just four days ago.

***

NOON. *PHILIPPINE CLIPPER* bobs at anchor just off Peale. During the long morning wait, passengers shuttle to and from shore to enjoy basking in the luxury of the Pan Am terminal.

The island is on high alert. Nothing is happening.

Suddenly, above the constant thunder of surf crashing onto reef, Captain Hamilton hears the din of something he knows a thing or two about: aircraft engines. One minute later, thirty-four Japanese Nell bombers approach at 1,500 feet. They are land-based and have flown from Roi-Namur, another of the Marshall Islands six hundred miles south.

The attackers drop 130-pound fragmentation bombs, destroying seven Wildcats parked wingtip to wingtip. Pilots racing to their planes are strafed. Shredded bodies lie in pieces on tarmac now covered in blood. The Pan Am sea base is also hit, killing ten employees. The nearby U.S. Marine airfield is bombed and strafed.

Floating unprotected in the lagoon, Hamilton's NC14715 is struck by twenty-six bullets. A bomb lands on the nearby shore, close enough to feel the blast wave. Luckily, the Clipper's topped-off fuel tanks do not explode.

The Japanese pilots are at the end of their tether. It's a long flight back to Roi-Namur and they can only hope they have the gas to get there. They turn for home, leaving behind an island wreathed in smoke from burning fuel stores. Dead marines. Shock. The attack happens so quickly that American antiaircraft batteries barely fire a single round. The dead are quickly transported by dump truck to a refrigeration unit, lest the island's crab population desecrate the remains.

Captain Hamilton can't stay here.

His Clipper can still fly. But there will be no reconnaissance. Hamilton requests permission from Wake's senior officer, Commander Winfield Scott Cunningham, to fly back to Midway. Permission granted, the captain orders the flying boat stripped of all seats and luxury items. Wake is home to several Pan Am employees. Hamilton aims to get them and those already on his passenger manifest home. Forty nervous men and women sit on bare metal as Captain Hamilton taxis out for his first takeoff attempt. Then his second. Finally, on the third try, *Philippine Clipper* lumbers into the air.

One thousand twenty-four long miles over open ocean. At first, Hamilton and his crew navigate by compass. As night falls, the position of the stars in the sky is their guide. Margin for error is minute. Midway will surely be as blacked out as Hamilton, making it hard to see from the Clipper's seventeen-thousand-foot ceiling. There is no radar to guide them in.

Nine hours later, far below, as stars and maps tell Hamilton Midway is near, a ship burns brightly on the sea.

Captain Hamilton takes note of the curious sight. Then he focuses on a safe landing.

It has been a terrifying day for Captain John Hamilton and his crew. He started his morning in one combat zone and will end it in another. He is overloaded with passengers and about to violate every rule in the Pan

Am safety manual by landing a seaplane in the dead of night, unsure whether or not enemy warships wait to shoot him down.

Hamilton is the ultimate pro. He not only lands safely but flies his shaken passengers to Honolulu in the morning. Then it's home to San Francisco for the captain and the rescued Pan Am employees.

***

CAPTAIN HAMILTON AND Pan Am Clippers leave our story now. Wake Island still figures prominently in our narrative, a sequence loaded with action, triumph, and surprise. "A cheery note comes from Wake, and the news is particularly pleasing at a time like this," the commandant of the marine corps informs Secretary of the Navy Frank Knox.

Those words will be premature.

First, let's close out the books on Captain John Hamilton—and Ernest Hemingway. Hamilton is an interesting man who will soon grow a thick mustache and wear his peaked white captain's cap at a jaunty angle— both of which make him look very much like Ernest Hemingway. It's worth giving the captain a proper send-off. Hamilton lives a long life with an illustrious flight career, based out of Hong Kong after the war, still working for Pan An, logging more than twenty-one thousand hours in the captain's seat, making the move from flying boats to jets.

His bio will claim that he "visited almost every major country in the world."

The war that begins with Captain Hamilton fleeing Wake Island right after "Pearl Harbor Day" means Pan Am's Martin M-130 will no longer fly commercial passengers. NC14715 and her sister ship NC14716 (*China Clipper*) will serve in the war effort. Both are operated by Pan Am personnel under the navy's transport wing command.

Each of the original three Clippers in Pacific service suffers a tragic fate. *Hawaii Clipper* is already gone, mysteriously lost in 1938. On January 21, 1943, *Philippine Clipper* will crash into mountainous terrain in California during a foul-weather flight from Pearl Harbor to San Francisco. *China Clipper* is lost in 1945. While landing in the Caribbean, she comes in too low, pitches forward onto her nose, and breaks in two.

As for Captain Hamilton, the escape from Wake is not his hairiest moment of World War II. He will also be forced down in the mid-Pacific, endure a forty-two-hour ordeal in twenty-foot swells, then somehow coax his aircraft into the sky again, piloting his seaplane safely to Honolulu.

A footnote to the "Pearl Harbor Day" escape is the amazing story of Captain Robert Ford's *Pacific Clipper.* The Boeing 314 flying boat was flying a new route from San Francisco to Auckland, New Zealand, as the attacks took place. The crew was forced to change flight plans. Ford will fly his Boeing 314 west across the Pacific, then the Indian subcontinent and Africa before finally returning to New York City on January 6, 1942. *Pacific Clipper* set a record for most miles flown in a commercial flight: 31,500.

Yet war in the Pacific is the beginning of the end for Clippers. Pan American's groundbreaking service becomes a grand footnote in aviation history. Luxurious flying boats are a romantic memory, never to be seen again. The Pacific skies once owned by Pan Am are theirs no more, the era remembered only on vintage travel posters and in nostalgic magazine advertisements—like the one featuring Ernest Hemingway and his fond memories of the Clipper, not to be published until 1956.

By then the noted adventurer will experience two plane crashes in small aircraft. He almost dies. The hard landings will take place in crocodile-infested waters just days apart. Fourth wife, Mary, will suffer broken ribs and Hemingway a skull fracture, a concussion, first-degree burns, crushed vertebrae, a ruptured kidney, as well as damage to his liver and spleen.

The incidents might sour anyone on air travel. But even after all that, the author never forgets the romance of flying on board the Pan Am Clipper.

There was the Pacific, when you took a day to Midway—another to Wake—one more to Guam—one to Manila—then Hong Kong.

One year after Hemingway's advertisement, Midway's Pan American Hotel is torn down.

MIDWAY UNDER FIRE

DECEMBER 7, 1941

MIDWAY ISLAND

9:31 P.M.

J apan returns to Midway, guns blazing.

Twelve hours after Pearl Harbor. Big naval guns belch fire from somewhere out in the total darkness of the nighttime ocean. This is Japan's "Midway Neutralization Unit." They are firing first and—like at Pearl Harbor—their firepower lands without warning.

George Ham Cannon is twenty-six years old. First lieutenant. Commander of Battery H, 6th Defense Battalion on Sand Island. ROTC graduate from the University of Michigan. BS in mechanical engineering. Square shoulders. Strong chin. Dark eyes and wavy brown hair. A walking, talking recruiting poster.

No man on Midway will forget December 7. News of the attack on Hawaii has made for a frantic day. At first, many thought the reports were a joke. Then came the call to "general quarters."

Clearly, this island home is next. Comm checks, foxhole digging, issuing of ammunition. The new technology known as "radar" has picked up "shapes." Then, just forty-five minutes ago, lights observed out at sea thought to be ship-to-ship communication between Japanese warships. It is not known if those are friendly. Just in case, long after twilight turns the island as dark as Pacific Mail Steamship Company coal, the searchlight battery keeps its blinking lights off to avoid giving away Midway's location.

Cannon's unit stands ready. Battery H has endured the rigor of Carthusian monks in the long, lonely months of transforming Midway into a fortress.

Duty is hard, though in a most unconventional sense. The marine corps tells him that his island barracks are 1,137 miles northwest of Oahu. Yet this is not a French Foreign Legion outpost in the middle of a remote desert where lonely men stand guard and long to be anywhere else. "This island is very pleasant and beautiful and should offer a happy outlook to married personnel. For single officers and men it will probably be better to rotate duty between there and Pearl Harbor at 3 to 6 month intervals during peacetime to avoid monotony and to give consideration to natural desires of the men," reported a 1940 reconnaissance in anticipation of increasing the defenses.

Days warm, nights cool. The white sand is so bright, its reflection burns men's retinas. Cigarettes are a nickel a pack. Authorized marine corps recreation is swimming, fishing, outdoor movies, and an occasional cold beer.

Like history's long list of Midway visitors, even the men of the United States Marine Corps find themselves amazed, even amused, by the albatross. The nest birds are nicknamed "gooney" birds for their lumbering gait and seeming lack of intelligence, which remind the marines of a bumbling cartoon character. One marine writes that they "were a considerable problem within the position-areas because once they fell into a gun pit they did not have the intelligence necessary to find their way out. Actually, the birds created quite a diversion for the men working on the guns; if paint were hereditary, I imagine that many a 'gooney' bird is still wearing the red-lead splotches so delicately given his ancestors by the Midway Detachment."*

To the marines' amusement, even the outdoor movies are watched by the albatross.

---

* The etymology of "gooney" dates back to England in 1895 when it was used as another word for a simpleton. The C-47 transport plane will adopt the same nickname later in the war, due to comparisons with the Midway albatross.

"The birds seemed to enjoy the movie as much as the men because the sooty tern and moaning bird would invariably flock around the sound box and emit their mournful wail. During the laying season the island was literally covered with eggs so that in certain areas it was almost impossible to walk without stepping on one."

The fortification of Midway is not done and new chicks are just hatching as the destroyers *Sazanami* and *Ushio* refuel at a tanker christened *Shiriya* fifteen miles off the thick coral barrier surrounding the island. They sail cautiously to a position southwest of Sand, 5-inch guns trained on the incomplete marine defenses. Chosen to protect the returning force and attack Midway, they departed Japan long after the rest of the *Kidō Butai*. Their job is to knock the airfield out of the war. The area is primarily home to VP-21 squadron's PBY Catalina search planes, the slow-moving "eye in the sky" for the U.S. Navy. A squadron of marine dive-bombers was supposed to arrive today but turned back for Pearl after news of the attack.

The first Neutralization Unit rounds fall short, landing in the water between coral and beach. Sharks and turtles are the main victims.

Lieutenant Cannon and Battery H man their .50-caliber antiaircraft guns from the nearby power plant. The aging structure is made of reinforced concrete and offers good enough protection from enemy shells. Cannon commands a small group of enlisted men. Corporal Harold R. Hazelwood mans the switchboard as communications chief. Platoon Sergeant William A. Barbour is Cannon's senior noncommissioned officer. They require permission to return fire.

This order has not arrived. The marines hold fast, their impatience growing with the deafening tremor and punch-in-the-gut percussion of each exploding enemy shell.

Out to sea, Captain Kaname Konishi is in charge of the Japanese attack. A rising star who will one day command aircraft carriers, he now leads aboard *Ushio*, an 1,800-ton destroyer. He orders both attacking ships to edge closer. At nine forty-eight, they resume firing.

The seaplane hangar is hit. Midway's skyline flares from utter darkness to flames, a world made suddenly visible.

Commander Konishi has waited for this bright profile. His gunners zero in on Midway's few but vital targets: the old Pan Am radio beacon, the laundry, the repair shops so vital to fixing broken aircraft.

Only now does Midway Commander Cyril Simard give his marines and sailors permission to discharge rounds. American searchlight batteries illuminate the destroyers twenty-five yards offshore. They train their beams on the ships, but only temporarily, losing that illumination when concussions from incoming rounds extinguish the red-hot feed mechanism. A brave marine shows why the corps has a reputation for reckless courage, using his bare hands to fix the problem in the dark. Searchlight back in action, Battery D opens fire.

The corps has been practicing. Captain Konishi orders his destroyers to move out of range, but it is too late. At least one Japanese vessel is on fire. This is the startling blaze in the darkness that Captain John Hamilton, flying in from Wake Island, witnesses thirty-five miles from Midway as he levels off for his final approach into the dark lagoon.

Even before Captain Hamilton successfully lands *Philippine Clipper* at Midway in the dark of night, the hour is nigh for First Lieutenant George H. Cannon and his men. He has been informed their location is "bombproof," though it is not, a fact he learns in a most unusual instance of bad luck.

A Japanese shell deflects off the aging laundromat next to the power plant. Rather than striking the unopposable might of thick reinforced concrete, the round hurtles into an unprotected air vent. The explosion rips through the opening, instantly destroying Lieutenant Cannon's position. His switchboard is knocked out, decimated by the blast and artillery fragments. Corporal Hazelwood suffers a broken femur. Sergeant Barber's ankle is shattered.

Lieutenant Cannon is the most hurt. Shrapnel crushes his pelvis. Blood gushes from his open wounds. Cannon grows more pale by the moment, but he is awake. Medical personnel race to the Michigander's rescue. Years of training take over. The lieutenant refuses to leave his position, waiting until communications have been established and his men evacuated.

Then Cannon is stretchered to a battalion aid station.

Where the marine from Detroit dies. Later, he becomes the first United States marine of World War II to be awarded the Medal of Honor.

***

FOUR OF THE six "heavy" carriers, as those mighty phantoms of the Combined Fleet are designated, bull through terrifying swells as they begin their return home. *Akagi, Kaga, Shōkaku,* and *Zuikaku.*

Hiryū and *Sōryū* lag far behind. Their job is not done. Pearl Harbor was only the start. Their mission, post-Hawaii, is ambitious.

First, bomb Midway. The American defenses must be neutralized before the island can be captured.

The same two carriers will then sail straight for Wake Island. Troop transports will be waiting offshore. *Hiryū*'s and *Sōryū*'s aircraft will overpower the small atoll before the landing.

Hard weather alters the plan. No one can fly in this shit. The Midway mission is scrubbed. Yet Wake Island is still a prime target, the next American outpost on the journey home. The Americans have been under attack since Captain John Hamilton fled on December 7. That will not change. Air strikes will kill, maim, eviscerate, annihilate, or—in less sympathetic military terms—*soften* the defenses. Invasion troops will go ashore when the defenses are butter. *Hiryū* and *Sōryū* will remain on station until the island falls.

Taking Midway will wait.

***

FROM N. C. Brooks' unnoticed arrival in 1859 to this unforgettable Sunday morning in 1941, Midway has slowly evolved from a sand spit to a luxury stopover to an extremely modern naval base: a pier for loading and unloading large ships; fuel tanks; barracks; telecommunications facilities; a dredged channel entrance; deepwater space for massive warships to turn completely around inside the atoll; airplane hangars; runways on land; runways on the sea; mines capable of blowing the lower limbs off tens of men speckling the sandy beachfront; and guns capable of sinking ships ten miles out to sea waiting to be fired.

Just like the seabirds that Japanese poachers once coveted and then the cable service that they almost claimed as their own, the new naval base at Midway is ripe for Japanese ownership.

It's a ready-made collection of runways, hangars, and barracks on a tactically perfect island just waiting for them to move in and expand their control of the Pacific.

If there's one thing the island's American defenders realize right this moment, it's that the first battle of Midway is over.

The second Battle of Midway is coming—date and time sure to be a surprise.

FRANKLIN AND WINSTON

Winston Churchill hears the news about Pearl Harbor.

The prime minister is spending the weekend at Chequers, forty miles outside London. Dignitaries from Britain and America fill the dining room. The Christmas tree is already up, decorated in ornaments, candles, and baked cookies, the smell of pine twining with Churchill's cigar smoke.

Churchill is in a foul mood, consumed in worry. Intelligence reports tell of Japanese movements near Singapore. He ponders whether or not to send an official warning to Tokyo.

Noting the time, the prime minister turns on the radio and shushes the room.

"Here is the news, and this is Alvar Lidell reading it."

Everyone in England knows the cultured voice of the BBC broadcaster. He has narrated the war for the nation, once even continuing on the airwaves as bombs fell outside his London studio on Portland Place. Now, wearing coat and tie despite the fact that no one can see him, Lidell begins to read the day's happenings.

Winston Churchill is among Lidell's regular listeners. Reception is poor here in the country. Through the static, the gathering of diplomats and secretaries hears words like "Japanese navy" and "United States."

"Pearl" something.

Naval envoy Tommy Thompson suggests the "Pearl" is a river in China.

Then Lidell clarifies the report, repeating the news in its entirety.

Sawyers, the butler, steps from the kitchen. "It's quite true. We heard it ourselves outside. The Japanese have attacked the Americans."

The prime minister is not horrified. Far from it. Churchill is ecstatic. This is the moment for which he has waited two years. The Americans have been broadsided. President Roosevelt has no choice but to fight. Finally, England does not stand alone.

"We shall declare war on Japan," Churchill announces.

American ambassador Gil Winant is among the dinner guests. "Good God. You can't declare war on a radio announcement. Don't you think you'd better get confirmation first?"

So Churchill calls the White House.

President Franklin Delano Roosevelt gets on the phone.

"It's quite true," the president tells Churchill. "They have attacked us at Pearl Harbor."

Roosevelt pauses a beat to let Churchill absorb the news. "We are all in the same boat now."

***

THE NEXT DAY, FDR sends Churchill a telegram confirming that the United States is at war.

"For The Former Naval Person," writes the president. This is their pet phrase, FDR reminding the prime minister they once shared high-level navy jobs.

> The Senate passed the all-out declaration of war eighty-two to nothing, and the House has passed it three hundred eighty-eight to one. Today all of us are in the same boat with you and the people of the Empire and it is a ship which will not and cannot be sunk.
>
> F.D.R.

EPISODE FOUR

———

PRINCE OF WALES

———

(FINALE)

ATTACK

DECEMBER 10, 1941
SOUTH CHINA SEA
0010 HOURS

It's been many pages since we stood with Captain John Leach on the bridge of the colossal *Prince of Wales*.

To recap: *Wales* has been sent to Singapore as a symbol of British saber-rattling. In the words of Prime Minister Winston Churchill, "Nothing like having something that can catch and kill anything."

Then, immediately after the ship's arrival, Pearl Harbor. All hell breaks loose across the Pacific. Almost immediately, London demands *Wales* engage the enemy. Britain is at war with Japan. Tom Thumb, Captain Leach, Jonah, Blackie the cat. Admiral Phillips sallies forth from Singapore to punish the enemy. After a century of the British Empire ruling over citizens of other nations, most Britons consider those "Japs" and others of different ethnicities racially inferior. Phillips and *Wales* will make short work of them.

A long night and day of sailing. Sailors melting belowdecks, the big steel boat a cauldron in the tropics. The lack of ventilation meant for protection from the cold in winter climes makes *Wales* a tropical hell. After twenty-five hours at sea, the admiral, unused to commanding a ship and not seeing much of the enemy, turns his flagship fleet back to Fortress Singapore. The days get fuzzy here, the international date line obscuring the actual number of hours between right now and seven fifty-five a.m. in Pearl Harbor on December 7, 1941.

Doesn't matter.

What matters now is Admiral Tom Phillips' insecurity about those orders from London. The enormous power of his flagship and her many stupendous guns, the weight of his new Churchill-appointed command after years as a bureaucratic tactician ("armchair admiral," some in the Admiralty call Phillips), and the sheer uncertainty of the moment give him pause. Tom Thumb needs to fulfill prophecy. Docking back in Singapore without catching and killing something means disgrace.

So he changes his mind.

HMS *Prince of Wales* is no longer heading back to Singapore.

Here, we resume our story.

Four hours after doing the one eighty, an exhausted Phillips receives new information on Japanese battle plans. There appears to be a landing planned at the small port of Kuantan. The fishing harbor is also home to an RAF base and a spiderweb of roads leading inland and then due south to Singapore. Obviously, not *straight* to the British stronghold, for capturing the naval base and surrounding city by land is ludicrous. But apparently, based on their landings, the Japanese have some sort of offbeat plan.

No matter. Admiral Phillips is a naval man. Pulverizing from the sea is his business. Beaches are a specialty, because everyone is exposed. Roads and farms and jungle are for the army.

Looking at a map, Phillips sees that Kuantan is not out of his way. It's actually on the route home. *Wales* can divert toward land, open fire on Japanese landing craft at dawn, then resume the dash to Singapore.

This is a chance to see action—and there is an extremely good chance of success.

Phillips immediately orders the task force to set a heading for Kuantan. The command is relayed once again by the blue signaling lamp, because Phillips is unwilling to break radio silence.

Japanese submarine *I-56* follows at a distance.

***

THERE IS NOTHING at Kuantan. No ships, no soldiers. As morning sun burns through the clouds, Force Z meanders along the Malayan coastline, searching for an invasion that does not exist. Admiral Phillips orders a thorough investigation, his warships sailing back and forth in absolutely no hurry to be underway to Singapore. A Walrus amphibious scout plane catapults from *Prince of Wales* at 0738. The pilot flies over Kuantan and reports "complete peace" on shore.

Phillips keeps hunting. He still labors under the misbelief that *Wales* is out of range for Japanese bombers.

The crews are nervous, antsy, wondering why they aren't running hard for home. There is an unnerving quiet to the ship as men speak in low voices about their sense of foreboding. Breakfast was served prior to sunrise in anticipation of a prolonged battle. Now a second meal is served as the men stand down. Many walk leisurely on deck, enjoying the warm weather and the deep blue of the sea. A rum ration is issued.

Not even reports that *Tenedos*, now several hundred miles closer to Singapore than *Wales* and *Repulse*, is under aerial attack light a fire under Admiral Phillips.

***

FIVE HUNDRED FORTY miles away in Saigon, ninety-four Japanese bombers prepare to find Force Z. Fifty-one Mitsubishi Nells and Bettys armed with Model 91 torpedoes, thirty-four with eleven-hundred-pound bombs, and nine flying in a search role. Fuel stores topped off. Plans made to reroute to the newly captured airfield at Kota Bharu if anyone runs low on gas. Recon flights shouldn't have an issue but those armed with bombs and torpedoes will travel with less fuel to compensate for the weight. The long flight over water will require a rapid deployment of payload and a quick turn to home. Ditching in the vast sea will most likely not result in rescue.

The preflight briefing goes long. Pilots grow bored. Finally, fortified by canteens of sweet black coffee and rice cakes slathered in bean paste— *ohagi*—Japanese fliers climb into their planes. First takeoff is at 0625. Time to target is just four hours.

***

THREE HOURS AND fifty minutes later.

Prince of Wales takes no evasive maneuvers when a Japanese scout plane appears overhead at 1015. Admiral Phillips orders a course correction, though only to inspect a cargo vessel sailing south. She turns out to be British, the *Haldis*, escaping to Singapore from besieged Hong Kong.

At 1040, *Wales'* radar screens show an incoming flight of Japanese bombers. A bugler blows the order to action stations. Watertight doors and hatches are slammed shut topside. In just two minutes, every man is in position. Despite the threat of incoming aircraft, Admiral Phillips still chooses not to break radio silence and call upon the RAF for help.

The first bombers are heard before they are seen. This first wave of eight Mitsubishis is nine miles out, traveling two hundred miles per hour at an altitude of ten thousand feet. High-angle guns on board *Wales* and *Repulse* train on those targets.

At 1109, Force Z opens fire.

There are several types of firing platforms on board *Wales*. Her monstrous 14-inch MKVII guns are meant to fire the broadsides Admiral Phillips intends to rain down on the Japanese landing fleet. At full strength, those extraordinary pieces of firepower can launch eight tons of explosive shells every forty seconds. But the MKVII can be elevated to only forty degrees. *Wales* is also in possession of eight Unrotated Projectile rocket launchers specifically designed for antiaircraft work. These have proven faulty during sea trials.

Instead, *Wales* fires her sixteen QG 5.25-inch MKI guns. Twin-mounted on eight platforms weighing eighty-one tons each, they can be elevated to seventy degrees. Maximum effective range is almost fifteen miles, up to an altitude of forty-nine thousand feet. Gunnery officers trained to perfectly plot angle and range give the orders to fire, sure in the knowledge the thirty-inch, eighty-pound shells launched from the twenty-one-foot barrels will blast the bombers from the sky.

But there is a problem. Admiral Phillips has ordered an aggressive course correction to keep his ships from being easy targets. Yet this comes after control officers in charge of plotting the angle and range of each 5.25-inch gun on *Wales* and the 4-inchers on *Repulse* have already made their calculations. Fuse settings depend upon the ships' bearings. So shells are exploding far to the right of approaching aircraft. The *Repulse* guns are of World War I vintage but *Wales* features the very latest in modern technology. There is no excuse for missing the targets by such a wide range.

At first puzzled, the gunnery officers soon realize they are not at fault. Course correction is to blame. The solution immediately makes its way up the chain of command. Admiral Phillips quickly orders a return to the original course.

But that takes time. As the eight Nells approaching from the south draw closer to *Wales* and *Repulse*—*Vampire*, *Electra*, *Express*, and *Haldis* being of little interest to the Japanese—it is unclear if the crew can execute the correction quickly enough.

***

LIEUTENANT YOSHIMI SHIRAI's eight-plane squadron takes off almost last. He directs his men to attack with the sun at their backs. This morning's briefing presented his pilots with photographs of *Wales* and *Repulse*, along with the news that *Repulse* has a much thinner main deck than the more heavily armored *Wales*.

Shirai directs his men to aim for *Repulse*.

Each Nell is armed with a pair of 250-kilogram bombs.

Shirai's path to his target takes him directly over *Prince of Wales*. The call to action stations means British decks are crowded. Men crane their necks skyward, watching low-flying planes with their open bomb-bay doors fly directly overhead. There is a sense of relief when nothing falls out of the sky, followed by the stunning moment when bombs *do* tumble out of the twin-engine Nells, this time falling straight down on *Repulse*. Seven explode in the sea, sending great white fountains of water high into the air. But a single bomb pierces *Repulse*'s main deck, punching down through the marine mess deck.

There it explodes.

One sailor dies. Several more wounded. The ship's Walrus seaplane is mangled beyond repair and pushed overboard. Damage-control parties rush belowdecks to control the blaze. The heat is intense, but the blast effects are superficial. *Repulse* continues under her own steam.

The bombers turn for home. Admiral Phillips does the same for Force Z. Now disabused of his belief that airplanes can do no damage to a ship at sea, Tom Thumb gives the order to sail at full speed for Singapore. The distance is 150 miles.

***

TEN MINUTES LATER, British radar shows a much larger formation of Japanese planes heading in their direction. These are the aircraft that originally overflew Force Z and attacked *Tenedos*. One squadron is composed of Nells meant to bomb from ten thousand feet like the flight that hit *Repulse*. But the other two are armed with torpedoes. Anticipating this moment, Japanese flight crews are radioing back to base for information about the ocean depth in this region. Minimum depth for a torpedo is twenty-five feet. Too shallow and the "fish" will strike the bottom and explode.

A quick response: The water is plenty deep.

Shortly after 1100, Japanese pilots visually identify *Wales* and *Repulse*. They level off at 7,500 feet and divide into two sections, one squadron focused on *Wales* and the other on *Repulse*. In the compass room on *Wales'* bridge, torpedo specialist officer R. F. Harland tells Admiral Phillips that he believes a torpedo attack is forthcoming.

"No, they're not," Phillips responds calmly. "There are no torpedo aircraft about." The admiral mistakes these powerful, fast-moving Japanese aircraft with the Royal Air Force's lumbering torpedo planes, perhaps the Fairey Swordfish that helped sink *Bismarck*. But these Japanese aircraft are far more modern than those outdated British biplanes. The enemy pilots are also unlike anything the British have ever seen, flying straight and low, impervious to antiaircraft fire.

Admiral Phillips sends a message requesting help to the RAF by wireless.

Finally.

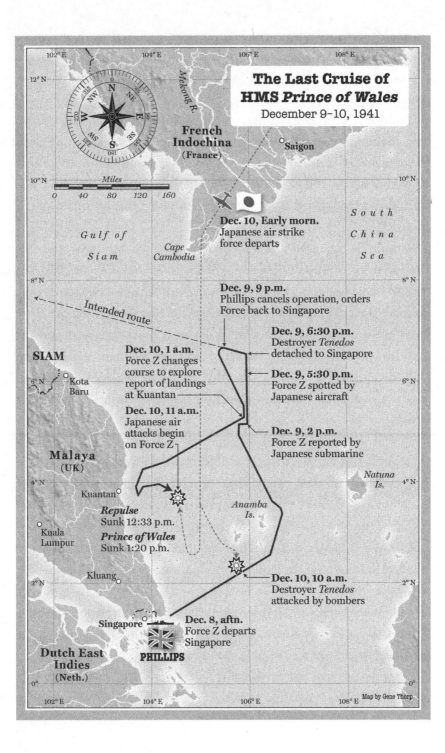

The Last Cruise of HMS *Prince of Wales*
December 9–10, 1941

French Indochina (France)

Saigon

Dec. 10, Early morn.
Japanese air strike force departs

South China Sea

Gulf of Siam

Cape Cambodia

Dec. 9, 9 p.m.
Phillips cancels operation, orders Force Z back to Singapore

Dec. 9, 6:30 p.m.
Destroyer *Tenedos* detached to Singapore

Dec. 9, 5:30 p.m.
Force Z spotted by Japanese aircraft

Dec. 10, 1 a.m.
Force Z changes course to explore report of landings at Kuantan

Dec. 10, 11 a.m.
Japanese air attacks begin on Force Z

Dec. 9, 2 p.m.
Force Z reported by Japanese submarine

SIAM

Kota Baru

Malaya (UK)

Kuantan

Natuna Is.

Anamba Is.

Repulse
Sunk 12:33 p.m.

Prince of Wales
Sunk 1:20 p.m.

Kuala Lumpur

Kluang

Dec. 10, 10 a.m.
Destroyer *Tenedos* attacked by bombers

Singapore

Dec. 8, aftn.
Force Z departs Singapore

PHILLIPS

Dutch East Indies (Neth.)

Intended route

Miles

0 40 80 120 160

Mekong R.

Map by Gene Thorp

At 1141, the torpedo attacks begin. Japanese pilots drop down low to release their payloads, aiming for broadside hits.

On *Wales*, the order to open fire is slow to come. Gunners are late in shooting. Japanese pilots take note.

At 1144, a torpedo slams into *Prince of Wales* on the port side, badly damaging a propeller. Her steering gear is bent and twisted, unable to function. *Wales* lists heavily to port. By 1158, the mighty battleship is staggering across the ocean. Captain Leach orders a flag bearing two black balls to be hoisted at the yardarm, indicating that his ship is out of control.

Meanwhile, *Repulse* is sinking. Nineteen torpedoes miss the vessel completely, but two hit home, knocking men off their feet "like the ship had crashed into a well rooted dock." The order to inflate life belts comes over the loudspeaker: "Prepare to abandon ship, and may God be with you."

Sailors leap into the water, then swim hard to get clear of the downdraft that will suck them under as the ship sinks. Journalist Cecil Brown and his expensive new shoes step into the sea. *Electra* and *Vampire* are now rescue vessels, sailing in close to pluck men from the congested waters.

Blackie, *Wales'* lucky cat, is among those collected.

The Japanese bombers depart at 1230. *Repulse* sinks below the surface at 1233. *Wales* still lives, barely. Another wave of bomber attacks at 1240. *Wales* is hit three more times on the starboard side. Men will remember the ship lifting up into the air and bouncing on the water. Captain John Leach orders all wounded transferred to the destroyer *Express*. A frantic Admiral Phillips is on the radio with Singapore, demanding a tugboat be sent to tow the battleship back into port.

This is impossible. At 1300, nonessential personnel are also ordered to *Express*, which comes alongside *Wales* so closely that sailors step from one vessel to the other.

Wales begins to capsize in more than two hundred feet of water. Admiral Phillips has a decision to make. The naval tradition of a captain going down with his ship is falling out of fashion. But even though thousands of his men have successfully escaped, hundreds more still cling to the side of the hull as she begins to list. *Express* breaks away so *Wales* doesn't pull her under. Overcrowded decks fill with men looking across the void at their doomed comrades.

The Royal Air Force appears overhead in *Wales'* final moments.

There is nothing the pilots can do but watch.

At 1320, *Prince of Wales* founders. Now or never. Admiral Tom Phillips and Captain Leach stand side by side on the bridge. Men in the water call out to them. Leach waves, showing no fear. He shouts to his sailors: "Good-bye. Thank you. Good luck."

"Phillips and Leach," CBS journalist Cecil Brown will write in a story soon flashed around the world, "slid into the water together. It's probable that their reluctance to leave the ship until all possible men had left meant their deaths, since it's most likely they were drawn down by the suction when *Wales* was on her side and then settled at her stern with her bow rising into the air."

***

"THE TELEPHONE AT my bedside rang," Winston Churchill will long remember. "It was the First Sea Lord [Admiral Sir Dudley Pound]. His voice sounded odd. He gave a sort of cough and gulp, and at first I could not hear quite clearly.

"'Prime Minister, I have to report to you that the *Prince of Wales* and the *Repulse* have both been sunk by the Japanese—we think by aircraft. Tom Phillips is drowned.'

"'Are you sure it's true?'

"'There is no doubt at all.'"

Churchill's shoulders slump. The black dog of depression washes over him. Total devastation. The prime minister's decision to send *Wales* to Singapore will weigh heavily on him for a very long time. If not for the prime minister's choice of Admiral Tom Phillips to assume command of Force Z, the brilliant adviser might well be alive. Churchill should have known better.

And of course, the loss of the delightful Captain John Leach makes no sense at all. It was only a few months ago that the captain contrived the wondrous moment off Iceland when Winston, in all his glory, reveled to the sound of foghorns and cheering sailors on the dark gray waters, cold Arctic wind chapping his smiling face.

So it is that Winston Churchill tries to fall back to sleep but cannot, pressed down into his mattress by crushing loss.

"I was thankful to be alone," the prime minister writes of the moments after hearing about the unthinkable tragedy. "As I turned over and twisted in bed the full horror of the news sank in on me."

GOING HOME

Meanwhile, the Ghost Fleet takes the long way home.

North Pacific. Steel gray skies. Raindrops the size of shotgun pellets. Waves washing sailors off flight decks.

The thirty-three ships of the *Kidō Butai* have gone undetected, unseen, and unheard for weeks. The carriers *Akagi* ("*Red Castle*"), *Kaga* (for the province of the same name), *Hiryū* ("*Flying Dragon*"), *Sōryū* ("*Green Dragon*"), *Shōkaku*, and *Zuikaku*—"*Flying Crane*" and "*Lucky Crane*"—now steer far north of Midway Island, lest they blunder into American aircraft carriers thought to be prowling those waters.

In Tokyo, these mysterious ships and their men are overnight heroes. Citizens are overwhelmed with patriotic enthusiasm. Emperor Hirohito even walks around the Imperial Palace in a naval uniform.

Yet the world still does not know precisely who hit Pearl Harbor, where they came from, or where they disappeared to. Everything about their existence is rumor. "Japanese planes engaging in the Hawaiian bombing were believed operating from South Pacific islands," reports the *Honolulu Star-Bulletin*. "The Japanese force that attacked Oahu reached island waters aboard two small airplane carriers."

Adds the December 8 morning edition: "Reports that Japanese aircraft carriers were sunk off Honolulu were not confirmed."

NBC News in New York confirms that the sinkings are, in fact, true.

They are not. No Japanese carrier is sunk. No Japanese carrier suffers so much as a scratch.

On December 9, *The Honolulu Advertiser* alerts its readers to be vigilant. These mystery vessels are coming back. The newspaper claims the unknown ships are now racing back to Hawaii for a second attack.

The same edition reports something that is actually *correct*: The Commercial Pacific Cable Company's transpacific link between Honolulu and Manila has been cut near Midway.

In Washington, it is clear that the U.S. Navy hasn't a clue about where the raid originated. White House spokesman Stephen Early is asked by reporters to explain how Japanese aircraft could reach "the outer defenses of the United States stronghold in the Pacific."

Early's response is unusual. The former reporter is a veteran of eight years of working for FDR. He is fifty-two, experienced enough to know better than to play fast and loose with the facts. Yet he cannot find the words to properly state how Japanese aircraft carriers traveled so far from home, dropped bomb after bomb and torpedo after torpedo on America's vaunted Pacific Fleet, then escaped without absolutely anyone in the United States military having a single clue about where they had come from.

"Carriers would naturally have had all night under cover of darkness to approach," states Early as if the Japanese ships arrived from Tokyo in the span of a single evening. "Planes would take off, come in at high altitude to launch the attack—coming in from the darkness."

Then disappear without a trace.

Ghosts.

Now it's back to Japan's Inland Sea for the *Kidō Butai*. The anchorage at Hashirajima awaits. There, protected by a ring of the Shikoku Mountains overlooking the dark blue bay; a web of antiaircraft guns; and submarine netting no American vessel could possibly dream of penetrating, the men of the *Kidō Butai* will celebrate their great success with the rest of the Japanese fleet.

In a straight line at full speed in calm waters, the journey takes half a week. Yet the escape route is intentionally roundabout, meant to hide the

"Mobile Force" in the biting weather and cold, wind-whipped seas of the northern Pacific. The ships will not return to Japan for seventeen hard days.

The mood on board the carriers is jubilant. There is drinking, because the storms make flight operations impossible. Of 353 aircraft launched on Pearl Harbor, just 9 Zero fighters, 15 Val dive-bombers, and 5 Kate torpedo bombers did not return. This is a small price to pay for sinking the battleships *Arizona, California, Oklahoma,* and *West Virginia. Maryland, Nevada, Pennsylvania,* and *Tennessee* are badly damaged.*

So as the *Kidō Butai* follows a northwest course for home, there is still a sense of disbelief.

***

COMMANDER MITSUO FUCHIDA thinks the Pearl Harbor strike could have accomplished much more. Coordinator of the aerial mission, he is among the last to land on *Akagi* after the attacks. It is this thirty-nine-year-old who launched a single blue flare from the open cockpit of his Nakajima B5N Kate torpedo bomber at seven forty this morning, confirming to Japanese aircraft making landfall over Oahu that the attack is a go. At seven forty-nine, he sends the message *"Tora, Tora, Tora"* to *Akagi* as an indication that the attackers have achieved total surprise.[†]

Fuchida does not rush back to *Akagi* when all is said and done, instead circling over Pearl Harbor, observing from the middle seat until every last Japanese aircraft launches its ordnance. Antiaircraft fire strikes his fuselage and makes it hard for his pilot to steer the plane. But Fuchida is mesmerized. "A huge column of dark red smoke rose to 1,000 ft., and a stiff shock wave rocked the plane," will say Fuchida later. "It was a hateful, mean-looking red flame, the kind that powder produces, and I knew at once that a big magazine had exploded. Terrible indeed."

---

* The United States named each battleship for a state. USS *Utah*, a former battleship converted into a training vessel, was also sunk on December 7.

† *"Tora"* means "tiger" in Japanese. However, *"To"* and *"Ra"* also combine terms for "charge" and "torpedo attack."

The commander finally orders a return course to his carrier. Fuchida is elated that the Pacific Fleet rests on Pearl's shallow bottom.

Yet he knows there is more to be done. The American fuel depot, submarine base, and shipyard so vital to repairing those damaged vessels were not hit.

Commander Fuchida finally lands. Still in his brown gabardine flight suit, the young officer charges to the *Akagi* bridge. He respectfully confronts Admiral Chūichi Nagumo, requesting permission to lead an immediate follow-up raid to bomb Pearl's gas-oil tank farms. All 4.5 million barrels of that fuel have been brought from the mainland to Hawaii by ship. In a comparison dating back to the ages of coal and transpacific flight, nothing happens in the modern Pacific without fuel. Fuchida argues that Japan should destroy that stockpile while they can. Without this vital supply, America will be immobilized. The neutered U.S. fleet will be helpless to stop Japan from attacking fuel convoys from California.

Japan will own the Pacific.

But Admiral Nagumo, commander of the *Kidō Butai*, is a cautious man. Fifty-four. Small. Angry face. Afflicted with arthritis. Once an aggressive commander who practiced the martial art of kendo in his spare time, he is now extremely wary. Nagumo is not a true believer in airpower and carrier forces roaming the seas.

Nagumo is not even a pilot.

The admiral dismisses Fuchida, refusing to take further risks. The reasons are sound: No one knows the location of American carriers *Enterprise*, *Lexington*, and *Saratoga*. The nearest Japanese naval facilities are thousands of miles away.

Should a carrier be sunk, there is a good chance her sailors and officers will be lost at sea.

Should crew be rescued when a carrier goes under, the long ride back to Japan on smaller ships will test each vessel's capacity.

Should a carrier, in a third instance, be damaged but not sink, every effort will be made to tow the ship back to Japan. Yet salvage operations are almost an impossibility. The distance is too great and the seas are rough enough to snap tow lines.

Admiral Nomura tells his aerial coordinator no. Better to make a run for home.*

Now three tankers travel alongside the six carriers. Foul conditions make ship-to-ship refueling a problem. No American pursuer of any kind has been encountered, so other than dealing with the weather, transferring diesel is the largest logistical issue facing the *Kidō Butai*. As Hawaii gets farther and farther behind, even the U.S. carriers no longer pose a threat. The men can go hungry, but the warships cannot.

Sailors, pilots, and officers of the Imperial Japanese Navy are inured to hardship; these men, "used to negotiating the rip channel tides and foul weathers of their islands, are fine navigators," *Time* magazine will report in the weeks after Pearl Harbor. "They work round the clock. They service their ships smartly. They submit to living conditions at which U.S. sailors would mutiny . . . the crew lives, to save space, in quarters so crowded that most officers enjoy less room than U.S. enlisted men." *Time*'s reporting reflects a sudden American desire to know everything about the IJN. Column inches revealing unknown truths about the mysterious Japanese become paramount.

And while a curious world doesn't know the whereabouts of the *Kidō Butai*, the names and displacement of Japan's aircraft carriers are well-known to the navies of the world. Now it is just a matter of guessing which took part in Pearl Harbor.

"The Japanese navy has nine aircraft carriers," writes the *Chicago Tribune*, citing an incorrect number. Their partial list includes "the *Soryu*, *Hiryu*, and *Koryu*, all of 10,050 tons. The *Ryuzu* 7,100 tons. The *Akagi* and *Kaga*, 26,900 tons, and the *Hosyo*, 7,470 tons."

London's *Daily Telegraph* also struggles to fill the gaps. "Apparently, Japan has concentrated most of her energy on the completion of aircraft carriers of which at least eight are in service. These are the 26,900-ton

---

* Commander Fuchida's claim to have confronted Admiral Nomura will later be disputed.

Akagi and *Kaga,* which are probably the ships that carried out the air attacks on Pearl Harbour."

No one but navy men and military historians remember tonnage. The six vessels sailing home are best remembered by their ages and names of origin, for this is what gives them their character.

Akagi and *Kaga* are the oldest, children of the Washington Naval Treaty, former warships turned into carriers with the addition of flight decks. At one time, *Red Castle* and her sister ship named for a province even had three levels from which to launch planes, one stacked on top of the other. No other aircraft carriers in history can make this unusual claim.

Flying Dragon and *Green Dragon*—*Hiryū* and *Sōryū*—were built in the mid-1930s, shortly after *Akagi*'s and *Kaga*'s retrofits saw them shorn of the two useless flight decks that made them appear so tall and top-heavy.

Shōkaku and *Zuikaku*—*Flying Crane* and *Lucky Crane*—are the newest, not quite *Yorktown*-class but very close to being the most modern aircraft carriers in the world. Capable of thirty-four knots. Storage space for ninety-six aircraft. Range of 9,700 miles, with torpedo-resistant armor comparable to that on Japan's best heavy cruisers.

The one weakness all six carriers have in common is a true Achilles' heel: a wooden flight deck. One well-placed bomb will punch straight through the sanded teak and thin steel, igniting ordnance, gasoline, aircraft—and men—belowdecks as the explosion penetrates deeper and deeper into the bowels of each ship.

The Japanese are not concerned. They have more ships, better planes, and highly trained pilots. This could never happen.

YAMAMOTO

DECEMBER 10, 1941
HIROSHIMA BAY, JAPAN
DAY

Japan's ambitious admiral makes big new plans.

Standing on the deck of *Nagato*, flagship of the Combined Fleet, this very complicated individual eagerly awaits the sight of his triumphant gray carriers sidling back into port. Short days, gunmetal sky, low fog, and hard rain. Even now, in the shadow of his monumental victory, the short, powerful admiral is in deep thought, knowing the U.S. Navy is far from defeated. He is obsessed with planning the next attack, the one that will cement his reputation as the greatest naval tactician of his generation—if not of all time.

The solitary genius is Admiral Isoroku Yamamoto, commander in chief of the Combined Fleet. The champion of the ghost ships making their way home is now a celebrity. From this day until his brutal death two years hence—we will get to that in due time—the enigmatic admiral with the gray crew cut will be infamous in America and revered wherever the Axis powers fly their flags. Either way, he does not enjoy the attention in the slightest.

"Japanese leadership on the whole is remarkable for its anonymity. There is no counterpart of Hitler, of Mussolini. How many Americans can name the Japanese Goering, Keitel, Raeder?" shouts one Associated Press article.

"From Tokyo's accounts of the week-old war with the United States, just one name has emerged."

Admiral Isoroku Yamamoto
Public domain / National Diet Library, Japan

Everything about Yamamoto is fascinating—and enigmatic. He is a gambler who has won large sums on poker, bridge, shogi—Japanese chess—and the Japanese game of stones known as "go"; playing the last of those is said to be a spectacular way of learning strategy. He is married but favors the company of geishas. Smoker. Drinker. Known for his work ethic. An amazing ability to walk on his hands for great distances. Yamamoto lost the middle and index fingers of his left hand at the Battle of Tsushima when his cruiser was hit by Russian guns. He is proud of the disfigurement.

At fifty-seven, Yamamoto—the name means "base of a mountain"—was born into a simple rural family but has spent a lifetime in the Imperial Japanese Navy. Unlike his peers, however, the small man was among the first to see the value of naval airpower; he learned to fly and became an early advocate for aircraft carriers. He was outspoken in his defense of the Washington Naval Treaty, knowing it would elevate flight as a naval weapon. Yet he also fought for the Japanese to step away thirteen years later, thinking the terms no longer fair.

The Harvard graduate and former naval attaché to the United States is also a longtime believer in the words of Japanese General Kiokatu Sato:

> If we do not break the ambitions of the American people and do not punish it for its unfairness, our souls will know no peace, even when they leave this world. We fought China for Korea. We fought Russia for Manchuria. The circumstances will oblige us to fight America. The war between Japan and the United States is the inevitable fate of our nation.

Admiral Yamamoto has spent a lifetime admiring and fearing the United States. He is the naval official who "apologized" to America for the bombing of the Panay in 1937. Yamamoto planned Pearl Harbor, overcoming the arguments of other top admirals. The *Prince of Wales* sinking a few days ago? Yamamoto received a celebratory call from Emperor Hirohito himself.

Yet the brilliant strategist knows America will rise up if he does not strike another blow on its navy. A knockout punch. The industrial might of the United States will eventually overwhelm Japan. Not this month. Not even this year. But one, two, three years down the line, America will come roaring back unless Yamamoto stops them.

Already in 1941, the United States has laid down the keels for 436 new vessels. This is part of a $7-billion U.S. Navy program to build 2,831 new ships.*

And that was *before* Pearl Harbor. No telling how the Americans will overreact and over-appropriate now that her Pacific Fleet is filled with holes, salt water, and drowned sailors in their blue dungarees and white Dixie cup hats.

"Should hostilities once break out between Japan and the United

---

* In modern currency, it's $144 billion.

States, it is not enough that we take Guam and the Philippines, nor even Hawaii and San Francisco," Yamamoto writes to Ryōichi Sasakawa, leader of the ultranationalist All-Japan Labor Class Federation. "We would have to march into Washington and sign the treaty in the White House. I wonder if our politicians (who speak so lightly of a Japanese-American war) have confidence as to the outcome and are prepared to make the necessary sacrifices?"

But Pearl Harbor—not to mention the simultaneous strikes in the western Pacific—changes everything. Japan must act fast.

So Yamamoto asks: What's next?

Which is why yesterday, December 9, as the Ghost Fleet was still battling heavy seas en route to Hiroshima Bay, Admiral Isoroku Yamamoto ordered his chief of staff, Matome Ugaki, to make plans for a full-blown invasion of Hawaii—aerial attack, landing craft, soldiers storming ashore.

Ugaki's quarters are next to Yamamoto's, near *Nagato*'s stern. They spend hours together, though Ugaki knows better than to gamble on a game of shogi with his boss, who is described as having "a gambler's heart." The invasion of Hawaii will soon become known as the "Eastern Operation."

It is appropriate the two tactical commanders bunk on the same ship. *Nagato* will go down in history as the location of the war's great Japanese naval decisions. A year ago, right here on *Nagato*, Yamamoto became convinced his navy pilots were capable of a great surprise mission. Something in his well-trained eye told him they could pull it off. "I wonder if an aerial attack can't be made on Pearl Harbor," he told Ugaki.

Likewise, on December 2, in Yamamoto's conference room aboard this battleship behemoth, all 33,000 tons of her, the admiral ordered, *"Niitaka yama nobore"* ("Climb Mount Niitaka")—the code words confirming the attack would proceed. By then, the *Kidō Butai* was quickly approaching Hawaii. This simple sentence committed Japan to war—and ultimately condemned Yamamoto to death. Atmospheric conditions on the morning of the attack were just right, even allowing Admiral Yamamoto to hear the *"Tora, Tora, Tora"* transmission in real time as Commander Fuchida confirmed total surprise.

Also coming in loud and clear were the first American distress signals.

Yet staff officers will recall Yamamoto as downcast on that morning, upset that no American aircraft carriers were in port. This was just a case of bad luck; *Enterprise* had been due to arrive back in Pearl Harbor at seven thirty that Sunday morning. She was on her way home from Wake after dropping off a squadron of pilots and planes. A stiff headwind slowed her arrival by several hours; otherwise *Enterprise* would have been a significant Japanese trophy.

Thousands of congratulatory letters are being sent to Japan's new hero, as Yamamoto is being hailed. Yet the admiral is depressed. "I would rather you made your appraisal after seeing what the enemy does," he responds to one note, "since it is certain that, angered and outraged, he will soon launch a determined counterattack."

Isoroku Yamamoto has staked his career on Pearl Harbor. There is no *Kidō Butai* without the "frog-faced" admiral, as *Time* will describe him. Yamamoto developed this tactical ploy of carriers attacking en masse, just as he has long lobbied for advances in aerial torpedoes and aircraft carriers themselves.

Now, as Admiral Isoroku Yamamoto waits on this cold December day on the Inland Sea, the world is beginning to learn not just his name, but that he has changed naval warfare forever. Gone is the battleship.

American newspapers will soon confirm this.

Reporting from Washington on December 14, the Associated Press notes the loss of American battleships at Pearl Harbor along with *Prince of Wales* and *Repulse* in the South China Sea. "The impressive reports of aerial bombers," a reporter for the syndicate writes, "aroused Congressional demands today for a reappraisal of the warship-versus-airplane controversy."

The visionary pilot Billy Mitchell, who was almost court-martialed for warning the navy about the threat posed to ships at sea by aircraft, is vindicated. The battleship is kaput. There's no better proof of its demise than a Congressional investigation.

What's next? What will be Yamamoto's coup de grâce?

For certain, those carriers returning to port must go back to sea as soon as possible. Japan is undefeated. The IJN is in full attack mode. Nineteen forty-one is about to become 1942. The South Pacific is becoming a Japanese lake as troops successfully attack and conquer every objective. The oil and rubber Japan so desperately needs are within reach. If the next few months go according to plan, Japan will own an uncontested defensive perimeter stretching from the North Pacific down to Australia.

Yet the hard truth remains: Even if every conquest on Yamamoto's wish list occurs and islands and their resources are gobbled up by the IJN, victory will not be total until Japan contends with the United States. America is on the ropes in the Pacific. Guam is lost. The Philippines are falling. Wake Island is surely just days away from capitulation.

This leaves Midway and Hawaii.

Yet he also knows the key to America's strength is *not* island possessions.

It is those Pacific aircraft carriers.

"If we have war with the United States, we will have no hope of winning," the admiral believes, "unless the United States fleet in Hawaiian waters can be destroyed."

The *Kidō Butai* must sink them just like all those American battleships.

Yamamoto has every intention of doing just that.

EPISODE FIVE

ADMIRAL AND CODEBREAKER

THE CODEBREAKER

Commander Joe Rochefort has spoken with Admiral Yamamoto. And he is not impressed.

The outspoken career naval officer pulls open the thick unmarked door to his basement command center. Slim, six feet tall. Brown-haired, married, the intellectual cunning of an Oxford don. He leaves behind the sunshine and warmth of Pearl Harbor and the cacophony from the navy yard's 1010 Dock.*

Rochefort enters the "dungeon," as it is known to all the abnormally pale-skinned men who spend days and nights in this windowless enclave. Descends sixteen concrete steps. Burn bags filled with confidential documents awaiting incineration line his path. Pushes open a second door. Five inches thick. Heavy like a bank vault's.

Rochefort's disdain notwithstanding, Yamamoto is very much on the commander's mind this morning. Rochefort met the admiral more than a decade ago while stationed in Japan to learn the language. Other Americans found the ebullient pilot gregarious, even fun. Joe Rochefort thought the middle-aged Japanese gambler was hiding a lust for war.

---

* The Ten-Ten or 1010—both are used—gets its nickname from its 1,010-foot length.

Joe Rochefort   *Public domain*

Typical Rochefort: Just like the messages he decodes, no man, no matter the rank, is safe from his scrutiny.

A chief petty officer guarding the entrance wishes his boss good morning. Pale fluorescent lights. Dungeon cold as a walk-in refrigerator. Close, dank air smells of stale tobacco, tropical mildew, and body odor. Nonexistent ventilation never quite allows this crowded warren of desks to smell particularly fresh. Background clank of the monstrous IBM computers lining one wall floor to ceiling. These noisy behemoths never stop processing the alphanumeric data fed into them on punch cards. Urgent findings are sent to Washington via Pan Am Clipper.

The underground enclave in Pearl Harbor's old administration building is enormous, fifty feet by one hundred. Rochefort's army of twenty-two codebreakers dress informally and call one another by their first names rather than by ranks or "sir." The best minds in cryptology labor in this airless room. They are linguists, traffic analysts, cryptologists—men prone to obsession and passionate about crossword puzzles. Most admit to being "nuts." The office hums with activity seven days a week, twenty-four hours a day. Hypo—the moniker comes from the phonetic code for this area of Hawaii—is the name given to Rochefort's intelligence unit. The more formal title is Fleet Radio Unit Pacific. The information they gather is so precious that Rochefort answers only to Admiral Husband Kimmel, the burly commander of the Pacific Fleet.

Rochefort kicks off his shoes and slides his stocking feet into slippers. To keep away the cold, he wraps himself in a dark red smoking jacket slipped over his khaki uniform shirt. Pipe and tobacco occupy one large pocket. Then Rochefort sits at his desk.

A package waits for him—a package that could change the course of the war. Its arrival is long overdue.

Rochefort breaks the seal and opens the fat manila envelope from Washington that will change his life—and world history—forever. Now, there aren't any pictures of this moment, things being confidential and all. We don't know if the envelope was manila or even an envelope, but it doesn't take much imagination to visualize a military package with its seal and tape and twine in 1941. What's most important is that the sender is a longtime friend doing Commander Rochefort and America a very big favor.

Two items slide into Rochefort's large hands.

The commander makes a sharp distinction between his work and his homelife. His wife and children are enjoying tropical Hawaii, with its soft island breezes. Just months ago, he was arriving in the office at nine and leaving by five. But the package means he will soon be sleeping here on a cot most nights, working twenty hours straight, living on stale sandwiches and bad coffee.

Every three or four days, it will be time to shower. Rochefort will spend his small gasoline ration to drive home, lather, rinse, scrape a safety razor across his face, kiss Elma and the kids, then immediately return to the dungeon.

That is all to come.

Back to the newly arrived package.

Rochefort lays the contents on his desk. Foremost among them is a copy of the Imperial Japanese Navy codebook, known as JN-25B. The codes are unbreakable, or so the Japanese believe. The commander has wanted to hold this volume in his hands for a very long time.

The second half of the present is a three-hunded-page stack of additional data that gives the parcel its heft. The book and the pages belong together. The codes contain 33,333 five-digit groups. They are combined with that heavy batch of pages, each of which contains a hundred random numbers. These "additives" super-encipher each message. This means a single code group can have as many as fifty thousand meanings. Multiply 33,333 by fifty thousand and the word "impossible" does not begin to describe what it will take to break the codes.

Amazingly, given their location at the focus of Japan's Pacific ambitions, Rochefort's elite team has not been allowed to handle this vital information until now. Instead, they have been delegated the task of cracking Japanese weather codes and a lesser cipher known as the Flag Officers Code. Two other navy intelligence outposts—Cast in the Philippines and Negat in Washington—have been given primary access to JN-25B. Even though home to the Pacific Fleet, Honolulu is such a low priority for those in Washington's intelligence community who wish to believe they have absolute authority that the Purple machine intended for Rochefort's team was given to the British.

A big mistake, it turns out. Singapore appears to be doomed.

Yet as of December 15 Rochefort's staff at Hypo has been ordered by Washington to ignore the weather and flag codes to focus exclusively on breaking JN-25B.

Cast has had a similar package for months but made little progress. Now those codebreakers are holed up in a Philippines tunnel, preparing to evacuate to Australia. The invading Japanese army is marching ever closer to their headquarters. No one has informed Cast that Hypo is also taking a crack at JN-25B.

The package was meant to arrive on November 1. But the ship transporting the top secret information was delayed three weeks in San Diego, the mystery contents not considered a priority. There was no attempt to remove the package from the vessel and transport it by air, which would have taken half a day. Before the ship finally got underway, the parcel was placed in the vessel's vault—but so far in the back that it was almost forgotten upon finally reaching Pearl Harbor.

Had the top secret material arrived on November 1 as planned, Hypo might have succeeded where similar units had failed and broken enough of the code in time to predict the Pearl Harbor attack.

But the package did not arrive on November 1.

It did not arrive on December 1.

It certainly did not arrive by December 7.

Yet, while the package might have taken forever to land on Commander Joe Rochefort's desk, the code must be decrypted as quickly as possible.

Lives are at stake. Starting tomorrow, an American carrier task force is sailing to Wake Island. There, the garrison of several hundred U.S. Marine Corps infantry and aviators, the U.S. Navy and Army personnel, and the 1,221 civilian workers of the Morrison-Knudsen Company have been cut off for days with no hope of rescue. The Japanese are not just attacking the island from the air—invasion troops are already attempting to go ashore.

The cryptologists' mission is to stare at rows of five-digit numbers pulled from radio intercepts. Find shapes and patterns where normal people see gibberish and fall asleep from boredom. Names of ships, islands, military units, and pretty much every fact the IJN spreads by gossip from operator to operator or transmits as a formal order. All of these must be discerned from the web of letters and numbers contained within the codebook. The big IBM computers will help digest the information but the long, involved work of deduction is distinctly human. Rochefort calls it the "staring process." Relies on his powerful memory to store away nuggets of information for future use. "He had a photographic mind and never, to my knowledge, forgot a single detail," one Hypo staffer will long recall.

The patterns are then handed over to "strippers" who subtract the additives from the actual code to find its true meaning.

Finally, linguists will translate everything from Japanese into English. Their job is to give a word to every value in the codebook. It is not enough to find the right term. That is as easy as purchasing a tourist's Japanese–English language book. Instead, the codebreaking linguists must intuit the subtleties they are unveiling. Among other nuances, that means knowledge of the kana, a system of syllabic writing divided into two forms known as hiragana and katakana.

If Hypo is successful, the U.S. Navy will know in advance the locations of the Imperial Japanese Navy, its objectives, which ships will sortie, when they will sail, and where they will sail to. The navy hopes that Joe Rochefort and the men of Hypo can make a difference in the Wake rescue mission.

Admiral Kimmel is sending the carriers *Saratoga* and *Lexington* to relieve the garrison. *Enterprise* will cruise somewhere in between, in position to support the carriers and protect Pearl—whichever is more urgent. Should Japanese carriers arrive on the scene, the stage will be set for the first head-to-head clash between the great naval air fleets of the United States and Japan.

Then, just after Joe Rochefort opens the overdue parcel, everything goes to hell in a handbasket.*

On orders of the president, Admiral Kimmel is relieved of command

---

* Admiral Husband E. Kimmel is treated poorly by history, as if he were asleep at the switch during the December 7 attack. In actuality, Kimmel was a fine officer of long standing who thought Hawaii would never be attacked. Few in the U.S. Navy believed otherwise, despite the storms of war. He retired shortly after being relieved of command, and he went to work for a military contractor. His son, Manning, a submarine officer, would die in July 1944. It is alleged that after Manning escaped from a sinking submarine, the Japanese captured him, soaked his body in gasoline, and burned him alive. On May 25, 1999, the United States Senate passed a nonbinding resolution exonerating Kimmel for the Pearl Harbor devastation. Presidents Richard Nixon, Ronald Reagan, and Bill Clinton all refused to reinstate his rank as a four-star admiral during their time in office. Husband E. Kimmel died in Groton, Connecticut, on May 14, 1968, at the age of eighty-six.

on December 17. His interim successor, Admiral William Pye, is terrified the rescue mission will go horribly wrong and destroy his already descending career.

So he cancels it.

A devastated Joe Rochefort is left to wonder who the next commander in chief of the Pacific Fleet will be—and whether or not that man will have the balls to take on Japan.

THE ADMIRAL

Admiral Chester Nimitz has a new job.

The former head of the U.S. Navy's Bureau of Navigation—a unique term for "personnel office"—is exhausted. He has just left the White House. There, the admiral sat down with President Roosevelt and the commander in chief of the Atlantic Fleet, Admiral Ernest King. "Get the hell out to Pearl Harbor and don't come back until the war is won" was President Roosevelt's direct order.

Now a burdened Nimitz walks home to his family apartment on Q Street to tell his wife he will soon be gone for a very long time.

Fifty-six, his eyes as blue as the sea after a gale, the wavy brown hair of his youth replaced by a thick white thatch. Texan by birth, son of a widow. Nimitz's mother remarried when he was five. Her new spouse was her late husband's brother, Chester's uncle Bill. Chester matriculated to the U.S. Naval Academy at sixteen. Annapolis is where Nimitz suffered significant hearing loss from a poorly treated ear infection. He has since become an adept lip reader.

The three-star is married to the former Catherine Vance Freeman of Wollaston, Massachusetts. The couple has three girls and a boy. "He was the handsomest person I ever met," she will write of his appearance during their courtship. "Those beautiful blue eyes, and a lovely smile."

Catherine lies down in the bedroom as Nimitz steps inside the small apartment. He sits next to her. "Have you got a fever?" the admiral asks gently. It takes no creative license to describe his words that way. Nimitz is known for his steel, but compassion is his hallmark.

"No, sweetheart."

Twenty-eight years of marriage makes a man easy to read. "What is it?" she asks. "What's happened?"

"I'm to be the new commander in chief in the Pacific."

Left unsaid is that Nimitz turned down the job earlier in 1941, arguing he was too junior. Other flag officers would resent his leapfrogging their seniority.*

Then there is the matter of war, which Nimitz predicted long ago. He foresaw the impact it would have on men's careers.

"It is my guess that the Japanese are going to attack us in a surprise attack," Nimitz once confided in his son, Chester Jr., now a submarine officer in the Pacific. The two officers were speaking long before Pearl Harbor. "There will be a revulsion in the country against all those in command at sea, and they will be replaced by people in positions of prominence ashore, and I want to be ashore—not at sea—when that happens."

Which is also why, when offered the role of CINCPAC one year ago, Nimitz turned it down. Yet he spent considerable time in the Pacific earlier in his career, even helping build the submarine base at Pearl Harbor. He has longed for a return to the land of aloha, but not under these conditions.

"You always wanted to command the Pacific Fleet," Catherine reminds her husband.

Chester confides in his wife, sharing top secret information known by few outside Pearl Harbor.

"Darling, the fleet's at the bottom of the sea."

---

* Senior officers in the army, air force, and marine corps are "general officers." Senior officers in the navy are "flag officers," because they fly a standard to mark their presence on a ship or at their headquarters.

***

ADMIRAL NIMITZ REFUSES to fly directly to Hawaii. The new job must wait. He's been working twenty hours a day since Pearl Harbor. Nimitz is exhausted and needs to get his head straight.

So the admiral takes the train. The B&O *Capitol Limited* leaves from Washington on Friday, December 19. By order of President Roosevelt, Nimitz travels in street clothes to avoid the public scrutiny an admiral in uniform draws. He uses the assumed name "Mr. Freeman," taken from his wife's side of the family. His aide, Lieutenant Hal Lamar, travels at his side. It is Lamar who took the call from Roosevelt that sent his boss to Hawaii. Not recognizing the voice and more than a little offended that the person on the line referred to Admiral Nimitz as "Chester," Lamar demanded to know the caller's name.

"This is the president. Put him on the phone."

Now it is Lamar's job to make sure Nimitz gets enough rest. He carries a briefcase of confidential information not to be shared with the admiral until the exhaustion ebbs. Admiral James Richardson of the Navy General Board even insists the lieutenant ply the admiral with a stiff jolt of whiskey each night to facilitate the process—and he provides two bottles of Old Grand-Dad for that purpose.*

Nimitz and Lamar share a Pullman sleeping berth; their rooms are divided by a common door but their beds are so close that the lieutenant can hear his boss snore restlessly as the steel wheels sing.

Yet even before his train chugs away from Union Station, Chester Nimitz is thinking about his new command—Wake Island, in particular. On every leg of the trip during those chances to step outside the train and wander the platform for a few minutes between stops, Nimitz checks the newspapers for the latest updates.

In Chicago, Nimitz gets a haircut and changes trains to the Santa Fe

---

* The Navy General Board was an advisory panel of aging admirals, many near retirement. Their role was to offer expertise on all manner of naval operations. The board was abolished in May 1951 and replaced by the formation of the Joint Chiefs of Staff and a restructuring of the U.S. military following World War II.

Super Chief. Thirty-six hours. Stops in Kansas City, Newton, Dodge City, La Junta, Raton, Las Vegas (New Mexico), Albuquerque, Gallup, Winslow, Seligman, Needles, Barstow, San Bernardino, Pasadena, and, finally, a second Union Station, this one in Los Angeles.

Somewhere between Chicago and Kansas City, Lamar opens his satchel of top secret documents and hands the admiral photographs and files of the Pearl Harbor destruction. Nimitz is appalled. Never before has he seen such carnage. "I find it difficult to keep on a cheerful side," the admiral writes Catherine. "Perhaps when I actually arrive and get over the first shock things will be better."

Through the next few years, Chester Nimitz will write letter after letter home. Yet despite the deep love and connection between himself and Catherine, the admiral does not wear a wedding ring. Like his Japanese counterpart, Admiral Yamamoto, the American admiral is missing a finger. Nimitz's hand was pulled into a piece of machinery early in his career. The gold band of his 1905 navy class ring jammed the gears and brought them to a halt, saving his left arm—but only after the finger was torn off at the first knuckle.

Now, therapeutic rail journey bringing him ever closer to Hawaii, Nimitz relaxes by trying unsuccessfully to teach Lamar to play cribbage, drinking two fingers of Old Grand-Dad at happy hour, and enjoying long naps. Outside, farms, canyons, and a landscape transforming from early Rocky Mountain snow to California's pale winter sunshine.

Nimitz worries about Wake and ponders how in the world he can resurrect the Pacific Fleet. The job is monumental. Millions of men and thousands of ships will all be the personal responsibility of this admiral who was found guilty in a court-martial after running a ship aground in 1906. Nimitz is professional but not perfect.

Los Angeles comes soon enough. Lieutenant Lamar flies back to Washington. A driver takes Nimitz to Coronado, an island just across the bay from San Diego and home to a naval air station. There, he waits out the weather to board a military flight for Hawaii. "I only hope I can live up to the high expectations of you and the President and the Department.

I will faithfully promise to do my best," he writes Catherine. His words lack sentiment, despite the holiday season. Theirs has been a military marriage marked by long separations. Both know the gravitas of what lies ahead. Inserting false cheer would ring hollow.

It is December 24 as Nimitz finally boards a PBY-2Y-2 seaplane in San Diego Bay. Coincidental to his location, the plane is known as a Coronado. The flight to Pearl is thirteen long hours. Despite melancholy about the coming task in Honolulu, the admiral makes a point to thank the aircrew for taking time away from their loved ones at Christmas.*

Hawaii lies southwest of California, at the same tropical latitude as Mexico City. The distance from San Diego is twenty-five hundred miles by air. No landmass in between. The PBY pilots navigate by dead reckoning during the long, dark flight. Admiral Nimitz spends the journey in the cold, unpressurized passenger compartment behind the cockpit. The deafening drone of the four Pratt & Whitney R-1830 radial engines will make his poor hearing even worse for several days after landing.

The morning sun rises behind the admiral as his flight finally approaches the Hawaiian Islands. Fighter escort appears over Molokai to protect the Coronado those last miles into Pearl. She is as enormous and defenseless as a Pan Am Clipper.

The tropical sun blazes hot and insidious in summer, quickly burning exposed skin. But winter has come to Pearl Harbor. December 25. Seven a.m. Low clouds. Cool air. Raindrops streak fuselage portholes. Ford Island and the Battleship Row devastation are clearly visible on final approach. Nimitz's seaplane splashes down near the East Loch, the smoothest and broadest stretch of water in the harbor. Weather adds a few low swells

---

* Coronado Island is considered the "Birthplace of Naval Aviation." Its location on San Diego Bay is where the first simulation of a carrier landing took place. North Island is the current name of the naval air station located there. Before the air station's commissioning in 1917, aviation pioneer Glenn Curtiss ran a flying school in that location. It's worth noting that Coronado Island was also the winter home of Chicagoan L. Frank Baum, writer of the Wizard of Oz book series. To this day, in a nod to those stories, Coronado is known as the Emerald City.

this morning. The admiral is not greeted by tropical aromas as the aircraft doors open. Instead, the toxic smells invading his nostrils are those of oil slicks, smoke, and decomposition.

In an act of historical coincidence, *Akagi* and *Kaga* are dropping anchor in the black mud at Hashirajima as the admiral's seaplane skims to a halt in the oil-slicked black waters of Pearl.

Three senior members of the fleet staff pull up to the floating aircraft in a filthy admiral's barge. Deck and rails covered in oil. Nobody touches anything, a difficult task in the choppy channel. Nimitz shakes hands all around.

"What news of the relief of Wake?" the admiral asks, breaking the ice.

WAKE

Soul crushing.

At the same moment the seaplane carrying Admiral Chester Nimitz splashes down in Pearl Harbor, Japanese troops are making themselves comfortable in barracks that American marines once called their own—rifling through footlockers for souvenirs and fresh clothes, selecting which of the hundreds of perfectly made racks to lay their heads on, grinning at the novelty of shitting in American-style toilets that offer a bowl and a place to sit rather than just footpads and a hole in the ground.

Eighty years from now, the attack on Pearl Harbor will still be so well remembered that people with only a passing interest in history will speak in broad, knowing brushstrokes about what took place, complete with rueful allusions to how devastating the defeat feels all these decades later. December 7 truly is a date that will live in infamy.

Midway will be spoken of a little less specifically, and mostly because people saw one of the movie versions.

Maybe, just maybe, eighty years on, amateur historians looking back at the early days of the Pacific War will mention MacArthur and the Philippines, though perhaps unsure of the chronology between "I shall return," the Bataan Death March, and the grandiose, somewhat overrated return itself. Dwight Eisenhower never made a show of Omaha Beach. For those looking to enhance their CliffsNotes, Nimitz, not MacArthur,

Admiral Chester Nimitz
Public domain

was the man who took on all of the Pacific as his purview from his first hour on the job.

Let's not even talk about how quickly Guam has been overlooked. Most people can't find that tactically vital speck on a map, let alone remember the tremendous sacrifice to hold that floral fortress Magellan stumbled upon four centuries before.

And Wake Island? Completely, totally, utterly, absolutely, positively, horribly forgotten.

The men who fought, died, or were enslaved there deserve better.

***

THE WORLD HAS a short attention span, even for enormous tragedy. It's the way of history. There's so much to remember, especially in wartime.

Yet in December 1942, a time when major wartime events are taking place, Wake is the most famous bastion of good on earth.

In Washington, DC, Winston Churchill and Franklin Roosevelt are meeting for the Arcadia Conference. This is the follow-up to their

Newfoundland clambake sixteen months ago. The focus is developing an Allied military strategy. Churchill is FDR's guest at the White House, where they keep late hours and continue getting to know each other. The prime minister is devastated that Singapore is falling, but he is still selling out the Pacific.

Little does Admiral Nimitz know in far-off Hawaii, but his impossible job is about to become a whole lot more difficult. The prime minister is convincing the president to endorse the Europe first policy. Defeating Hitler is the priority. Japan is a distant second and won't take precedence until the job in Europe and Africa is finished. Nimitz needs to wait his turn and hope he can keep the fleet alive that long.

In the Soviet Union, the Nazi siege of Leningrad continues, with the loss of three thousand citizens a day. Here in the Pacific, Japan is invading Hong Kong and Borneo, and close to chasing the U.S. Army out of the Philippines.

Wake Island—or, as newspapers are calling it, the "Alamo of the Pacific"—is a symbolic affront to Japan's dominance, the only place on earth where the United States appears to have a chance of winning a fight—any fight, anywhere. This is the victory the American public and their new British allies so desperately crave as their Pearl Harbor hangover turns to hatred for all things Japanese.

Beginning in the hours after Captain John Hamilton and his Pan Am Clipper flee to the safety of Midway Island in America's first moments of war, Wake's thousand-plus defenders have been stranded halfway around the world from home, waging a fierce battle to repulse a much larger Japanese invasion force. Their daylight hours are spent desperately scanning the horizon in hope of rescue. Food and ammo are running low. They don't even have fresh drinking water.

The marines are not alone. All those construction workers from the Morrison-Knudsen civil engineering company are throwing down their shovels and picking up rifles to fight alongside their USMC island brethren.

After the embarrassment and loss of December 7, the people of the

United States desperately need good news—and the men on Wake Island
are national heroes for giving it to them.

The defenders are ferocious, their gunnery audacious. Before opening
fire, they wait for enemy ships to arrogantly come within a few thousand
yards. Four Japanese surface vessels and two submarines lie on the bottom as the price of hubris.

No need to hold Wake. Strategic impossibility. But the marines need a
helping hand to get off the island. A successful rescue is hardly a win, but
it would be the moral victory Americans crave.

The world can only wonder what would have happened to these men
if President Franklin Roosevelt had not fired Admiral Husband Kimmel.
The former commander in chief of the Pacific Fleet's decision to launch a
rescue mission was bold. American carriers were racing for Wake to
avenge Pearl Harbor.

Racing!

The officer community is small, as the reader can tell. All those references to academy graduates and the men with whom they share navy
lives speak to an insular society. These are not strangers. The marine
corps is a branch of the navy. Since 1881, midshipmen have been given
the choice of going navy or marines after graduation. The officers on carriers and Wake are Annapolis classmates, confidants, training partners,
men with whom they shared hours of drill, study, boredom, and cramped
bunk space as they moved up the navy pipeline from plebe to firstie to
ensign to command on the cruisers, battleships, and shore postings de-
fining their careers. Happy hours at the officers' club. Best men at one
another's wedding. They know their fellow officers' wives and the names
of their children. Who cheats at golf. Their religion, cocktail, brand of
cigarette. By all means, *full fucking speed ahead.*

Then no.

Critics of Kimmel's plan say those carriers might have been sunk,
confirming the admiral was taking too great a risk.

Or the flattops might have come through. There would have been a
true confrontation of aircraft carriers and pilots as fighters and

dive-bombers from *Lexington*, *Saratoga*, and maybe even *Enterprise* engaged their opposites on *Hiryū* and *Sōryū*. Maybe the marines on Wake would have reveled in a surge of patriotic pride as a battered Japanese fleet retreated back across the waters to lick its wounds.

The world will never know.

Admiral William Pye takes over for Kimmel. He will serve as interim commander of the Pacific Fleet until Chester Nimitz assumes command. But a man with absolute power can do a lot of damage in two weeks. Pye—who stated confidently on December 6, "The Japanese will not go to war with the United States. We are too big, too powerful, and too strong"—is suddenly terrified of the Imperial Japanese Navy.

The sixty-one-year-old Admiral Pye lives a life of tragedy, one naval aviator son killed in a plane crash in 1938 and another boy fated to die aboard the submarine USS *Swordfish* when it is lost with all hands in 1945. But his decision on December 22 to recall the Wake Island rescue mission consigns hundreds more good men to their deaths.

When the command to abort is received on ships throughout that relief convoy, devastated veteran naval officers actually break into tears at the thought of abandoning the marines. Another shellacking by Japan is unthinkable. On *Saratoga*, officers discuss the possibility of ignoring the order altogether. No matter the intentions, that's called mutiny.

In Washington, Chief of Naval Operations Betty Stark agrees that Pye is making the right choice. The rationale is simple: Losing even a single U.S. carrier is too great a risk. Woe to the admiral who believes otherwise.*

Once Pye's mind is made up and those deadly American carriers turn

---

* Admiral "Betty" Stark will suffer his own career misfortune after Pearl Harbor. Admiral Ernest King will replace him as chief of naval operations in March 1942. Stark will be reassigned to Britain, where he will oversee naval operations in Europe and coordinate the navy's role in the June 1944 D-Day landings. However, shortly afterward, Stark faced a court of inquiry that found him accountable for Pearl Harbor. Admiral King endorsed the report and Stark was relieved. He left the navy in 1946 and died in 1972. Admiral Stark is buried in Arlington National Cemetery.

around and steam back to the relative safety of Pearl Harbor, Japan is un-opposed in its invasion of Wake Island. The Japanese systematically re-duce the island's defenses through naval and aerial bombardment. Zeros from *Hiryū* and *Sōryū* strafe and bomb the marines and construction crews. The final blow is a successful amphibious landing that overwhelms the desperate Americans.

Two days before Christmas, two hours before dawn, nine hundred Japanese soldiers march out of the sea. The marines and hard hats are waiting. Fighting is personal, close. The enemy has plenty of ammunition.

Every marine and laborer is soon dead or taken prisoner. More than three hundred will remain on Wake to serve as slave labor, selected be-cause of their construction expertise. Hundreds more will be sent to Jap-anese POW camps throughout Asia, there to spend the war living under barbaric conditions that will slowly starve and kill many. The final ninety-eight Americans still alive on Wake in October 1943 will be marched into an anti-tank defense bunker and executed by machine-gun fire.*

***

JOE ROCHEFORT IS closely monitoring enemy radio traffic. He knows Ad-miral Pye has made a grave error by recalling the rescue force. "The Jap-anese," he is certain, have "no knowledge of the location of our carriers . . . any hostile action on our part by way of our carriers would have been a tremendous surprise to them."†

Yet lessons are being learned.

Angry as Commander Rochefort might be—and, make no doubt, rage consumes the normally calm officer—he is kept busy by the Japanese fleet which produces a boundless volume of radio signals as they lay siege and

---

* The Japanese commander on Wake, Admiral Shigematsu Sakaibara, will be hanged in 1947 for that war crime.

† Admiral William Pye's career is effectively over after the Wake debacle. He will be-come president of the Naval War College in November 1942 and is buried at Arlington National Cemetery in 1959.

invade. Rochefort and his cryptanalysts take full advantage. Every clue is retrieved and recorded for future help in breaking JN-25B.

Traffic analysis is the most common form of radio intelligence. Long messages usually imply a coming battle or something important. There are patterns in all transmissions, giving away the sender, the location, and the letters or numbers of a ship's call sign.

The second bit of "good" news is a top secret mission to rescue one very special officer. Two days before Wake falls, as it becomes clear the atoll will be overpowered, an American PBY-5A Catalina from Midway undertakes what appears to be a simple mail run. The aircraft lands in the lagoon, taking fire as it delivers the last letters from home the defenders will see until the end of the war. Having dropped those heartbreaking mailbags of love and desire and practical matters, like how the mortgage is going to get paid should the man of the house become a POW, the seaplane pilots hastily take off and return to Midway.*

Only now they carry a passenger, one Major Walter Bayler. The Annapolis grad earned his pilot's wings at Naval Air Station Pensacola and his graduate degree in communications engineering at Harvard. He has been on temporary assignment at Wake to establish an air-to-ground radio communication link. More important, Bayler is an expert in the top secret new technology known as "radio detection and ranging."

The navy calls it "radar."

The British used it with great success against Nazi Germany's Luftwaffe during the Battle of Britain. Also known as RDF—"radio direction finding"—this allows advance warning of enemy approaches by land and air. The major's knowledge is most extensive. Few men possess more. He must not become a Japanese prisoner.

So it is that Walter Lewis John Bayler of Lebanon, Pennsylvania,

---

* The PBY-5 Catalina is a seaplane. The "A" model is a seaplane that also has retractable wheels for landing on a hard surface. The PBY-5A, introduced in 1940, became the workhorse of the Pacific Fleet.

crouches within the hold of the cramped PBY fuselage with its eight crew members as it flies the long hours "home" to Midway. Upon landing, Bayler immediately gets to work building radar facilities for that island's own stranded marines.

Radar will ensure Midway has advance warning of *all* approaching enemy.

Should Joe Rochefort and his team at Station Hypo break JN-25B, Midway won't just have advance warning; they'll know who's coming, when they're coming, and where they're coming from.*

Lieutenant Colonel Bayler can be described as a romantic, a brother marine, or just a good guy. Perhaps all three. Either way, his last act before flying to freedom touches many lives. The night before his flight out, he offers doomed marines the chance to write letters home. He will make sure they get delivered. Wake warriors set pencil to paper. Some refuse, either too busy with working on defensive fortifications or, in the case of some single enlisted men, thinking there is no one to write to.

Bayler walks through hospital wards, trenches, hangars, and command posts, collecting mail. Many are love letters, hardened men gushing to their special girls. Others are words of reassurance. By seven a.m. on the twenty-first, Bayler is away. As promised, the letters make it safely back to America long after the islands fall.

"I am writing this under somewhat difficult circumstances," Captain Henry Talmage Elrod, a pilot, writes to his wife. "I'll think of a million things I should have said after I have gone to bed tonight. But I am now going to say that I love you and you alone always and always and repeat it a million times or so."

Captain Elrod is mortally wounded two days later. Once the Japanese destroy all American aircraft, the thirty-six-year-old Georgia native is

---

* For the rest of his life, Major Bayler will be known as the "Last Man Off Wake Island." He will rise to the rank of brigadier general, teach high school physics in Orange County, California, after retiring from the military, and pass on at the age of seventy-nine. He is buried in the Riverside National Cemetery.

killed defending his men as they bring ammunition forth to a gun em-
placement. A Japanese soldier pretending to be dead rises up and shoots
him. The captain receives the Congressional Medal of Honor for his
courage.*

Major Paul Putnam, in a letter to his wife, Virginia, expresses the
powerful sentiments each man is feeling for his loved ones back home.
Words of strength and love and reassurance for the tough days ahead.
"Keep the old chin up, girl. Don't know just when I can get home to see
you all, but I surely will get there. Give my little gals a great big piece of
my love but keep a piece as big as all of them for yourself. Take great big
pieces. There's plenty of it! Your Paul."

Thus inspired, Putnam takes off alone on the morning of December 21
in a vain attempt to end the invasion all by himself. He searches for the
aircraft carriers launching planes against Wake, hoping to initiate a one-
man attack. Sure suicide. But *Hiryū* and *Sōryū* are nowhere to be seen.
Putnam returns to base, resigned to what is to come.

Major Putnam is about to spend the next three and a half years in a
prisoner of war camp.

Not to get too far ahead of our story, but it might make the reader feel
uplifted to know the good news that the pilot will make it home alive to
his wife and three daughters in Michigan when the war is over.[†]

***

BACK IN HONOLULU as Wake Island falls, Joe Rochefort makes do with
news that the *Kidō Butai* has been located. Radio traffic tells the com-

---

* Captain Elrod's Medal of Honor is awarded posthumously to his widow, Elizabeth, in
1946. After his death during the war, she joins the U.S. Marine Corps Women's Reserve
and rises to the rank of major. She will remarry in 1950. In an unusual twist, Elizabeth
Elrod Carleson and Henry T. Elrod are both buried in Arlington National Cemetery, an
honor not often offered to wives. Her military service makes it possible. However, they
are not together. Henry is in section twelve and Virginia in section eight.

† Major Paul Putnam will remain in the marine corps after his return, rise to the rank
of brigadier general, and pass on at the age of seventy-eight. He and Virginia are buried
at Oak Grove Cemetery in Fairfax, Virginia.

mander *Akagi* and *Kaga* arrived back in Japan on December 24. *Shōkaku* and *Zuikaku* one day later.

Sōryū and *Hiryū*, Wake Island conquered and its defenders enslaved, drop anchor in Japan on December 28.

Rochefort is certain Admiral Yamamoto has immediate plans for each of these carriers.

Commander Rochefort must not only track their every movement, but also anticipate Yamamoto's attacks long before they launch.

Obsessed, driven, and not at all fond of losing, Joe Rochefort is determined to win this fight.

THE ADMIRAL

Admiral Chester Nimitz takes command.

Pearl Harbor. A year many would like to forget is just hours from coming to an end. Bloated glorious dead bobbing to the surface for burial, more than three weeks after the attack. Nimitz salutes as he accepts the role of commander in chief of the Pacific Fleet from fellow Admiral Pye. He addresses the sailors of his new command, all standing at crisp attention. The media hangs at the back of the formation, clad in tropical-weight suits, fedoras, and cloaks of cynicism.

"I have just assumed a great responsibility and obligation, which I shall do my utmost to discharge," the newly anointed CINCPAC promises.

"The Pacific Fleet is doing, and will do its utmost, to shoulder its load," the admiral states in the blandest terms possible. One reporter thinks Nimitz looks more like a banker in his choker whites than a navy man. Another disregards him as "fatherly." The admiral can, indeed, be stiff or paternal if a situation calls for it. He is also gregarious and deeply loyal.

Yet none of the reporters see much difference between Kimmel, Pye, and Nimitz—just another navy bigwig spewing the same boring bureaucratic speech.

This is by design. Admiral Nimitz's goal is to remain as vanilla as possible. A small target is not easy to attack.

The admiral describes himself to the press as a *"kama'aina"*—a local—in a joking reference to his service at Pearl Harbor three decades ago. It is two weeks since President Roosevelt personally gave Nimitz this pressure-packed job. The admiral is still adjusting to his new role.

He remains guarded while taking questions. Acknowledges that Japanese submarines shelled Kauai and Hawaii yesterday but leaves for "higher authority" any future plans about how to stop these incursions, knowing all the while that it is his job and his alone.

The press cannot see that this boring and unconcerned admiral is in fact tense, worried, and anxious. He has endured chronic insomnia and intestinal distress since his arrival. The muggy Hawaii climate adds to his sleep difficulties. He calms his insomnia by rising in the dark of night to study charts of the Pacific. He has been in Honolulu a week but delayed assuming command—by reading reports, taking tours of Pearl, getting to know the lay of the land—so his first decisions as commander will be the right ones.

Nimitz has also taken up residence in the spacious quarters on Makalapa Hill once occupied by Admiral Husband Kimmel.

The two men are old friends. As Kimmel awaits the consequences of his Pearl Harbor failure, he shares a house across the street from Nimitz with Admiral Pye. The three men, plus Pye's wife, spend evenings playing cribbage. If it is awkward to sit with his two heavily criticized predecessors each night, Nimitz does not say. Their behavior and fate are for others to pick over.

Now, his change of command ceremony complete, Nimitz steps aboard the submarine *Grayling* and orders his admiral's flag raised. Four white stars on a dark blue background. This act of symbolism formally gives him command. It also marks his promotion from three-star rear admiral to full four-star.

Nimitz built this submarine base in 1920, back when he was a thirty-five-year-old lieutenant commander. Infatuated with underwater technology, the future admiral led the change from gasoline to oil-burning diesel, believing that fuel more suited to automobiles and airplanes turned submarines into bombs. Symbolism aside, the more traditional policy of standing on a battleship to raise his ensign is out of the question, because there is none. The *Grayling* is chosen because Nimitz was once a sub man. He proudly wears the twin gold dolphins of the submarine insignia on his uniform.*

The anchorage was "algaroba and cactus," as the *Honolulu Advertiser* describes what Pearl Harbor looked like before its modernization. So yes, Nimitz is a *kama'aina* now returned home.†

As the admiral's change of command comes to an end, the shadow of Japanese victory hangs over the upturned battleship hulls littering the waters of Pearl Harbor.

But the new CINCPAC sees a silver lining in the devastating defeat: The raid would have been much worse if those ships were attacked out on the open ocean—with thousands of sailors drowning in the deep waters rather than making the short swim to the dock, there to fight again.

***

A FEW FINAL bits of business this morning.

The senior officers who served under Admiral Kimmel and Admiral Pye are beaten men. In the last three weeks, they have endured the double defeats of Pearl Harbor and Wake Island. Their humiliation could not be greater. Most are sure the once promising careers that brought them flag duty are at an end. Many are attempting to transfer to ships as a means of righting that wrong. Nothing restores a foundering career like sea duty.

Admiral Nimitz calls these men into his office as a group. The room feels formal, everyone wearing the starched, high-collared whites from the change of command. The admiral privately believes America might not recover from the "terrible defeat" of Pearl Harbor. He worries the

---

* The "dolphins" are actually mahi-mahi, also known as the dolphinfish. They are not the marine mammals of the same name.

† Algaroba is also known as the carob or kiawe tree. Its sweet, edible pods are often used as a chocolate substitute. South American in origin, the tree was introduced to Hawaii in 1827 by a Catholic priest who used a seed from the royal garden in Paris. It is legend in Hawaii that the thorny branches were used as whips by missionaries to keep native Hawaiian schoolchildren from misbehaving in class.

situation could "not get more chaotic and confused, and appear more hopeless."

Nimitz hides his fears but his priorities are clear: restore morale, keep Japan away from the rubber and oil of the East Indies, maintain communications between Pearl and Midway, and halt Japanese expansion.

One man. Four extraordinary challenges.

Add an unspoken fifth: find a way to attack.

Defense won't work. Nimitz needs to strike *hard*. Ponderous hours on the train and plane drilled that into his head.

But before all this, he must address this dire personnel issue.

The admiral takes a seat at his new desk.

"I know most of you here and have complete confidence in your ability and judgment," Nimitz tells them. The admiral's tone is calm and direct. "We've taken a whale of a wallop but I have no doubt of the ultimate outcome."

Tension eases as the men in the room slowly realize no one is getting fired. The word "we" says it all. These men will soon learn "the man with the blue eyes" is a most accessible boss.

The room clears. The intelligence officer in the bunch remains behind. Surely, this is the man who will get the ax. If anyone should be fired, it is the officer who couldn't predict Pearl Harbor. His name is Lieutenant Commander Edwin T. Layton. Thirty-eight, dark black hair, can't see without glasses. Speaks fluent Japanese. Has not only met Admiral Yamamoto but also played bridge with him several times. Coincidentally, a very good friend of Commander Joe Rochefort of Hypo, both men posted to Japan in the 1920s.

Layton asks that Nimitz assign him to sea duty as commander of a destroyer.

But the lieutenant commander is vital to Nimitz's plan for success.

The admiral's years at the Bureau of Navigation give him a keen eye for talent. He tells Layton he'll be far more effective at Pearl Harbor than on a destroyer. Then he offers Layton a promotion. Layton is now the fleet's principal intelligence officer. He will work closely with Joe Rochefort to provide the admiral with concise daily analyses of enemy intentions. This is such a priority that an intelligence briefing will be the first item on Nimitz's daily agenda each morning at eight a.m.

There's a caveat: Nimitz demands that Layton assume a new identity.

"I want you to be the Admiral Nagumo of my staff," Nimitz explains a few days later, referring to the *Kidō Butai* commander. This is typical of the admiral's leadership style. Since his days as captain of the USS *Augusta*, Nimitz has given younger officers enormous responsibility, believing high pressure and even mistakes are essential to personal growth. He has observed Layton and knows he is a cautious man, reluctant to give a superior information that is not completely accurate. This must change.

"I want your every thought, your every instinct as you believe Admiral Nagumo might have them. You are to see the war, their operations, their arms, from the Japanese viewpoint and keep me advised what you are thinking about, what you are doing, and what purpose, what strategy, motivates your operations.

"If you can do this, you will give me the kind of information needed to win this war."

Lieutenant Commander Edwin
T. Layton   *Public domain*

THE ADMIRAL AND
THE CODEBREAKER

Time for Admiral Nimitz to meet his notorious codebreaker.

The admiral needs to see Joe Rochefort in person. Having spent the last week playing cribbage with Kimmel, Nimitz has gotten an earful about the commander. He knows about Rochefort's disdain for authority. Stubborn independence. Unusual manner of dress.

He's not certain he wants the officer to stay on.

Nimitz enters the dungeon through the inconspicuous street-level door and walks the sixteen steps down into the basement of the admin building. The chief petty officer points him to Rochefort's desk.

Nimitz makes his way over and stands before the commander.

The Hypo leader ignores the admiral.

Rochefort has a full agenda. There is the matter of JN-25B, which haunts his every waking moment. In addition, there is the emotional duress that comes with the upcoming separation from his family. Like all other nonmilitary personnel, Rochefort's wife and children are being evacuated to the mainland. Rochefort will move out of their rented bungalow and take a room at the bachelor officers' quarters here on the yard, walking distance to the dungeon.

Then there is the workload. The Japanese are sending more messages in JN-25B, all of which need to be studied for some method of breaking the code. Sheer volume alone makes this task almost more than Hypo can handle.

And right this very minute, with a four-star admiral standing on the other side of his desk, Rochefort is in a state of hyperfocus, consumed with translating a Japanese message into English.

So Joe Rochefort does not spare a single moment from his obsessive day to answer questions from the new commander in chief, Pacific Fleet. Not at first. He does not rise as Nimitz stands before him.

Nimitz begins talking, unaware he is invisible.

Annoyed, Rochefort *finally* puts down the intercept and reluctantly begins answering the admiral's questions.

Nimitz's biographer writes of a brief tour of the facility that follows: Admiral Nimitz was "shown around by the officer in charge, Lieutenant Commander Joseph J. Rochefort. There was not much to see except rows of desks and filing cabinets. . . . Admiral Nimitz showed polite interest, asked a few questions, and departed."

Rochefort's biographer will venture his own guess about why the commander is so rude, stating, "Admiral Nimitz had caught Rochefort on a bad day, clearly fatigued. Even after the *Kidō Butai* had slipped away and the threat of another Japanese invasion had faded, he had continued to put in long hours."

Rochefort has his own version. "I may have been a little abrupt, in that I wasn't paying too much attention to what he was saying to me or stuff like that. I couldn't recall any of that stuff at all because I was interested at that stage of the game in what was in this message. That's all I'm interested in. I don't care about any commander in chief or anybody else."

All three versions agree on one thing: Admiral Nimitz is not impressed.

"Came down and made us a little inspection, and this was probably completely unsatisfactory from his point of view," Rochefort admits. "Because at that time I had only one object, which was to read Japanese traffic."

Nimitz says nothing about the smoking jacket and slippers, the lack of naval decorum. The arrogant officer giving him the brush-off is said to be good at his job, which is precisely why Nimitz is making it a priority to see Rochefort on Day One of his administration. But this same officer and all these men under his command did not predict Pearl Harbor. Exactly how good can he be?

Rochefort says one smart thing in the admiral's presence.

Just one.

This saves his job.

Nimitz asks Rochefort what he considers to be the primary objective of Hypo. The commander's response is simple: "Making sure CINCPAC knows today what the Japanese are going to do tomorrow."

This is what Nimitz wants to hear.

The admiral says his goodbyes. He leaves Rochefort to his translation and walks back up the steps into the light of day.

As disastrous as the first meeting with Hypo's commander might have been, Nimitz makes the choice to give him the same leniency about Pearl Harbor that he gave senior staff earlier this morning. Commander Rochefort can stay.

The unlikely, often rocky, and ultimately world-changing partnership between Chester Nimitz and Joe Rochefort has begun.

THE ADMIRAL

Admiral Chester Nimitz strikes.

Not hard. Not with great might. But doing something is better than doing nothing.

USS *Enterprise*, the mighty flagship of Admiral William Halsey's task force, sails from the calm protected waters of Pearl, bound for American Samoa. Nimitz has ordered a series of hit-and-run attacks on Japanese outposts. They won't do much but raise morale.

The pinprick raids are risky. Top officers on Nimitz's staff have angrily debated the wisdom of such attacks every moment of the nine days since the plans were unveiled. Aircraft carriers are Hawaii's mobile defense force. The mantra that losing even one will give Japan a far greater advantage has been repeated ad nauseum.

Admiral William Pye's legacy is alive and well.

"Nimitz immediately faced opposition from other flag officers at Pearl Harbor," Lieutenant Commander Ed Layton writes. "They believed it was trying to achieve too much with our limited forces. Admiral Bloch, whose responsibility for defending the Hawaiian sea frontier was an essential part of his duty as Fourteenth Naval District Commander, argued that it was too risky to island bases with carriers whose losses would leave us wide open to a Japanese rampage."

With a gentle nudge from Admiral Chester Nimitz, Admiral Claude

Bloch will shortly leave Hawaii for good, then the navy altogether long before the end of 1942.

Yet Bloch's concern about America's short supply of aircraft carriers is well-founded. The United States currently has three in the Pacific: *Enterprise*, *Saratoga*, and *Lexington*—"Lady Lex."

Romantics might also say that USS *Langley*, as the former CV-1 is known, makes four.*

Sort of.

Langley, America's first-ever aircraft carrier, is stationed off the Philippines. So old that President William Howard Taft attended her christening. The original design even featured a homing pigeon coop for state-of-the-art communication. Once the *Jupiter*, she was converted into a flattop in 1922 and renamed. She *had* a capacity for thirty-four aircraft.†

Then *Langley* was repurposed as a seaplane tender right around the time the modern, marvelous *Yorktown* was christened. Her large, elevated flight deck has been effectively neutered—cut in half and covered in derricks. The pigeon coop is an officer's quarters. Deck cranes lift seaplanes to and from the water. Technically, *Langley* is now AV-3, though the logic of "A" to describe seaplanes makes no more sense than the mysterious "V" appended to carriers of all sorts.

Regardless, no one forgets their first, including the U.S. Navy. To the men who have long served on *Langley*, she will always be CV-1.‡

---

* The USS *Langley* was named after Samuel Langley, who had attempted unsuccessfully to launch an aircraft from atop a houseboat in 1903. Langley was the secretary of the Smithsonian Institution at the time. Langley, Virginia, best known as the home of the Central Intelligence Agency, is named for a different Langley—Langley Hall, home of Thomas Lee in Shropshire, England. Lee was the crown governor of the Colony of Virginia from 1749 to 1750.

† *Jupiter*'s sister ships were *Cyclops*, *Proteus*, and *Nereus*. All three vanished without a trace at sea in the same waters two decades apart under mysterious circumstances. One theory blames the Bermuda Triangle.

‡ A collier is a large cargo ship that carries coal. The first such vessels date back to the fourteenth century. Carrying coal is not glamorous, but it's worth noting that all four vessels utilized by Captain James Cook on his three voyages of discovery—*Endeavour*,

A true fourth carrier—CV-5, USS *Yorktown*—glided through the Panama Canal over Christmas. She missed Nimitz in San Diego by a week. Her theater of operations has permanently changed from Atlantic to Pacific, where she will serve the rest of her days.

Whether it can be argued the United States has three carriers in the Pacific, or four, or even five, the sobering truth is that Japan has eleven.

An almost four-to-one ratio. Or, at the very least, more than two to one.

And it's not just numbers. A brief glance shows that America's flattops are just plain old. The *Lexington* (CV-2) is ancient, converted to a carrier way back in 1922. Her deck capacity is seventy-nine aircraft.

The *Saratoga* (CV-3) is the same age, capable of carrying the same number of planes. Both are former battle cruisers with elevated flight decks. *Langley*, so recently put out to pasture, is just three years older than both of them.

But there's good news.

Enterprise (CV-6) is one of the modern new *Yorktown*-class carriers. Room for ninety-six planes. *Yorktown* herself carries ninety fighters and dive-bombers. The third vessel in this modern style of CV is the *Hornet* (CV-8), currently undergoing sea trials off the Virginia coast.

Should *Hornet* sail to the Pacific when she finishes those tests, all three *Yorktown*-class vessels will be at Admiral Chester Nimitz's disposal. These are the equal of any carrier in the Japanese fleet. If Nimitz can put those three into battle at the same time, the Imperial Japanese Navy just might be in for a surprise.*

Adventure, *Resolution*, and *Discovery*—were colliers, chosen for their ample holds and easy handling on high seas. The famous HMS *Bounty* of mutiny fame was also a collier.

* For those who are keeping track by number and have noticed missing aircraft carriers in the sequence, CV-4 is the USS *Ranger*. She serves in the Atlantic Theater. *Ranger* will survive the war and be sold for scrap in 1947. CV-7 is the USS *Wasp*, currently serving in the Atlantic but soon to arrive in the Pacific. The United States will commission twenty-three heavy aircraft carriers during World War II, concluding with CV-31, the USS *Bon Homme Richard*.

Of course, all this is predicated on the Pacific Fleet fending off the unstoppable *Kidō Butai* until that day arrives.

Nimitz does the best he can to protect his carriers. Each is so massive and home to so many sailors and officers and planes and bombs and torpedoes and hopes that it seems extraordinary to believe these floating air fields made of more than two dozen tons of steel could ever perish. Brobdingnagian, *in extremis*. Yet each is also as precious and fragile as the eggshell of a Laysan albatross. So *Titanic* in their unsinkability. Nimitz protects them with an expendable but vital complement of destroyers, cruisers, tankers, and submarines. They surround the flattops like secret service around the president, ever ready to take a bullet.

The smart plan would be to keep these precious aerial assets in a safe location until the Japanese fleet is located. Yet instead of caution, Nimitz assigns *Enterprise*, *Saratoga*, and *Yorktown* to perform these quick hit-and-run operations to harass Japanese strongholds in the Central Pacific. At this stage of the war, his fleet literally at "the bottom of the sea," Nimitz knows American attacks against the superior Japanese force are like a mosquito attacking an elephant.

On January 11, *Enterprise* sails from Pearl Harbor. She will rendezvous at sea with *Yorktown* and *Saratoga* before launching raids.

Hours later, 480 miles southwest of Honolulu, the unthinkable happens:

America loses a carrier.

And it's not CV-1.

USS *Saratoga* is torpedoed en route to her rendezvous with *Enterprise*. Japanese submarine *I-16* punches a hole in her side, killing six sailors. Extensive flooding. Fires. *Saratoga* turns back for Pearl, limping into port two days later. The damage is more severe than thought. She continues on to the mainland for months of work. *Saratoga* is of so little use for now that her big deck guns are removed before she sails from Hawaii. They are quickly installed on land in shore defenses.

Hornet can't get here fast enough.

THE CODEBREAKER

A lot going on in the world.

In the Soviet Union, "100,000 Nazis Are Caught in a Crimean Trap," according to the wire services.

Closer to home here in Honolulu, Lieutenant General Delos C. Emmons, military governor of Hawaii, is defending martial law as the best way to protect the islands and not as a reflection on the Hawaiian people.

"Air Raid Alarm: Series of Short Siren Blasts," the *Star-Bulletin* reminds its readers. "All Clear Signal: One Long Blast. (There are no practice alarms)."

Gone With the Wind, *Citizen Kane*, and *The Maltese Falcon* still linger in theaters.

Commander Joe Rochefort and the men of Hypo, sequestered in the dungeon near 1010, know nothing about these events.

Their entire existence is this basement room with its cold concrete floor, deafening IBM mainframes, and the battle to learn everything there is to know about the Imperial Japanese Navy.

Rochefort divides the dungeon into sections, one for each of codebreaking's four disciplines: translation, traffic analysis, ship plotters, and cryptanalysts. The men in these quarters have been hand selected for genius. The commander prefers self-starters, individuals comfortable taking initiative. Excess chattiness and watercooler socializing are discouraged. Lieutenant Commander Joe Finnegan is a linguist and codebreaker. Former submariner Jasper Holmes has transformed into an intelligence analyst. Captain Jack Holtwick, a cryptographer, never lets the dank basement interfere with dressing impeccably in a starched uniform. Lieutenant Tex Biard, a linguist. Lieutenant Commander Wesley "Ham" Wright, a codebreaker. Colonel Red Lasswell, who likes cigars. Lieutenant Commander Tommy Dyer, a savant with the sign "You don't have to be crazy to work here, but it helps" posted over his desk.

Dyer, a Kansan who graduated from Annapolis in 1924, is a man prescient enough to have suggested months ago that the basement of the 14th Naval District admin building would be the ideal hideaway to maintain Hypo's independence from navy hierarchy. Previously, the group was in a much smaller room located upstairs. Little differentiated the eccentric codebreakers from the staid military bureaucrats wandering the halls. Security was sloppy.

The team moved in mid-August. From that day forward, outsiders have rarely been allowed into their midst. Even Admiral Nimitz doesn't just walk in off the street.

"Nobody came in without our knowledge," Joe Rochefort will state.

These are just a few of the men trying to break JN-25B, among the many impossible new tasks handed down by Admiral Chester Nimitz. The basement even has new additions that add to its eccentricity. At the invitation of gruff Chief Petty Officer Tex Rorie, Joe Rochefort's top enlisted man and guardian of the dungeon's main door, members of the USS *California*'s band now work at Hypo. Their battleship was sunk on December 7; their instruments are underwater. Though *California* has since been raised, the musicians are eager to perform any task required to be part of the Rochefort team. It turns out, there is an unknown but amazing correlation between music and codebreaking.

It is one month since Hypo began work on JN-25B. The staring process is slow, and just a morsel of the code has revealed itself. But the team is relentless in its scrutiny. "If you observe something long enough, you'll see something peculiar," Dyer believes.

An uptick in radio traffic helps but these dedicated men believe their unique skills will eventually help win the war. Sometimes a thousand messages a day. Rochefort and his men compare transmissions from ships at sea with the codes before them for similarities. There is evidence, for instance, that *Akagi* and *Kaga* might be anchored at the Japanese bastion on the small island of Truk, based on fewer signals from Hiroshima Bay.

As with Morse code technicians everywhere, each Japanese operator has a signature style of delivery—a "fist." By charting each of these enemy sailor's location, Hypo can track the ships at sea.

So the job is not just cracking codes. It is providing the most up-to-date information on the location of the Japanese navy to Admiral Chester Nimitz.

Because he demands to know everything.

Nimitz has been on the job only two weeks, but the admiral already leans heavily on his intelligence specialists. They are his eyes. When it comes to subjects like radio traffic and cryptology, most flag officers still have one foot in the homing pigeon age. Not Nimitz, a man who has always had a fondness for the latest technology. CINCPAC doesn't just request data; he demands specific omniscient information from Hypo. Carriers, submarines, battleships, Japanese air force, disposition of reinforcement troops.

Joe Rochefort will not have all the answers until he breaks JN-25B. Many of his conclusions are guesses right now. But Hypo does not operate in a vacuum. Their connection with the outside world comes in the form of Admiral Nimitz's daily eight a.m. intelligence briefing, delivered by fleet intelligence officer and Rochefort's longtime friend Lieutenant Commander Edwin Layton. Hypo is Layton's primary source of information. A secure telephone line next to Rochefort's desk connects the two men immediately. They speak several times a day.

And at the desks all around Rochefort as he converses on the scrambler, the staring continues.

***

ANOTHER ROUND OF newspaper headlines focuses on Japan's ongoing conquest of the Pacific. But unlike news reports from Europe and the United States, Joe Rochefort and Hypo know *everything* that is going on in this part of the world.

They even know it first.

Intercepted radio messages tell of planes from four of Japan's big carriers attacking New Guinea on January 20. The Japanese hope to capture the large island and position their military within striking distance of Australia. *Akagi* and *Kaga* launch air groups against Kavieng the following day, even as planes from *Shōkaku* and *Zuikaku* bomb airfields at Madang, Lae, Salamaua, and Bulolo. The four carriers will take turns bombing targets throughout New Guinea for the next week.

Meanwhile, *Hiryū* and *Sōryū* batter defenses at the small Dutch naval base on Amboina Island in the Dutch East Indies. One week later, Japanese landing forces come ashore to claim this lucrative stronghold of oil and rubber.

Much to his chagrin, Joe Rochefort predicts none of these attacks. JN-25B is still unbroken. On his watch, Japan has taken almost total control of the southern and western Pacific. It is as if they are waiting to finish that job before turning their attention once again to Honolulu.

Hypo needs to work faster.

And now let's take a few pages to check in on Midway.

Because Midway is under attack.

MIDWAY

Dusk. U.S. Marines at general quarters—or "battle stations," as the navy likes to say. "This is not a drill!" comes the order. A Japanese submarine abruptly surfaces between Sand and Eastern. Nautical twilight was twenty minutes ago. The startling silhouette rises in stark profile against the orange sky.

I-73 sails aggressively toward the Brooks Channel entrance, preparing to fire upon the island's radio station, whose masts make a prominent target—and connect Midway to the world. This matters more than ever since the underwater cable has been cut—though the connection still exists between Midway and Honolulu

Japanese submarines have been spotted throughout the Pacific. This arrival is unique, but not a surprise.

Thus, the marines are ready.

More than ready.

"Within less than one minute," the official marine report will state, "Battery D (3-inch) had a two-gun salvo on the way."

The men of the corps have been spending considerable time preparing for this moment. This is their post. There can be no running away in fear, for there is no place to go.

Radar calibration is a focal point, and there is a great hurry to train inexperienced radio operators in this new technology. The official marine corps report notes that they were "fortunate in having" Major Walter L. J. Bayler, "the Marine aviation officer who had been sent back from Wake with that atoll's last reports."

Radar is like faith: knowing that something is real even if it cannot be seen. Gunnery has its own very visual belief system—that of target, meteorology, firing unit, and accuracy. This particular religion says that if a target exists, it can be destroyed.

It is gunnery, not radar, that saves Midway right now. Within three minutes, the marines fire twenty-four rounds on the submarine, bracketing it in the water. These aren't sniper rifles killing with pinpoint bullets. "Area fire weapons" value accuracy over precision. A healthy deviation makes them more lethal than hitting the same spot every time.

I-73 sailors firing from exposed deck guns launch a dozen salvos of their own. Then they scurry back into the 343-foot boat and slam shut the hatch.

The Japanese submarine crash dives.

The marines cheer, even as they continue scanning the darkening sea for signs of the enemy's return. Yet they would have preferred a kill. Their disappointment subsides thirty-six hours later. The American submarine USS *Gudgeon* comes across *I-73* 240 miles northwest of Midway. The sixty officers and crew on board *Gudgeon* are returning home to Pearl after their first war patrol. Running at periscope depth, they spy the Japanese sub exposed on the surface, recharging her batteries, letting a little fresh air into her cramped quarters, and maintaining a comfortable sixteen knots in the mistaken belief she has no enemies in these remote northern waters.

Gudgeon launches her fish. Three torpedoes run straight and true.

Imagine the chaos on *I-73* as her hull bursts open two minutes later. Thick metal skin burst like an overripe tomato. Deafening thunder of cold ocean water roaring in. Flames and smoke. Gut-wrenching screams of panic. The world goes sideways, then vertical. The inevitable moment gravity pulls her down, down, down.

The *Gudgeon* crew feels the percussion of each distant detonation. Yet

the American submarine flees the scene before confirming whether the
Japanese ship is damaged or destroyed. There's no telling if another lurks
nearby.

Commander Joe Rochefort and Hypo provide the answer. JN-25B radio intercepts show that *I-73* is the first Japanese warship sunk by an
American submarine.*

***

LIEUTENANT COLONEL HAROLD D. Shannon takes pride in Midway's
combat readiness. Forty-nine. One year to live. The atoll's marine corps
commander. A World War I veteran who began his career as an enlisted
man, then rose through the ranks. Shannon has served on several conti-
nents during his nearly three decades in the corps. Brown hair parted on
the left, taut smile when he smiles at all, wire-rimmed glasses. Silver Star.
Croix de Guerre. Shannon's knowledge of tactics and what it takes to defend a position runs deep.

Shannon drinks two dozen cups of coffee on a typical 1942 winter day.
He bunks in a small room off the underground combat operations center
with the entrance camouflaged so thoroughly that Japanese patrol planes
do not know where to look. This command post operates around the
clock. Even in the dark of night, the colonel's subconscious wakes him up
to listen in on phone calls and discussions about the latest events demanding his attention. A staff officer rouses Shannon for good a half
hour before dawn, then immediately launches into a detailed report about
sea conditions, size of waves breaking over the reef, tide, wind, cloud
cover, and any recent radar developments.

"And woe to the officer who didn't know every one of those things accurately and in the specified terminology. After the report was properly
rendered, the colonel would relax and start his coffee marathon with the

---

* The U.S. Navy makes this claim but does not take into account the mini submarine
sunk by the USS *Ward* an hour before the main attack on Pearl Harbor. Ironically, this
was the first shot fired in the Pacific War. Another first was prisoner of war Ensign
Kazuo Sakamaki, a crew member of the HA-10 midget submarine that washed up on
Bellows Beach, Hawaii, on the morning of the attack.

cup that was always hot and ready for his awakening," one marine will recall.

The coffee consumption begins before the briefing. Shannon demands a hot pot be ready from the time he rises at 0500 all the way to the last three servings he drinks at midnight before falling into brief, exhausted slumber.

Shannon's marines mimic the colonel's obsession. Underground personnel shelters allow them to sleep without fear of a stray round killing them in the night. Conditions are cool in their bunkers during these winter months, but lack of sunlight makes for better shut-eye. Breakfast, dinner, and a midnight snack with—what else?—hot coffee are delivered to them at their gun positions, which are also manned around the clock. The food is prepared in the main galley, then placed on trucks for delivery. The fortifications are so strung out that there is no time to also serve lunch.

"The lack of a noon meal was quite disconcerting to the new arrivals, but they soon became accustomed to it and actually were in better health," one report states.

"When conditions permitted, movies were held in a blacked-out warehouse during the day and men off watch could go. But the high point of each day was the noon libation of two beers at the PX."

The only recreation in these tense times is swimming, though in small groups—and always wearing helmet and sidearm until wading into the surf. One favorite cartoon floating around the island is that of a lone nude marine wearing nothing but a gun belt and helmet while dipping his toe into the sea.

Sand and Eastern both have significant numbers of gun batteries facing north, south, east, and west. Sand is home to the seaplane base, radio station, fuel tanks, and command post. Eastern, with its mile-long runways, is almost completely devoted to flight.

But the smaller island is still not ready for war. Facilities need to be expanded to make room for not just the navy and marine aviators, ground crews, and support personnel, but also incoming army bombers and their many squadron members who will help defend the islands. Bunkers are built along the runways, adding protected parking spots for fighters, dive-bombers, and heavy B-17 Flying Fortresses. Aviation gasoline in fifty-gallon drums is buried in the ground nearby, their upper portions poking out of the sand for easy access. These are topped off by gas trucks after each flight. Reserve water and emergency rations are distributed for storage in each bunker. Slit trenches for daily ablutions. More underground concrete shelters are constantly being dug and poured

Through all this, there is the repetition and rigor of daily training. Readiness must not be compromised. As the submarine attacks show, Japan could appear on Midway's doorstep any day—as it has since the decades of bird poop and poachers.

***

So IT IS that *another* Japanese submarine returns two weeks to the minute after *I-73*. As before, the goal is cutting off Midway's communications with the outside world. Surfacing a scant thousand meters off Sand, the Japanese vessel fires three quick rounds. A concrete bunker filled with small-arms ammunition is hit but fails to explode.

Firing just as rapidly, the guns of Battery A on the southernmost tip of the island chase away the intruder with two quick rounds.

Yet *another* Japanese submarine surfaces two days later. Nobody on shore can tell for sure if it is the same as last time, but it reveals itself in the same location off Brooks Channel and at the same time of day. This time, two Brewster Buffalo F2-A2 fighters patrol in the skies above for this very reason. This fighter is no match for the Japanese Zero, German Messerschmitt Me-109, British Spitfire, or even the U.S. Navy's F4F. It is extremely slow, heavy, unstable at any speed, climbs poorly, dives even more pathetically, and has the enormous turning radius of an aircraft carrier. It is such a horrendous aircraft that, as arms manufacturers and aircraft developers make fortunes that will tide them over for generations in this wartime economy, its manufacturer, the Brewster Aeronautical Corporation, will soon be out of business. In short, as the British learned in the Malay Peninsula fighting on the first day of the war, the Brewster is only five years old but functionally obsolete.

That does not matter on the night of February 10, at two minutes before six. Marine pilots John F. Carey and Philip R. White drop down low and strafe the long gray hull. The 6th Defense Battalion's shore batteries open up soon afterward. It is not sure whether the intruder is hit, but that is the last Japanese submarine Midway will see for a very long time to come.

***

MEANWHILE, THE GHOST Fleet is on the move.

Japan's carrier force remains far from Japan and its cold winter climate. Since mid-January, they have made port at a Central Pacific refuge in the Truk Islands, where the air is balmy, the bay is 150 feet deep and clear blue, dense green jungle-covered hills rise straight up from the sea, and the tactical targets of New Guinea and the Philippines are a hard day's cruise in the distance.

Now the *Akagi* and *Kaga* leave Truk and steam due west for Palau, a few hundred miles off the Philippines. They arrive on February 8.

Within a week of dropping anchor, the four battleships; carriers *Akagi*, *Kaga*, *Hiryū*, and *Sōryū*; six cruisers; and perhaps twenty destroyers under Admiral Nagumo's command steam through the Molucca Passage, sailing east of Timor by February 19.

One week later, Japan permanently cripples a most sentimental American flattop. The USS *Langley* barely floats after nine Japanese bombers drop their payloads on her short flight deck. The old girl absorbs five hits. Sixteen sailors die. The ship is in flames, engine room flooding. The order is given to abandon what used to be known as CV-1.

As the crew transfers to nearby destroyers, the wounded and empty *Langley* lists in tropical waters, a great tilted pile of rust and memories.

Her loss is shocking.

Torpedoed *Saratoga* is out of the war for the foreseeable future. Her rebuild on the mainland will last six months.

Langley is gone for good. All that remains is for someone to put her out of her misery.

Because she is no longer seaworthy but still a prize, two torpedoes and nine 100mm shells are fired into her hull by the *Whipple* and *Edsall* to keep her from falling into Japanese hands. She comes to rest in deep waters off Java.*

It is the horrific fate of *Langley*'s crew that once again shows the overwhelming strength of the Imperial Japanese Navy. Just as the sailors on *Prince of Wales* and *Repulse* learned three months ago, no place in the Pacific is safe from the IJN—and surviving the sinking of a ship is no guarantee of safe passage home.

Langley survivors are transferred from *Whipple* and *Edsall* to the oiler *Pecos*—485 men in all. *Pecos* has already filled her decks with survivors of the USS *Stewart*, damaged while in dry dock less than a week earlier. Add in *Pecos*' complement of 314 officers and sailors, and more than a thousand men cram the oiler's decks. She is bound for Australia, two days' sail across the Timor Sea. *Pecos*' top speed is fourteen knots. The slow, overcrowded tub is easy prey.

On March 1, *Pecos* blunders into *Akagi*'s path and is sighted by Japanese reconnaissance pilots when she is just thirty miles south-southwest of the vaunted Japanese carrier. Planes immediately launch from nearby *Sōryū*. *Pecos* is hit but remains afloat, sending emergency calls to any Allied ship that might offer assistance.

But Admiral Nagumo's carriers are too many and too swift. A second blitz of enemy ordnance is soon dropped on *Pecos*, this time by dive-bombers from *Kaga*. As *Pecos* sinks, sailors leap into the water and race to swim clear. Japanese aircraft strafe the men treading water as they await rescue. *Whipple* tries to help, yet only 232 sailors are plucked from the sea. *Whipple* is forced to leave hundreds more behind to drown when threats of enemy submarines force her to leave the vicinity. These sailors

* *Langley* rests in deep seas off the southern coast of Indonesia, in what is known as the Java Trench.

can only watch as the destroyer's diesel smoke disappears. Soon they will have to make the terrible decision of whether to end their lives immediately by taking a deep breath and sinking forever below the surface—or to continue treading water in heavy, waterlogged clothes and a life vest that will only prolong their agony as they pray until their bodies give in to exhaustion for the rescue ship that will never come.

***

FROM EAST TO west, north to south, the *Kidō Butai* owns the Pacific.

The first months of the war are proving extremely successful, allowing Admiral Yamamoto to turn his attention to the Hawaiian Islands from time to time. He begins keeping a close eye on Midway Island. On March 10, a Japanese patrol seaplane is caught snooping just offshore. Four marine fighters splash the spy.

Yet this is the risk Yamamoto must take to achieve ultimate victory. He has his own codebreakers, but nobody with the expertise of a Joe Rochefort or a Hypo to predict what the Americans will do next. All he can do is attack.

Back to the admiral and the codebreaker.

But first, the fate of Singapore.

SINGAPORE

FEBRUARY 15, 1942
SINGAPORE
7:50 P.M.

Singapore falls.

Lieutenant General Arthur Ernest Percival sits in a windowless room at the Ford factory in the Bukit Timah suburb of the island, looking across a wooden table at Japanese officials in suits and dark uniforms. Fifty-four. Snaggletooth overbite. Rail thin. The general wears wrinkled khaki and rests his elbows on the hard surface. Reaches out his right hand. Picks up the pen that will seal his fate.

A Union Jack on a small flagpole leans in the corner, now the property of Lieutenant General Tomoyuki Yamashita. The "Tiger of Malaya" needed just seventy days to drive his outnumbered Japanese army five hundred miles down the Malay Peninsula to capture Singapore. A force of thirty-five thousand Imperial Japanese Army overwhelmed eighty-five thousand Commonwealth troops.

The war is now over for General Percival and the three fellow British officers sitting by his side. The surrender documents are pushed across the table for him to read. Upon signing, Percival and his officers will be led to a prisoner of war camp.

Since Yamashita's men invaded the island one week ago, his soldiers have killed without discrimination. Even hospital patients are bayoneted in their beds. By agreeing to have his soldiers lay down their arms, Percival believes he is sparing the lives of his men and the thousands of civilians now under Japanese control. He is wrong. Massacres of local citizens, particularly those of Chinese ethnicity, will soon take thousands more lives. Half his men will die in POW camps from hard labor, disease, malnutrition, or execution.

Just as the Imperial Japanese Navy is rampaging throughout the Pacific, Japan's army is proving an unstoppable force. Singapore will now be the southern capital of Japan's Greater East Asia Co-Prosperity Sphere. Once the Philippines fall, as they will any day soon, the British and American presence will be all but eradicated.

Winston Churchill will one day take the blame for the Singapore debacle. The warning signs have been there since long before *Prince of Wales* sinks: lack of modern airplanes, inadequate defenses. It is Churchill who thought Singapore, his "Gibraltar of the East," would never fall. Who could ever believe that the Japanese army would attack by land, shielding itself in the jungle? The big guns protecting the island all point out to sea, from where every British military planner has assured the prime minister an invasion would come. They have a full 360-degree traverse, so theoretically they should have punished the Japanese, no matter where they attacked from. In the end, the guns served their stated purpose of preventing invasion by sea—but failed to stop the army coming from the jungle.

So now the fortress that was supposed to hold out 180 days has fallen in seven.

The sword in the heart is removed.

General Percival presses the nib of his pen down on the surrender documents and carefully signs his name.

***

IN LONDON, A devastated Winston Churchill broadcasts the news to his nation. "I speak to you all under the shadow of a heavy and far-reaching military defeat. It is a British and Imperial defeat," he tells the nation, speaking into a BBC microphone. His voice is that of a eulogist and, for once, uninspiring.

"Singapore has fallen," Churchill tells England.

He believes this moment of disgrace is "the worst disaster and largest capitulation in British history." The prime minister cannot bring himself to use the word "surrender."

"This, therefore, is one of those moments when the British race and nation can show their quality and their genius. This is one of those moments when it can draw from the heart of misfortune the vital impulses of victory.

"We must remember that we are no longer alone," he adds, reminding his listeners and himself that as bad as this loss might be, Britain has an ally in these dark times. One year ago, the nation was being bombed day and night by Nazi Germany. Her army was being pushed out of North Africa. The loss of Singapore is catastrophic. Thirty thousand British soldiers were captured before the surrender. Now sixteen thousand British, fourteen thousand Australian, and thirty-two thousand Indian soldiers are also taken prisoner by the triumphant Japanese army.

"Here is the moment to display the calm and poise combined with grim determination which not so long ago brought us out of the very jaws of death. Here is another occasion to show—as so often in our long history— that we can meet reverses with dignity and renewed accessions of strength."

Yet even as he utters these words, Winston Churchill knows Great Britain will never recover from this loss. Her global prestige and empire are forever gone. The Japanese have proven Britain's once formidable army to be weak and confused. For months afterward, the prime minister will lapse into dark depression at mention of the word "Singapore."

Churchill's personal physician, Lord Moran, is one of the few individuals with regular personal access to the prime minister. He is witness to the effects of Singapore's loss. "Though his mind had been gradually prepared for its fall, the surrender of the fortress stunned him. He felt it was a disgrace. It left a scar on his mind," Moran writes of this fateful day. "One evening, months later, when he was sitting in his bathroom enveloped in a towel, he stopped drying himself and gloomily surveyed the floor: 'I cannot get over Singapore,' he said sadly."

The countdown to Midway accelerates.

THE ADMIRAL AND
THE CODEBREAKER

Admiral Chester Nimitz is discouraged.

His carriers have prowled the Pacific for two months. Their hit-and-run raids in the Marshall and Caroline Islands are effective, though not overwhelming. The admiral is melancholy, fearing that he is failing. He speaks often with his boss in Washington, Admiral Ernest King, now promoted to chief of naval operations. But it's been ages since Secretary of the Navy Frank Knox has reached out. Knox is a confidant of President Roosevelt. The admiral has every right to feel his job is on the line.

"I have not received anything from K. recently, so I believe he is lying low," Nimitz writes home to Catherine. "Am afraid he is not so keen for me now as he was when I left but that is natural. Ever so many people were enthusiastic for me at the start but when things do not move fast enough they sour on me. I will be lucky to last six months.

"The public may demand action and results faster than I can produce."

Now, on this warm Monday, Nimitz sits in his office reading a dispatch from Commander Joe Rochefort and his basement warriors. They have decrypted a message showing that Japanese bombers will attack "AK" in two days. Nimitz is pleasantly surprised that the codebreakers are adept enough to know the location of the sender, the type of aircraft to be used, and the date of the attack.

Yet the identity of AK is unknown.

Nimitz demands Hypo give an answer.

So Joe Rochefort makes an educated guess. The commander believes Pearl Harbor is the target known as AK—and doesn't bat an eye when telling Nimitz precisely that. The Japanese are calling this raid "Operation K." It is already known that Wake Island is "AA," based on the extensive traffic before the invasion. An intercepted radio message from AA to Japan's Fourth Fleet confirms AK's "Aviation facilities repairs completed" and "three battleships present."

This fits the description of activities currently underway at Pearl Harbor.

Nimitz is impressed by Rochefort's predictions. Admiral King in Washington is not. Codebreakers there are telling him the communiqués are Japanese misdirection.

Nimitz's faith in Hypo is rewarded.

Rochefort's vindication comes on the night of March 4, as two enemy flying boats approach Honolulu. Their target is the Ten-Ten Dock, right next to Rochefort's underground command post.

Y-71 and Y-72 are each classified as an "Emily," a type of four-engine seaplane with a range of three thousand miles. Weather conditions predict a clear sky and full moon, but as the slow-flying aircraft approach the target, they fly straight into a tropical rain deluge and thick, puffy clouds. Visibility is almost zero. The planes become separated. Y-71's pilot drops his bombs at two ten a.m. Y-72, now separated from his wingman, drops his own ordnance twenty minutes later.

The bombs fall way off course.

In his bed at home, top codebreaker Tommy Dyer hears the explosions from a distance. His wife is alarmed but he falls right back into a deep sleep, content in the knowledge Hypo accurately predicted that AK is Honolulu.

Admiral Nimitz, his own comfort level with the dungeon predictions rising, quickly dispatches a seaplane tender to patrol off French Frigate Shoals. Rochefort's men claim this location halfway between Pearl and

Midway is where the Emilys refueled before their bombing run. Nimitz has every reason to believe the Japanese have secretly taken control of this tiny atoll.

Indeed, two days after Operation K, Rochefort reports to Nimitz with more information: Japan is no longer interested in attacking Honolulu. Their submarines are lingering in the gap between Midway and French Frigate Shoals.

Now, in addition to AA and AK, Rochefort's cryptologists increasingly see another set of letters: "AF."

On March 9, a radio message alerts Hypo that Japanese air commanders are requesting data about wind strength and direction near AF. Rochefort guesses again, telling Nimitz Midway is AF—and about to be bombed.

Once again, Admiral King in Washington believes this is Japanese subterfuge. He radios Nimitz that another attack on Pearl Harbor is coming. Commander Rochefort, in his usual defiant way, quickly sends a message to Nimitz and King: "AF is probably Midway."

Nimitz is by now used to Rochefort's arrogance. King, a hard-drinking serial adulterer whose fiery command style could not be more different from that of CINCPAC, reluctantly defers to Nimitz, allowing him to believe or disbelieve the self-righteous codebreaker at his own peril.

The stage is set for Rochefort and Hypo to be very right or very wrong.

Once again, the commander is right.

At eleven a.m. the following morning, Midway's radar staff under the command of marine corps Major Walter Bayler spots two incoming aircraft on their screens. Four fighters are launched to intercept. The Buffalos come across none other than Y-71, the Emily whose bombs missed Pearl Harbor by ten miles one week ago.

The seaplane doesn't have a chance. All four American planes take part in downing the enemy bomber. "Fighters engaged an enemy plane last seen in a vertical turn losing altitude with white smoke pouring from outboard engines. Fighter pilot observed object resembling burning plane in water immediately thereafter," Midway radios to Nimitz.

The admiral's faith in Hypo is now complete. Command Rochefort rides a wave of success as his men learn more and more about the unbreakable Japanese code each day. After just three months of work on JN-25B, Hypo celebrates the slow unfolding of its mystery. "By January and February we were well into the breaking process," Rochefort will admit in all honesty.

On March 11, Rochefort capitalizes on his triumphs. He sends a message to Admiral King and Admiral Nimitz stating once and for all the Japanese codes for each American-controlled Pacific Island. Using the navy standard of the letter "X" as a form of punctuation, Rochefort writes: "Recoveries of code place designations as follows X AF is Midway X AH is Hawaiian Islands X AI is Oahu (probable) and AG is Johnston (question)."

Later the same day, radio intercepts provide Rochefort further proof of the designations for Oahu and Johnston Atoll. They are, indeed, AI and AG.

Amazingly, months go by before the Japanese make another reference to "AF." It is as if they forget the island exists.

Overwhelmed by the volume of data piling into a mountain of paper and reports on his messy, unorganized desk, Commander Joe Rochefort pushes AF to a far-off corner of his mind. The man who doesn't forget anything will soon remember little about what those two letters mean.

***

ON MARCH 10, *Lexington* and *Yorktown* surprise a wave of Japanese ships landing soldiers on New Guinea's northern coast. One hundred four American planes launch, then fly high over the Owen Stanley mountains before diving down and strafing the Japanese invaders without warning. Four enemy vessels sink; fourteen others are severely damaged.

The Japanese invasion was predicted by Hypo.

Thanks to Commander Rochefort's men, Admiral Chester Nimitz finally revels in a major naval victory.

The win has meaning. This is more than a hit-and-run. America's stunning success shows that Admiral Nimitz is unafraid of using his carriers as offensive weapons.

A relieved Nimitz finally settles into his new command, knowing he's going to be here awhile. Nights are still a sleepless time, but he brings exercise back into his regimen, taking long walks or time in the evening for a set of tennis. He has a horseshoe pit built in his backyard. Nimitz also begins entertaining at his residence, getting to know his officers outside of work.

Lieutenant Commander Layton, the young officer delivering Nimitz's daily intelligence briefing, is an eyewitness to the transformation of his boss from unsure to supremely confident.

"In just three months we had established a reliable basis for tactical and strategic intelligence to support the Allied war effort in the Pacific. It was our ability to intercept and break significant portions of the enemy's operational traffic that gave us the edge."

That ability is about to be put to the test.

EPISODE SIX

COUNTDOWN TO BATTLE

YAMAMOTO

APRIL 5, 1942

HIROSHIMA BAY, JAPAN

DAY

Admiral Isoroku Yamamoto is restless.

The admiral turned fifty-eight yesterday. Now he fidgets in his headquarters aboard his new flagship *Yamato*. A restless man on a very big ship. She is the most enormous battleship in history, measuring more than a hundred feet longer than the late HMS *Prince of Wales* and weighing twenty percent more than any American fighting vessel. Her nine main guns, situated in three turrets, are also the largest ever built. Her name is painted in gold on the hull. A chrysanthemum shield six feet wide, also gold, graces the bow. This emblem of the imperial family symbolizes royalty, rejuvenation, and longevity.

Yamamoto's behemoth battleship is safely ensconced at the south end of Hiroshima Bay. Few places in the world say "navy" as much as this port in the Kure Naval District, with its naval air group, naval prison, naval fuel depot, naval hospital, naval arsenal, naval drinking establishments. Submarines, minesweepers, cruisers. Navy planes. A world of ships and the men who sail them.

Yamamoto's thoughts are on two closely related topics. The first is the effectiveness of the *Kidō Butai*. The British Eastern Fleet has moved from Singapore to Colombo, on the island of Ceylon, off the southern tip of India. Modern-day Sri Lanka. Yamamoto has ordered Admiral Chūichi Nagumo and his carriers on a Pearl Harbor–style surprise raid to destroy the Royal Navy ships in their berths. Five carriers are making the journey: *Hiryū*, *Sōryū*, *Akagi*, *Shōkaku*, and *Zuikaku*. All took part in Pearl Harbor. *Kaga* is the only member of the *Kidō Butai* not in attendance.

Should Operation C prove successful, Japan's sphere of influence will extend from the Central Pacific into the Indian Ocean—roughly one-third of the globe. This will be a symbolic victory. Just like with the admiral's dreams of invading Oahu, which he has had to set aside temporarily, occupying even a small piece of the Indian subcontinent for any length of time is impractical. But destroying the British fleet can only increase Japan's global naval superiority.

"If it is necessary to fight, in the first six months to a year of war against the United States and England I will run wild. I will show you an uninterrupted succession of victories," Yamamoto boasts.

Thus, the admiral eagerly awaits news of yet another glorious triumph.

***

THE SECOND ITEM is the admiral's obsession with the United States Navy's carrier fleet. Their attacks in New Guinea last month show that Admiral Nimitz is willing to gamble with his most precious commodity. Since February 1, *Enterprise* and *Yorktown* have successfully raided the Marshall Islands, Wake, and Marcus Island. No attempt was made at conquest.*

If American flattops can appear out of nowhere to launch aircraft thirty-five hundred miles from Pearl Harbor, then they are more than capable of committing the unthinkable: an attack on Japan. Admiral Yamamoto's greatest fear is American bombs falling on Tokyo. On his orders, fishing boats now patrol six hundred miles off the home islands on

---

* The reader will recall Marcus Island—also known as "Southern Bird Island"—from earlier in the text, when poachers reduced the bird population from hundreds of thousands to just seventeen. Its only tactical significance was its proximity to the Japanese home islands. A garrison of seven hundred Japanese soldiers occupied the island during World War II.

the lookout for aircraft carriers sneaking into Japanese waters. He calms himself by reading the weather reports, taking pleasure in days when overcast skies prevent flight over the nation's capital.

Japan's control of the Pacific is still inviolate. Since December 7, Japan has crushed all Allied resistance—the "United Nations" as Americans, Brits, Aussies, Kiwis, and Dutch call themselves. Her navy is unstoppable. America's random victories aside, Admiral Yamamoto dictates this war.

Yet Yamamoto knows he must eventually grapple with those United States Navy aircraft carriers. He doesn't know where they are, how many there are, or even which are in the Pacific. He wrongly believes that *Lexington* has been sunk and that *Hornet* is already here. In all, Admiral Isoroku Yamamoto believes there are five American carriers somewhere in the thousands of square miles of this vast blue ocean. Finding and destroying the floating fortresses is his greatest ambition.

Yet a seek-and-destroy mission is not Yamamoto's style. Like in a good game of shogi, deception is central to his mindset. Thus, the admiral favors a trap of the most clever design.

Which is why, at this very moment in Tokyo, one of the admiral's favorite aides is in meetings to decide which of two American installations Japan should attack next. The Naval General Staff favors American Samoa. These same officers tried to block Yamamoto's Pearl Harbor attack a year ago, lacking the admiral's visionary mindset.

Their rationale for an attack on Samoa is the severing of communications between the Americans and the Australians. A future Japanese invasion of the land down under could follow, which would secure the entire western Pacific for Japan.

Captain Yasuji Watanabe, arguing on behalf of Admiral Yamamoto and his Combined Fleet, states that attacking Midway is the wise move. Evicting Americans from the Pacific must be the priority.

The admiral endorsed the outline for this battle plan one week ago. Yamamoto still holds a candle for a future Hawaii invasion, believing "continued initiative," such as that follow-up after a successful Midway invasion, is the secret to "a short, decisive war." He will lure the American carriers into a trap off the atoll, destroy them, and secure Japan's Pacific dominance for generations to come. Samoa and Australia can wait.

The debate is violent. Condescending arguments against Midway make Yamamoto's plan seem foolish. Chief among these, states Commander Tatsukichi Miyo of the Naval General Staff, is that America will not care enough to send a carrier task force to her defense. Look at what happened to the stranded marines on Wake Island. Admiral Yamamoto's trap will be ignored.

The stalemate becomes certain victory for the pro-Samoa contingent.

Just when it seems Watanabe has lost, he places a call to Admiral Yamamoto.

The phone rings on *Yamato*. Watanabe hands the line to Commander Miyo.

Yamamoto will not hear a word about American Samoa. The admiral states with all confidence that Midway is the only solution. The man now famous throughout Japan for his tactical genius threatens his mind is "firmly made up."

The Naval General Staff knows what this means: Yamamoto will threaten to retire. This will make the Japanese public and the emperor most unhappy. The general staff will bend the knee, just as they were ultimately forced to do over Pearl Harbor. Commander in Chief of the Combined Fleet Isoroku Yamamoto gets his way.

On April 18, Emperor Hirohito, Japan's supreme authority, approves of Admiral Yamamoto's audacious plan to waylay America's carriers. To add a further layer of deception, Japanese troops will simultaneously invade the Aleutian Islands near Alaska.

By the time he receives the emperor's approval, Admiral Yamamoto's raid on Colombo is over, with the sinking of the British aircraft carrier *Hermes* and two Royal Navy cruisers. In all, a hundred thousand tons of British shipping are underwater. Japanese losses are minimal. The sinking of HMS *Hermes* and the earlier demise of USS *Langley* remove two of the first three aircraft carriers in world history from the wartime stage.

The remaining vessel is Japan's *Hōshō*, soon to engage in Yamamoto's next big battle.

The stage is set for Midway.

A document titled "Imperial Navy Operational Plans for Stage Two of the Great East Asia War" is drawn up, beginning the planning process.

Admiral Yamamoto writes to Niwa Michi, the geisha with whom he spends many an off-hour when he can get away to Tokyo. "The first stage of operations has been a kind of children's hour and will soon be over; now comes the adults' hour, so perhaps I'd better stop dozing and bestir myself."

He is well aware that Japan's many victories possibly make him over-confident, but he cannot shake the feeling that he and his navy are destined for another round of glory.

> The thing that worries me slightly is that, although the war's only been going on for something over three months, a lot of people are feeling relieved, or saying they're grateful to Admiral Yamamoto because there hasn't been a single air raid. They're wrong; the fact that the enemy hasn't come is no thanks to Admiral Yamamoto, but to the enemy himself.
>
> Anyway, my advice is that it would be safer, if only it were possible, to keep half one's property and half oneself somewhere outside the city.

Admiral Yamamoto's words are prophetic.

On the morning of April 18, American bombs fall on Tokyo.

HORNET

Hornet arrives.

In most dramatic fashion.

And Admiral Isoroku Yamamoto's worst fears are soon to be realized.

Sixteen days after sailing from California. Nobody knows she's here. Sixteen olive drab army B-25 bombers lashed to her flight deck. Towering swells. Heaving bow. Bitter cold. Uniform of the day for any man out in the open means gloves, wool cap, and ten-button peacoat.

The newest sibling in the *Yorktown*-class is escorted off the port beam by USS *Enterprise*. The support vessels of the "Big E's" Task Force 16 and her own Task Force 18 clutter the sea for miles around. They sail in the same cold northern latitudes the *Kidō Butai* utilized on December 7—only these warships are traveling *away* from Hawaii.

As Bull Halsey informs the crew of *Enterprise*, "this force is bound for Tokyo."

Halsey will remember the moment for the rest of his life. "In all my experiences in the Navy, I have never heard such a resounding cheer as came up from the ship's company."

Enterprise's job is fighter support. Her planes circle over the combined task force as protection against surprise attack. *Hornet*'s own fighters are consigned to her hangar bay because the big bombers only fit up top on the flight deck out in the open. Brought aboard by crane back in Alameda and roped in place, the B-25s have withstood the thousands of miles since then exposed to the elements. A gale just a few days ago is the worst of it, corrosive sea spray coating each thin metal fuselage. Weather so bad that two men are swept overboard—and somehow rescued.

Five hours to the noon launch. The B-25s will not be coming back. Taking off from an aircraft carrier in such a large plane is barely possible. Landing is out of the question.

The pilots' commanding officer, U.S. Army Lieutenant Colonel Jimmy Doolittle, will lead them at an extremely low level to Tokyo, where each will drop his one-ton payload. Radios, gun turrets, and even the heavy Norden bombsights have been removed so they can carry more fuel.

This raid is not the brainchild of Admiral Chester Nimitz. It is Franklin Roosevelt who decided Tokyo needed a wake-up call. That inspiration came all the way back on December 7, when everyone in America—even the patrician president—lusted for Japanese blood. But the problem facing the navy was "How?" A carrier force would have to get within a few hundred miles, then pray Japanese pilots didn't find them during the anxious hours awaiting their aircraft's return.

The solution is a long-range bomber that will fly clear across Japan after dropping its death blow, then continue west to land somewhere in China.

Halsey is boss. He wants to launch planes 250 miles off the Japanese coast. But at seven forty-four a.m., the plan changes. *Hornet* and *Enterprise* are spotted by one of Admiral Yamamoto's early-warning fishing boats. The Japanese skipper does his job, radioing back to Japan that not two, but *three* American carriers are approaching. On board *Yamato* in Hiroshima Bay, Admiral Yamamoto is confused but not completely surprised. There has been an increasing number of American submarines sighted in Japanese waters. Intelligence reports also show increased activity around Pearl Harbor, indicating enemy ships leaving port for an operation.

Yamamoto immediately orders land-based aircraft to launch and find the Americans.

"Enemy task force containing three aircraft carriers as main strength sighted . . . 730 miles east of Tokyo," Yamamoto signals. "Operate against American fleet."

The *Kidō Butai* are a very long way away, somewhere off Taiwan in a group of islands known as the Pescadores. *Akagi*, *Hiryū*, and *Sōryū* scramble east to find the American carriers. Their pilots end their daily ritual of sunbathing on deck in folding chairs as the eve of a great battle looms.

Meanwhile, back on *Hornet*, these bombers need to get going. Each B-25, so large that its wings and tail hang over the side of the ship, is wheeled into position for immediate launch. Fuel tanks are topped off. Each B-25 receives its allotment of four bombs—three high explosive and one incendiary. Taunting messages to Japan and Yamamoto are written in chalk on the smooth metal casings. *Hornet* turns into the wind to increase airflow coming across the deck.

A navy officer steps into the ready room one deck below to tell the army guys it's time. They lounge in padded chairs with metal frames. Months of training have prepared them for this moment.

"Come on, fellas," Doolittle tells his flight crews. "Let's go."

Pilots race to the flight deck, absorb the hit of a bitter north Pacific wind as they step out into the open, find their aircraft, then climb up into cockpits through a door in the nose, strap into their seats, run checklists, start engines. Navy deck personnel undo tie-downs as the big propellers cough to life, then spin hard. The carrier rocks in thirty-foot waves, gale-force gusts soaking the decks, planes, and aircrews in torrents of spume. Rain squalls abruptly start, then stop, then start again, adding to the misery. *Hornet*'s thirty-two-knot speed combines with the Pacific's bluster for a seventy-five-knot headwind, creating maximum lift. The up and down of the deck will require each pilot to time his takeoff with the moment the bow turns upward, lest he bury his nose in the sea.

From *Enterprise* comes the flashing light of ship-to-ship Morse communication, Admiral Halsey telling Doolittle and his men, "Good luck and God bless you!"

The veteran is tough as stone. But the message touches him like a minor gospel of hope.

Nobody on *Hornet* or *Enterprise* has seen anything like what is about to take place. Sailors and officers hold their breath, unsure if the lumbering B-25s will make it into the air.

Hornet's deck officer stands near the bow, holding both corners of a checkered flag to keep it stiff. Doolittle, in the lead aircraft, revs his throttles to maximum capacity while standing on the brakes. The deck vibrates from the torque of sixty-four Wright Cyclone engines powered up to full throttle. Lined up behind Doolittle, the fifteen other pilots do the same.

The flight officer drops his flag. Lieutenant Colonel Doolittle lifts his feet. Propellers scream so hard, it feels like engines are about to explode. A sudden sprint down the length of the flight deck. The pilot times his roll as the bow faces down into the waves. The big ship rocks upward by the time he chunders past the flight officer, a man who looks very much like someone about to be blown overboard.

Slowly, ever so slowly, barely faster than *Hornet* itself, the heavily laden B-25 lumbers into the gray sky like a great winged beast.

Jimmy Doolittle is away.

One by one, every bomber launches. Elapsed time just under one hour. Admiral Halsey wastes no time escaping the area. He orders a course change for the combined task force. Soon, *Enterprise* and *Hornet* are sailing northeast at twenty-five knots, leaving Japan behind.

There, in the high northern waters, they vanish, the new Ghost Fleet.

The next day, long after Doolittle and his raiders drop bombs on Japan for the first time in the war, setting off air raid sirens throughout Tokyo, the entire Imperial Japanese Navy continues searching for *Enterprise* and *Hornet*. Admiral Yamamoto is so enraged and embarrassed that even Russian trawlers are boarded in the search for American pilots who might have splashed into the sea.

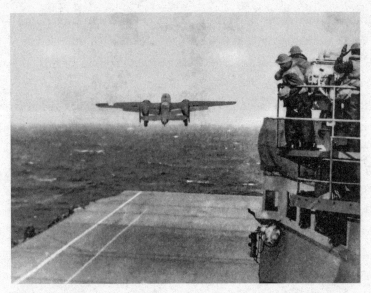

A B-25 launching off *Hornet* (Doolittle Raid)   *Public domain*

Finally, Yamamoto angrily admits defeat. As he feared, the Americans are proving to be worthy adversaries.

"Cease operations against the American fleet," the admiral reluctantly orders two days later.

It is beyond belief that large American bombers took off from a carrier. The only base close enough for them to launch on Tokyo is Midway—which provides yet another reason for Admiral Yamamoto to execute his invasion plan.

Now, more than ever, Yamamoto needs to destroy the American carriers. The construction of new flattops and the repair of battleships raised from the mud of Pearl Harbor will soon be concluded. Japan will face an even more powerful threat when that day comes.

The Japanese Ministry of War quickly issues a full report of the Doolittle Raid. The document reaches five conclusions. The first three focus on morale, losing face, and the necessary diversion of Japanese forces to prevent a second raid.

Yet the desire for revenge is coursing through the Japanese military, an emotion no less furious than the one a stunned FDR felt on December 7. So the final two bullet points reflect an outcome Admiral Yamamoto could never have predicted: The Japanese army is now clamoring to join the navy as part of the Midway operation; and his old rivals at the Imperial General Headquarters are "unreservedly behind [the] Combined Fleet Midway-Aleutians operation plan."

***

AT HYPO IN Pearl Harbor, the enormous flow of radio traffic brought on by the Japanese search for *Enterprise* and *Hornet* reaps a proportional windfall. "The radio traffic brought a bonus of intercepted messages that updated and confirmed the latest call signs of ships and shore stations," Lieutenant Commander Ed Layton writes.

Intercepting radio transmissions is not difficult. As the number grows during this crucial time, the recurring patterns begin to make themselves known. With more pieces added to the puzzle every day, the dungeon's residents grow closer to a full understanding of the Japanese code.

Yet JN-25B is still not broken.

As events rapidly approach confrontation, that top secret data holds the key to victory or defeat.

NIMITZ

A PBY-5A Catalina glides to a halt in the lagoon and taxis to the Sand Island seaplane dock. It's not one of the planes stationed at Midway. Must be coming from Pearl Harbor. Curious marines pull the aircraft up the ramp onto land. The doors are situated behind the high wings and twin engines, in the middle of the bulbous fuselage.

The port hatch opens. Commander of the Pacific Fleet Chester Nimitz emerges, much to the marines' shock. Most wear swimming trunks for the recovery operation and snap to attention, bare chests and legs tanned by hours in the sun. The admiral wears rumpled khakis over a white T-shirt, no tie, no sweat rings beneath his arms, the four stars on his collar denoting a rank so high that most of these men have never seen such a sight up close. Nimitz stretches his legs and arms after six hours in the cramped plane. He's glad to stand up straight again. There was no flush toilet on board, just a bucket with a seat located back near the tail. The fuselage smelled heavily from the tar-impregnated paper of airsickness bags. Though warm and heavy, the fresh island air is most welcome.

The over-caffeinated Lieutenant Colonel Harold Shannon steps forward and salutes. Summoned to greet Nimitz, the commander of the Sixth Marine Defense Battalion is prepared to leave his command bunker and spend the day leading the admiral on a tour of this well-fortified island home.

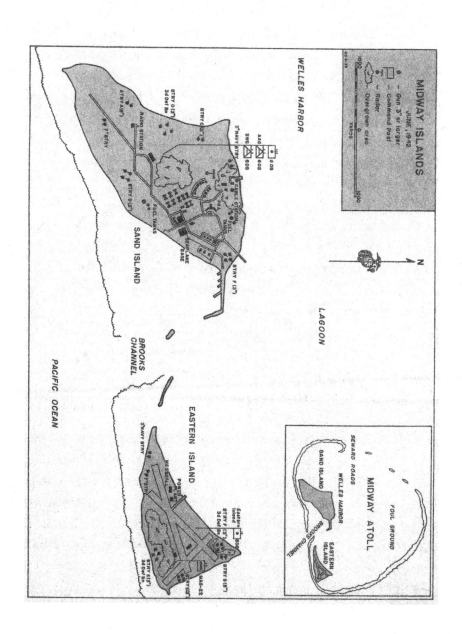

MIDWAY ISLANDS
JUNE, 1942

● — Gun 3" or larger
□ — Command Post
◆ — Radar
⬭ — Overgrown area

1000   0   1000
YARDS

WELLES HARBOR

BTRY A(6")

● 7" BTRY

RADIO STATION

BTRY D(3")

BTRY C(5"-51)

3" NAVY BTRY

SW6 608
AA6 608
● 608

CABLE STATION

FUEL TANKS

FUEL TANKS

BTRY B(3")

SEAPLANE BASE

BTRY F (3")

SAND ISLAND

LAGOON

N

BROOKS CHANNEL

PACIFIC OCEAN

EASTERN ISLAND

S"NAVY BTRY

BTRY "D"(3")

MESS HALL

POWER PLANT

BTRY F (3")
3d Def Bn

BTRY E(3")
3d Def Bn

BTRY S(5")

AA0-22

Eastern Island
● 608

MIDWAY ATOLL

SEWARD ROADS

SAND ISLAND

WELLES HARBOR

BROOKS CHANNEL

EASTERN ISLAND

FOUL GROUND

The colonel is quickly impressed by the admiral's attention to every last detail.

"The Commander-in-Chief inspected every installation on Midway with the greatest thoroughness," the official marine corps report will state. "At the conclusion of a hard day's climbing, ducking, and keen observing, the admiral asked Colonel Shannon to enumerate the major items he would require to hold Midway against a large-scale attack. After Shannon had stated his requirements—which were necessarily considerable—Admiral Nimitz asked, 'If I get you all these things you say you need, then can you hold Midway against a major amphibious assault?'"

"Yes, sir," replies Colonel Shannon.

Nimitz nods. No mention of a great plan involving aircraft carriers and their task forces. Just a subtle reminder about avoiding a second Wake. The admiral requests a detailed list of all supplies and equipment.

Hypo has still not broken the JN-25B code. Midway is strongly believed to be the location of the coming attack, but there is still no absolute proof. In lieu of certainty, Nimitz errs on the side of readiness.

So just to be safe, Nimitz states that D-Day is May 28.*

The admiral is going full Rochefort, growing more and more confident with the gray areas of intelligence gathering. So the date is not a lie, not a guess, but something hopeful in between.

May 28. In marine jargon, that's twenty-four days and a wake-up. Time is of the essence. Nimitz flies back to Pearl Harbor the next morning. Tasks his staff with a thorough study of the Wake Island debacle. Nimitz believes Midway will be an expanded version of what happened there. The study "may indicate procedure which the Japs will follow," he instructs. Nimitz insists airpower is the key to victory. Reinforcement of antiaircraft defenses is of the utmost importance.

Wake had neither, and so was lost.

---

* Though the designation "D-Day" is famously synonymous with the Normandy landings on June 6, 1944, the military labels every amphibious assault, from North Africa to Sicily to the Pacific, as such.

***

COLONEL SHANNON MAKES his list. No item is overlooked. On May 7, he submits the long, specific, and outrageous litany of requests: twelve new 3-inch antiaircraft guns, eighteen 20mm antiaircraft guns, eight 37mm antiaircraft guns. All of which will come from the 3rd Defense Battalion at Pearl Harbor. The colonel desires two more rifle companies, a platoon of five light tanks.

Shannon also requests an aircraft upgrade, leaning less on the obsolete Brewster Buffalo fighters and the equally useless Vought Vindicator (nicknamed "Vibrators" by their pilots). Instead, pilots of Marine Air Group 22 are requesting the more trustworthy SBD-2 dive-bombers and Grumman's new F4F-3 fighter, with its amazing top speed of 328 miles per hour and range of 845 miles. A Japanese Zero, by comparison, maxes out at 320 miles per hour, though it can fly an astounding 1,600 miles without refueling.

A big ask. Colonel Shannon has been in the military long enough to know he won't get everything he wants—and he may never hear from the busy admiral at all. So he is startled to receive an immediate follow-up letter from Admiral Nimitz. The typewritten note on the commander in chief's letterhead is addressed to Shannon and his navy equal on Midway, Commander Cyril Simard.

Colonel Shannon will receive every item on his wish list.

Nimitz also writes that Simard and Shannon are immediately promoted to captain and full colonel, respectively. The admiral sends a joint personal letter of congratulations and affirms their exemplary work.*

Then Nimitz writes in detail about the enemy units and what their

---

* A captain in the navy and a colonel in the marine corps are equal in rank. In terms of comparison across other services, both are considered O-6. The "O" is for officer. The "6" is for the level of rank. The difference stems from the navy adopting the British rank system and the army, marines, and army air corps (known as the air force since 1947) selecting French traditions. It's worth noting that "colonel" is pronounced with an "r" because when the English started using the word in the sixteenth century, they followed the pronunciation of the French word *"coronel"* but the spelling of the Italian word *"colonello."*

roles will be. Nimitz reminds the two commanders about "steps being taken to reinforce the atoll, and assured both officers of his complete confidence in the Marines' ability to hold Midway."

The admiral's simple plan is based on *Hiryū* and *Sōryū*'s strategy at Wake Island. He believes Japanese carrier aircraft will dive-bomb and strafe as a prelude to invasion. This will leave their flattops without planes—or defense.

In the meantime, marine corps pilots taking off from Midway before the Japanese arrive will bomb the Japanese carriers. Colonel Shannon and his well-fortified marines here on the island have the big guns necessary to fend off any invasion.

Admiral Nimitz does not mention the American carrier task forces that will lie in wait for the Japanese.

Nimitz reiterates that D-Day will be May 28. Using Midway's code name of Balsa, Nimitz states: *"Balsa*'s air force must be employed to inflict prompt and early damage to Jap carrier flight decks if recurring attacks are to be stopped. Our objectives will be first—their flight decks rather than attempt to fight off the initial attacks on *Balsa*. . . . If this is correct, *Balsa* air force . . . should go all out for the carriers . . . leaving to *Balsa*'s guns the first defense of the field."

These are orders. Not suggestions. There can be no mistaking the admiral's intentions.

The official marine corps report on what happens next:

That evening, Colonel Shannon assembled his key subordinates and warned them in general terms of the impending enemy attack. Additional defensive measures and priorities of final efforts were outlined, including special measures of advance reconnaissance and preliminary preparations to enable the 3d Defense Battalion's forthcoming batteries to occupy positions in minimum time. All recreational activities within the marine force were suspended, and 25 May was set as the deadline for completion of the measures

ordered. To insure maximum effort by all hands, this information
was disseminated in general terms to all Marines in the garrison.

Slowly but surely, Admiral Chester Nimitz is preparing the perfect
surprise for Admiral Yamamoto and the Combined Fleet. He will have
four aircraft carriers at his disposal when the Japanese attack Midway.
For the first time since taking this job, he will fight toe to toe with Admiral Yamamoto, his fighting force a true equal to the *Kidō Butai*.

Then he loses two more flattops.

YORKTOWN AND *LEXINGTON*

N O BATTLESHIP OR CARRIER LOST BY U.S. AT CORAL SEA." The *Star-Bulletin* Saturday-morning headline shouts at the reader. Bold block letters. All caps. Loads of black ink.

"The Navy department today officially denied Japanese claims that any American aircraft carriers or battleships have been lost in the United Nations–Japanese air battle in the Coral Sea."

Reports out of Tokyo boast, "Japanese forces sank the aircraft carrier *Saratoga*, another carrier of the *Yorktown* class and a battleship of the *California* class."

Optimists in Washington are calling what happened in the Coral Sea the biggest battle in U.S. naval history. Yet no one can explain why President Roosevelt canceled his morning press conference yesterday.

Washington and Tokyo rarely tell the truth. Hearsay is a daily part of war news. Blackouts and censorship mean that very little of what appears in print is completely accurate. Delays in reporting are standard. Much of what really happens is not printed for months. As of this morning, for instance, the American people know little about the Doolittle Raid and who took part. It is still just a rumor.

In the case of the Battle of the Coral Sea, taking place in waters just east of Australia's Great Barrier Reef, the Japanese claims are true. Some of their facts are not correct but the actions occurred.

The USS *Saratoga* is nowhere near the Coral Sea.

USS *Lexington* is.

In fact, right now she is at the bottom of the Coral Sea.

Yorktown is nearby as Japanese planes strike CV-2. Two torpedoes in the port side of her hull just below the waterline as well as bombs to her flight deck and superstructure do her in. Burning and beyond salvage, she is abandoned. Two thousand seven hundred seventy officers and sailors are rescued by the rest of the task force before the destroyer *Phelps* is ordered to fire five torpedoes into her just before six p.m.

Lexington sinks with the sun.

The Japanese pilots turn their full attention to *Yorktown*.

A long-standing argument in the world of aircraft carrier design is whether or not to armor the flight deck. Extra steel plating—usually three inches—can prevent a bomb from piercing this uppermost portion of the ship, then detonating in the hangar deck below, triggering a wave of explosions and towering flames as airplanes, aviation gas, and ordnance are consumed.

Those extra two thousand tons also make carriers top-heavy. To balance the ship, the size of the hangar deck must be reduced. This means room for fewer planes. The Japanese, who do not park aircraft on the flight deck and whose Zeros lack folding wings for easier storage, actually need *more* hangar space. *Akagi, Kaga, Hiryū, Sōryū, Shōkaku*, and *Zuikaku* lack an armored flight deck.

As does *Yorktown*. Like on her Japanese counterparts, CV-5's pilots land on a thin sheet of steel topped by a layer of sanded wood—teak for the Japanese, pine for the Americans.

The crucial blow comes at eleven twenty-seven a.m. on May 8. A Val dive-bomber pilot weaves through clouds of antiaircraft fire to lay a five-hundred-fifty-pound bomb smack in the middle of *Yorktown*'s flight deck. The Douglas fir and Appalachian steel immediately give way. The ordnance leaves behind a series of gaping holes as it punches straight down through five more decks into the very bowels of the ship, then explodes. Fires travel down the narrow passageways, blistering paint and burning men. Fuel tanks rupture. *Yorktown* pours oil into the sea. A massive black slick stains the blue waters. Every hand fears the surprise submarine torpedo that will finish the vessel.

Yet unlike what Tokyo radio now claims and the conviction of the Japanese pilots who are quite sure they sent CV-5 to the bottom, *Yorktown* is still afloat and carefully making her way for Pearl Harbor. Admiral Chester Nimitz, who is demanding an accurate damage assessment, flies a team to the carrier to pick through the destruction. He needs answers now. Should *Yorktown* sink on the way back into port, Nimitz is left with just *Hornet* and *Enterprise*. The pending Midway attack suddenly tilts wildly in favor of Japan and Admiral Yamamoto. And yet Nimitz must engage the enemy. Keeping his carriers in port while Midway is overrun will not just be another Wake. It will be a crushing blow to morale in the Pacific and at home—and perhaps the end of his career.

If there is good news in this tragedy, it is that the Japanese have lost their first carrier of the war. *Shōhō* also rests at the bottom of the Coral Sea. American pilots also succeed in severely damaging *Shōkaku*, forcing it to retire from battle.

"JAPAN BLAMES WEATHER FOR CORAL SEA FAILURE," the *Advertiser* prints on May 13. After four months of victory after victory, anything else is a loss to the Imperial Japanese Navy. Follow-up articles to the Battle of the Coral Sea will continue for another week.

Yet not another word is written about *Yorktown*.

Admiral Nimitz strictly censors the Honolulu press. The fate of *Yorktown* is nobody's business.

Better that the enemy believe she's sunk.

ROCHEFORT

Joe Rochefort trusts his memory.

A mountain of paper covers his desk. Not in neat piles but in random scraps, dropped one on top of another. A less complicated mind might see the mess as confusing. Rochefort, who cares not at all for organization, knows precisely where to put his hands on important documents when he needs them. "Because I could remember," he will explain years from now when he is asked to recount those heady days before the Battle of Midway. "I could remember back three or four months."

That callback kicks into gear as he stares at the latest decrypted message.

Using what is known of JN-25B, the cryptologist has personally translated a vital communiqué from the Imperial Japanese Navy to the supply ship *Goshu Maru*. She is to proceed to Saipan, where the invasion force is gathering. Her hold will then be filled with "base crews and ground equipment." *Goshu Maru* will "advance to Affirm Fox . . . military supplies which will be needed in the K campaign will be included."

Affirm Fox.

AF.

To Rochefort's busy mind, that geographic designation is a distant phantom. It's been two months since AF appeared in Japanese transmissions. That would be March 23, shortly after the Emily seaplane attacks on Honolulu. All clues back then pointed to AF being Midway. Japan has not changed its code since. A hundred thousand facts have passed across Hypo desks in these last eight weeks. Its sudden reappearance is definite cause for concern.

Yet, if his recall proves correct and he is right about AF, Commander Joe Rochefort can prove beyond the shadow of a doubt Midway is Yamamoto's target.

Rochefort asks around the office if anyone else remembers.

Joe Finnegan, a fellow linguist, confirms Rochefort's hunch. The Massachusetts native also worked on the translation in March. He validates Rochefort's memory that Midway is AF.

Joe Rochefort is extremely excited.

"I've got something so hot it's burning the top off my desk," marvels Rochefort, placing a call to Ed Layton at CINCPAC. In addition to AF being Midway, he is certain that the "K Campaign" refers to the invasion fleet on Saipan. For once, Rochefort is eager for an intruder to join him in the dungeon. "You'll have to come over and see it. It's not cut and dried but it's hot."

Rochefort even shows enthusiasm for his four-star boss, adding, "The man with the blue eyes will want to know your opinion of it."

Layton descends, joining Rochefort to scrutinize the new findings. The intelligence analyst is convinced Rochefort is on to something. He relays the news to Nimitz in his own excited and cautious way, allowing himself to have an opinion without having an opinion.

The admiral is skeptical. He wants to be completely sure. Nimitz orders Layton and his war plans officer, forty-six-year-old Captain Lynde McCormick, to visit the dungeon first thing in the morning to analyze every morsel of data.

McCormick shares a birthday with Finnegan. He will one day become a four-star. He was born in Annapolis and stayed in town to attend the academy. Above all else, he has a reputation as the consummate professional. So McCormick is thorough, not a man to immediately praise or criticize.

Rochefort, for once in his career, shows tremendous respect for a superior officer. Sensing a fellow intellectual, the commander places his stacks of information on an impromptu table of plywood laid over sawhorses. He briefs the captain on signals traffic, the interwoven flow of Japanese data, the evolution of Roman letters as Japanese regional locators. Rochefort builds his case carefully, like a courtroom prosecutor. He shows that at least four *Kidō Butai* carriers will be traveling with the invasion force.

Captain McCormick remains in the dungeon all day. Sorts through data, pores through files, asks questions. McCormick held a similar position as war planner before Pearl Harbor. He is among the Kimmel staff retained by Nimitz. That largesse will be forgotten if McCormick makes the wrong call about AF. His carefully plotted career depends upon getting this right.

McCormick's report to Admiral Nimitz is unequivocal: Midway is AF. The date and time are still unknown, but the IJN is definitely coming. "Seeing the raw data at firsthand has reinforced my own conviction of an impending invasion of Midway," McCormick tells the admiral.

Midway.

Not Australia, New Guinea, or Honolulu.

Japan will hit Midway.

Admiral Nimitz was not impressed when he met Joe Rochefort more than four months ago. Rochefort's peculiarities are at odds with the rest of the admiral's staff. But give credit where credit is due: Admiral Chester Nimitz has given the commander plenty of slack. Day by day, that faith is rewarded.

Nimitz zips up the new finding. He begins by restricting access. For months, Lieutenant Commander Layton's morning intelligence briefing to Admiral Nimitz has been passed on to the British, Australians, and New Zealanders. But even the closest allies have spies. He won't take chances of Japan learning their vaunted code is slowly revealing itself like a flower in bloom.

"If I were you, I would not put anything about Midway in your intelligence," Nimitz cautions Layton. "I think the thing to do is hold this one very close, so there will be no leaks."

But a leak, of sorts, has already taken place. And it's not with America's allies. As part of his standard procedure, Joe Rochefort copied the Office of Naval Intelligence in Washington on his message to Layton concerning AF. They agree with him.

Yet there is another group of intelligence analysts in Washington, DC. This highly political group is known as OP-20-G—20th Division, G Section—or more simply Office of the Chief of Naval Operations. Their leader is Captain John Redman, a former Olympic wrestler and naval academy graduate who used his connections to get a pioneer in cryptanalysis and early mentor of Joe Rochefort's fired.

We're about to go deep into the historical weeds here, so buckle up. The genius on whose story we're about to spend a couple paragraphs is more than worth this detour into minutiae.

Captain Laurance Frye Safford was born in Somerville, Massachusetts, in 1893. Like so many in our story, he attended the naval academy, from which he graduated in the class of 1916. Intelligence analysis was not the cloak-and-dagger world it would become. Quite the opposite. Many considered it unreliable, a voodoo-like work of magic no admiral trusted.

So when Safford was assigned to a research desk at the Code and Signal Section of the Office of Naval Communications, it was not a harbinger of rapid career advancement. The year is 1924. A Japanese naval codebook is stolen by U.S. agents from Japan's consulate in New York City. Safford is ordered to find a way to make use of the information. Working with the Underwood Typewriter Company, he designs a special code machine for the interception of Japanese radio messages.

He promotes this new form of intelligence throughout the navy, searching for individuals with minds for patterns and code. Among the first young men hired (there is also a woman, the brilliant Agnes Meyer Driscoll) is Joe Rochefort.

Now forty-eight, Safford is the father of naval intelligence. Thanks to politics, he is also out of a job. It is Safford who sends Joe Rochefort to Hypo in the summer of 1941. It is Safford who introduces IBM computers to codebreaking. It is Safford who heightens radio-traffic analysis by extending a high-frequency direction-finding net across the Pacific.

And it is Laurance Safford who sends Joe Rochefort the JN-25B package to decode.

Safford actually predicted the Pearl Harbor attack based on radio-traffic analysis. He was ignored by the director of naval communications, an admiral named Leigh Noyes. The admiral is demoted and reassigned for this failure—to Honolulu, of all places. Captain John Redman—a man with no background in cryptology—uses his connections to take control of naval intelligence.

Laurance Safford is not promoted for being right about Pearl Harbor. Redman sees him as a threat. The father of naval intelligence is reassigned to be the assistant director of naval communications for cryptographic research. His new job gives him no power at all.

Captain John Redman now focuses his sights on destroying Safford's acolyte in Honolulu.

Commander Joe Rochefort.

Not only does Rochefort contradict the opinions of OP-20-G in Washington, but he is correct in those contradictions. He has an enemy in Redman just for being extremely good at his job.

***

REDMAN'S CODEBREAKERS CLING to the belief AF is not Midway but Johnston Island, located between the Marshalls and Hawaiian Islands. The confusion grows as cryptologists at Cast, the intelligence equivalent to Hypo in the Far East, is now safely removed from the Philippines to Melbourne. They believe AF is a place known as Jaluit Island.

Rochefort continues to disagree. "AF has to be under American control. It is a place which is in close proximity to the place the Japanese used as a refueling for their attack," he argues, referring to the March seaplane strike.

Admiral Nimitz backs Rochefort one hundred percent. The admiral's

May 16 staff meeting focuses on a Midway attack. "Unless the enemy is using radio deception on a grand scale, we have a fairly good idea of his intentions," Nimitz tells his top officers. The admiral's conviction is infectious. Even Admiral King is coming around to Rochefort's "AF as Midway" theory.

But Washington is Washington: bureaucrats, placeholders, climbers. Men thousands of miles from the action who care more about politics and a window office than the hard work of staring at mountains of data to find the right answer.

OP-20-G refuses to lose this battle. With his independent ways, Rochefort has always been a burr in their saddle. Now they spread rumors among high-ranking generals and admirals that Rochefort is leading the United States into a trap. These cryptologists can't look past the debacle at Pearl Harbor. They still cling to the belief that Hawaii and the mainland are the next targets. These whispers travel the navy grapevine all the way back to Hawaii, where Admiral Nimitz feels increasing pressure to present stronger evidence that AF is Midway.

After almost a week of second-guessing, Nimitz sends his top intelligence officer downstairs to have a talk with his basement-dwelling friend.

"As commander in chief, I cannot be satisfied as to Rochefort's or my guess about where AF is. You are to tell Rochefort to do everything within his power to try and solve this problem and pin down the fact that AF is or is not Midway," Nimitz instructs Layton.

So it is that Lieutenant Commander Ed Layton and Joe Rochefort have a long talk on the afternoon of May 18. Monday. Rochefort listens to the criticisms. Together, both men seek a solution. None is forthcoming.

Commander Rochefort does not sleep well that night in his small room at the bachelor officers' quarters. At dawn, he walks down the sixteen steps into the dungeon, slips on his smoking jacket, lights his pipe, walks across the basement, and pulls up a chair at the desk of Wilfred "Jasper" Holmes. The New Yorker is a former submariner who resigned his commission before the war and taught at the University of Hawaii until being recalled to active duty. A naval academy graduate with a master's in engineering from Columbia, forty-two-year-old Holmes also pens underwater adventure stories for *The Saturday Evening Post* under the pseudonym Alec Hudson. All of which is to say, this polymath is a perfect fit at Hypo.*

Over the clank of the IBM computing machines, Rochefort calls over a few other staffers. A top secret meeting begins. Conversation is obscured by the din. "We've got to prove to the world that AF is Midway," the commander begins.

Jasper Holmes brings a unique perspective to the discussion. During his time as a professor, he once studied the effects of mixing coral and salt water for the runways at Midway. Holmes has been there. Knows the hardships and routines. His brain noodles as he seeks a connection between his past and this immediate call to action.

"Fresh water is a constant problem at Midway. A breakdown of the new freshwater distilling plant would be a serious matter," Holmes theorizes. He adds that if the Japanese found out Midway was low on fresh water, the intercepted news would be relayed to Tokyo immediately.

Rochefort immediately sees what Holmes is getting at.

"Very good, Jasper. Very good."

The impromptu meeting concludes. The commander hatches a plan, then shares it with Ed Layton, who receives approval from Nimitz. A simple but unique message will be sent to Captain Simard on Midway via the underwater cable link with Honolulu. The Japanese do not have access to these communications because they do not use airwaves. Simard's instructions are to reply by broadcasting from Midway to Pearl Harbor an uncoded radio message telling of a broken freshwater system.

---

* Holmes will go on to serve as the dean of the University of Hawaii at Mānoa's College of Engineering from 1947 to 1965. Under the pseudonym Alec Hudson he wrote a book titled *Up Periscope! & Other Stories* that fell into the hands of Gene Roddenberry, creator of the *Star Trek* television show. The series has been compared to "a space version of submarine warfare" and several episodes are thought to have been inspired by Holmes' Alec Hudson stories.

The transmission will go like this: "At the present time we have only enough water for two weeks. Please supply us immediately."

Simard sends the message on May 19.

On May 20, Wake Island radios Tokyo telling of a broken water system at "AF."

***

JOE ROCHEFORT MIGHT have shared this coup with his naysayers. His accomplishment is nothing short of remarkable. Not many men in the history of the world can claim they predicted a major military campaign. The whispering against him might come to a quick end. Instead, he lets them find out for themselves. The codebreakers in Melbourne and Washington know nothing of Rochefort's ruse. So when Cast—now renamed Belconnen for their new location—comes across the Japanese message, their mystified response is to send it along to the Office of Naval Intelligence. "If authentic it will confirm identity 'AF' as Midway," writes one cryptologist.

Now comes the time for Rochefort to let everyone in on his plan. "Affirm Fox is confirmed here as Midway."

He closes with a sharp reminder that this problem was cleared up two long months ago:

"As stated previously."

Washington will make him pay for being right.

INVASION REHEARSAL

Boats and coral don't mix.

In the brutal heat and humidity of Guam, Japanese landing troops practice invading Midway. The reef forming the atoll presents the biggest obstacle to their landing. It is known that the coral surrounding Sand Island and Eastern Island is 110 meters wide, submerged beneath three feet of water. Once past this barrier, troops must wade through waist-deep water for a quarter mile to reach the beach.

Fifteen hundred Special Naval Landing Force troops practice the rigorous series of events they will execute in less than two weeks' time. First, a group numbering a hundred soldiers is placed in a landing barge and ferried out beyond the reef here at Tumon Bay. The Daihatsu turns around after reaching open ocean, taking care to avoid the "washing machine" effect of surf pounding on the coral, which forces the bow under water.

Secured within the well deck are twenty-three-foot-long collapsible landing boats or inflatable assault boats. The Daihatsu draws too much water to pass over the reef. Instead, soldiers place the smaller landing craft in the water and step out onto the reef in waist-deep water. Every man has passed a swim test.

During the invasion, the SNLF expects to overwhelm the Americans. They will attack Sand Island. Another elite group known as the Ichiki Detachment, numbering two thousand elite soldiers under the command of namesake leader Colonel Kiyanao Ichiki, will attack Eastern. Intelligence reports show 750 marines, 500 construction workers, and a small armory of 5-inch guns, antiaircraft guns, and machine guns. That lightweight American defense should already be obliterated by the time these men file into Daihatsus for the early-morning attack, which is why these soldiers will continue this drill well into the night.

The men know they will spend their next few days on a transport ship that will sail from an unnamed port in Japan and deliver them to a location near Midway. When the morning of battle arrives, assault teams will assemble on decks. The order will be passed to step over the side, then lower themselves by cargo nets or Jacob's ladders into their appointed landing craft. The Daihatsu will navigate toward the reef, just as they are doing time and again today and tomorrow and the day after, repetition to the point of redundancy being the beginning of the life-and-death ballet that will play out as they find the reef and make their way to the beach.

Results so far are not as cut-and-dried. In fact, they are downright discouraging. Boats get stuck on the reef. The coral is unstable, and soldiers fall underwater as they struggle to keep their footing on the gnarly, sharp organisms. When the reef is finally left behind, men attempt to fire their rifles toward the shore with some measure of accuracy as they march. The rations in their small packs get soaked in salt water, making them inedible. There is little water with which to refresh themselves under the scorching midday sun.

Then, once they reach the sand, the men of the SNLF are placed back on a Daihatsu to do it all over again.

The landing boats, whether inflatable or made of canvas and wood, are the invasion's weak link. They get stuck when the water is too low. Paddling ashore is slow, and there is little hope of self-defense, because firing a rifle and rowing are difficult to accomplish at the same time.

So every possible method of getting to the beach is being investigated. Lengths of bamboo are known to float well, but it is hard to hang on and fire a gun at the same time. Tire inner tubes solve this problem, allowing men to rest their weapons while taking aim. A sudden swell, however, can send a shot in the wrong direction—most likely into the backs of soldiers wading in front of their compatriots.

And this is only for men with rifles. The SNLF considers itself "naval infantry," an oxymoron that does not stop them from also carrying flamethrowers and mortar launchers.

This training will continue for three days and nights.

Then straight on to Midway.

For all their solitary training, the men know they are part of something far bigger than themselves. The upcoming mission is still a mystery to them, but the enormity of the invasion fleet is unlike anything these men have seen before.

THE ADMIRAL AND
THE CODEBREAKER

J oe Rochefort knows the location.

Now the commander needs the date.

He thinks he's found a clue.

His codebreakers have decrypted a missive named "Occupation Force Operational Order No. 4." The message orders these invaders to sail from the port at Kure on the date "N–5"—the landing date minus five days—whereupon they will join the "main body of the occupation force."

But what's "N"?

The commander orders Hypo to focus exclusively on chronology. The group goes through old punch cards and printouts looking for date-time codes. The room is smokier than ever, with pipes, cigars, and cigarettes. Everyone is drinking too much coffee. No one dares suggest anything more than a few hours of refreshing sleep. The day is long and seemingly without end.

Then Lieutenant Joseph Finnegan, the thirty-six-year-old who survived the bombing of the USS *Tennessee* on December 7, finds the pattern.

Lieutenant Commander Layton explains what Finnegan sees: "It was a neat simple substitution cipher, with garble check involving a 12x31 (12 for months, 31 for days) garble table," Layton writes. "At the left, representing the 12 months was a column of 12 kana, different from those in the table—SA, SI, SU, SE, SO, TA, TI, TU, TE, TO, NA, NI (SA for January, NI for December). To encipher, for example 27 May, one picked the fifth line (May = SO), ran across to the twenty-seventh column, HA, and recorded the kana at the intersection. The encipherment, then, was SO HA HO, the third kana proving the garble check."

For men like Joe Rochefort, Ed Layton, and Joe Finnegan, such logic is elemental—as are the conclusions. Now they must sell it to those who don't think this way.

On May 26, Rochefort uses Finnegan's sample to decipher a radio intercept. It's from Japan's Combined Fleet to a group of destroyers transporting soldiers to Midway. They are ordered to leave port in Saipan on May 28, then "at 1900 6 June arrive at AF." Allowing a few days for the Japanese navy to soften Midway for invasion, this proves the actual attack will take place at least one day earlier, perhaps two.

June 4.

Rochefort relays this news to Layton, who immediately hands it to Admiral Nimitz. The admiral doesn't want any more guessing. So Nimitz turns to a man two decades younger and six pay grades lower to promise him when and how Midway will come under fire. The admiral needs to know that Layton has complete trust in the latest intelligence.

Nimitz asks Layton to name the "dates and dispositions the enemy intends to take up around Midway."

The lieutenant commander has been preparing for this moment. As he will write in his memoirs, "The latest Hypo information had enabled me to make a more precise estimate of the distance-time factors . . . working backwards from the sailing dates, and the decrypted orders for the June 6 arrival of the invasion force transports, I reconstructed a tentative plot that was accurate enough to predict when and where the transports carrying assault troops should be located . . . when it came to the carrier striking force . . . I could not be so certain."

Now Layton stands before Admiral Nimitz, reluctant to answer the question.

"I have a difficult time being specific," he tells his boss.

"I *want* you to be specific," Nimitz shoots back. He reminds the younger officer of his wish that Layton should stand in as a proxy for Admiral Nagumo. "After all, that is the job I have given you—to be the admiral commanding the Japanese forces and tell us what you're going to do."

Layton is uncomfortable. He prefers to speak in generalities. Yet this is an order.

"Alright then, Admiral. I've previously given you the intelligence that the carriers will probably attack Midway on the fourth of June, so we'll pick the fourth of June for the day. They'll come in from the northwest on the bearing of 325 degrees and they will be sighted about 175 miles from Midway, and the time will be 0700 local time."

To Lieutenant Commander Layton's relief, Admiral Nimitz takes the bold risk of agreeing completely with this estimate.

"The next seven nights were sleepless ones for me," Layton will remember. "I knew very well the extent to which Nimitz had staked the fate of the Pacific Fleet on our estimates, and his own judgment, against those of Admiral King and his staff in Washington."

NIMITZ

Today is challenging for Admiral Chester Nimitz.

The morning starts with his high-level conference. This is the most important meeting Chester Nimitz has conducted since taking over CINCPAC.

The purpose is final approval of Midway plans.

All business. Spit and polish. Nimitz sits at his desk, with assorted other officers gathered around in chairs. Maps taped to the walls. Windows closed. Nimitz's desk is just large enough for a blotter, two phones, an ashtray for his cigarettes, and another for anyone else who might light up. Everything is tidy, but not obsessively so.

"There was a general discussion of the Midway problem conducted by the admiral," his official staff log notes. It is known as the Graybook, for its color and cover. "General Emmons and General Richardson (from War Dept., and intimate of General Marshall) were present, as so were Rear Admiral Spruance, who will be C.T.F. [commander, Task Force] 16 until Vice Admiral Halsey returns to the job from the sick list. While nothing new was brought out, all hands expressed views and were given a very clear explanation of the problem by Admiral Nimitz. General Emmons said he hasn't near enough planes to defend Oahu. That is, of course, nothing new."

All jokes about the army and its reluctance to allow its bombers to participate at Midway aside, the star of the meeting is a very tardy Joe Rochefort.

Leave it to Commander Rochefort, with his ongoing lack of enthusiasm for chain of command, to show up thirty minutes late. In his desperate desire to bring the most up-to-date intelligence, he loses track of time. Clearly, the commander has not slept. "Looking disheveled and bleary-eyed," Ed Layton writes, "well aware that he had kept the commander in chief waiting, he could not escape the icy gaze that greeted his brief apology."

Commander Rochefort is abashed by the lack of a warm greeting. "The atmosphere was very impersonal," he says, mildly offended.

Rochefort hands Nimitz his latest findings, making sure to add that they are extremely important.

"Admiral Nimitz asked me a question, and I would look over there and see four stars," Rochefort remembers of the meeting. "I was sure of my facts but stressed that they were only deductions. I could not have blamed him if he did not accept my estimates . . . it was obvious that when Nimitz sent for me, he had already decided on his course of action."

Rochefort is correct. Gambling his entire career, and the future of the Pacific Fleet, on the guesswork of Joe Rochefort and Ed Layton, Admiral Chester Nimitz is luring the *Kidō Butai* into a trap of his own making off Midway.

The meeting of May 27 is just to let everyone in Hawaii and back in Washington know that the admiral's next course of action will be full speed ahead. *Enterprise* and *Hornet* sail in the morning.

Two carriers against the entire Japanese fleet. Will this be enough?

***

IT IS JUST over six months since Admiral Nimitz's seaplane landed in Pearl Harbor on Christmas morning. *Enterprise* has been at sea almost that entire time. She made port yesterday but her crew did not receive leave, despite those many months aboard ship. She sails again in a matter of days. Readiness is more important than revelry right now. There's a lot to do before she sails for "Point Luck," as the Midway rendezvous is code-named.

Her skipper, the beloved Admiral William "Bull" Halsey, will not be on board. He returned from sea twenty pounds lighter, overcome by exhaustion, and suffering from severe dermatitis. Halsey is now in the hospital, where he will remain until long after *Enterprise* sails for Midway in less than a week. Nimitz immediately chose Admiral Ray Spruance as his replacement.

First, Nimitz loses *Lexington*. There's no telling whether or not he has also lost *Yorktown* for the Midway battle.

Next, the admiral loses his top sea dog. Halsey is Nimitz's alter ego on the ocean, a fighting man with the guts and confidence to win a complex fight like Midway. Spruance is known to be competent, though he lacks even a day in command of an aircraft carrier.

What else can go wrong?

Well, the Japanese can alter their naval code. JN-25B is now JN-25C. Just when Hypo is on the verge of breaking the entire IJN code, the vast majority of it is altered.

"A body blow," Ed Layton calls the setback. "Months of hard work had to be abandoned overnight and the grueling work of assembling additive groups had to begin all over again."

The good news is that the change takes place after Hypo has full knowledge of Japanese battle plans. The bad news is that they won't know of any alterations.

Layton and Joe Rochefort know their contributions to whatever happens at Midway have been enormous, but from this day forward, the Japanese are "effectively blacking out our ability to make last-minute changes."

Says Rochefort: "You might say a curtain went down and we weren't reading anything."

***

ADMIRAL NIMITZ PAYS a personal visit to *Enterprise* on the next stop of today's hectic schedule. The band plays "Ruffles and Flourishes" as the admiral steps onto the flight deck—"ruffles" played on drums and "flourishes" on bugles. The entire ship's company stands at attention. A short speech, then Nimitz awards the Navy Cross to Messman Doris Miller, who shot down four Japanese planes from the deck of the USS *West Virginia* during the Pearl Harbor attack.

The admiral also singles out three pilots for the Distinguished Flying Cross. "I think you'll have a chance to win yourself another medal in a few days," he tells Lieutenant Roger Mehle, a fighter pilot.*

The next recipient is Lieutenant Dusty Kleiss, a dive-bomber aviator and naval academy graduate who has seen enough of the war. *Enterprise*'s long months at sea have the twenty-six-year-old doubting how much more he can take. Kleiss longs to return to the States and marry his girl. He overhears Nimitz's remark to Mehle and gives a surprised "sideways glance" while remaining at attention.

After moving over to where Kleiss stands, Nimitz reads his citation aloud. "Well done," the admiral tells Kleiss.

"Nimitz gave me the most careful look I ever experienced in my whole life," Kleiss will long remember. "His stare jolted me like a shot of whiskey, his eyes penetrating and honest. I wanted to impress him. When he reached out to shake my hand, I felt emboldened, ready to go back into battle and fight for him . . . I experienced something I never thought possible. A leader had put the fight back in me."†

Yorktown isn't due back in port until tomorrow. But Nimitz is in for a nice surprise on this busy day. She arrives early, a sight for sore eyes dragging herself into Pearl in the afternoon. She clears the harbor entrance trailing a ten-mile-long oil slick. Her crew parades in whites on the flight deck. The vast space is empty of aircraft; planes launched for Hawaii once *Yorktown* was assured of safe arrival.

Tugboats guide her toward Dry Dock #1. The concrete basin reinforced

---

* Twenty-six-year-old Lieutenant Mehle will survive the Battle of Midway and go on to a fruitful naval career. He will retire in 1970 as a rear admiral. Before the war, he married Aileen Elder, who would go on to become the famous gossip columnist Suzy Knickerbocker. His second wife was Dorian Leigh, considered by many the world's first supermodel. Mehle died single on August 30, 1997. He is buried at Princess Anne Memorial Park in Virginia Beach, Virginia.

† Miller later died in action. The USS *Doris Miller*, now under construction, will be CVN-81, the first aircraft carrier named for an enlisted sailor and an African American.

with steel is one thousand two feet and five inches long. A hundred thirty-eight feet wide. Thirty-five feet deep. The lock gate is lifted. *Yorktown* pulls in. Blocks are set in position to hold her in place. The caisson, as the lock gate is also known, shuts. The air becomes cacophonous as pumps roar to life, sucking out all the water. It takes a day and a night, but Dry Dock #1 is almost completely dry as she receives visitors. The mighty keel of *Yorktown* laid down so long ago at Newport News is exposed. Admiral Nimitz temporarily voids an order stating that the ship's tanks of aviation fuel must be drained, a process that takes a full day. This will allow work to begin as soon as he gives the go-ahead, risk of explosion be damned.

***

ONE DAY LATER.

May 28, a Thursday. Wearing waist-high waders, Admiral Nimitz walks through the knee-high water pooled at the bottom of the dry dock. *Yorktown* is vital to his Midway plans. Attempting to take on the *Kidō Butai* with just two carriers would be an act of foolish arrogance. He is familiar with the action report from Coral Sea detailing *Yorktown*'s damage. The 551-pound armor-piercing bomb that punched a hole in the flight deck and exploded fifty feet deep into the ship, just above the forward engine room, ripped through six compartments, refrigeration systems, radar, a messing space, and lighting on three decks. Crucially, the number two elevator that lifts aircraft from the hangar deck up to the flight deck is not functioning. Seams in her hull are split. Several fuel oil compartments are ruptured.

Small wonder that hard-luck Rear Admiral Aubrey Fitch, who has had both the *Saratoga* and *Lexington* shot out from under him, is not optimistic. Repairs will likely mean returning to the shipyard at Puget Sound in Washington, like *Saratoga*. Fitch moved his flag to *Minneapolis* after *Lexington* sank and spent the three-week journey back to Pearl assessing the damage. His testimony bears a great deal of weight. Fitch, a fifty-eight-year-old pilot who also once commanded USS *Langley*, can stake a claim to being the most experienced carrier admiral in the fleet. Fitch believes it will take ninety days to fix *Yorktown*.*

But Joe Rochefort predicts the Japanese will attack in a week.

A small army of shipwrights and engineers walk alongside Nimitz as he surveys the bare hull. Outside the dry dock, fourteen hundred shipyard workers stand ready to go to work. These tradesmen, most of Hawaiian descent, have repaired several battered warships since December 7. *Yorktown* will be their first carrier. Most expect to work all summer inside this cavernous warren of tight quarters, endless miles of wiring, and horizontal and vertical pipes crisscrossing the interior. Their motto is simple: "We keep them fit to fight."

Alongside Nimitz is Captain Claude Gillette, Pearl's yard superintendent. The admiral flew Gillette and a small team to *Yorktown* on her way home from the Coral Sea. The superintendent made a thorough study of the damage. He radioed back his twofold findings: *Yorktown* can be fixed but it will take a monumental effort.

Nimitz inspects the gaping seams torn open by explosion. He already knows what he's going to say.

"We must have this ship back in three days."

"Yes, sir" comes the reply.

The tradesmen get to work.

---

* Fitch's extraordinary record of commanding America's first three aircraft carriers was not the high-water mark of his career. The trim, dapper admiral became commander of all U.S. Navy aircraft in the Pacific, then deputy chief of naval operations. Following the war, Fitch was named superintendent of the naval academy, the first aviator so honored. He died in Maine at the age of ninety-four in 1978.

MIDWAY

Morning on Midway. D-Day. No sign of Japanese attack—yet.

In Pearl Harbor, around-the-clock repairs for USS *Yorktown* are underway at Dry Dock #1. In the Libyan desert, a brave band of French freedom fighters is surrounded by German General Erwin Rommel's Afrika Korps in what will become a fight to the death. In Hollywood, *Casablanca* is in its first week of filming.

So many things going on in the world, but none matter more to the men on Midway than being ready. Stranded with thousands of birds, surrounded by nothing but water, alone in every way, the inhabitants of Midway Island await the inevitable. All week long, men old and young, officer and enlisted, single and married wonder if this could very well be the day they die.

A message arrives from Admiral Nimitz: Today is actually *not* the day.

Yet make no mistake, the attack is still coming. Only now the window is June 3 to 5. The marines, still racing to assemble their defenses, called this "a welcome change"—one of two on this pivotal day.

"The second was arrival, partially via the light cruiser, *St. Louis*, of the first reinforcements: The 3d Defense Battalion's 37-mm. antiaircraft battery (Captain Ronald K. Miller), together with Companies C and D, 2d Raider Battalion (Captain Donald H. Hastie and First Lieutenant John Apergis). The 37-mm. guns were promptly emplaced, four on each island, while one raider company (C) went into bivouac in the woods on Sand

Island, and the other (D) was sent to Eastern Island," reads the official marine corps report.

The next day brings more good news. The USS *Kitty Hawk* is a smaller version of an aircraft carrier known as a tender. She parks at the Midway dock bearing not just more big guns, but several brand-new airplanes. Sixteen SBD-2 Douglas dive-bombers, seven F4F-3 fighter aircraft.

"The planes," one marine marvels, ". . . were unloaded, wheeled over to the short seaplane apron, fueled, and flown off to Eastern Island with a simplicity and rapidity that was so characteristic of those superbly led and well-trained Marine air units."

The following day brings even more aircraft, "a period of the most intense activity. Army and Navy aircraft arrived at Eastern Island until it seemed that the field could accommodate no more," states the official synopsis of events. "One aviation report seriously complained that even the numerous birds overhead were being crowded out of the air by the concentration of traffic."

***

So IT IS, the Midway garrison grows stronger and more prepared with every passing day. A total of 107 aircraft on Eastern Island. Colonel Harold Shannon's marine corps force now numbers more than two thousand armed with mortars, antiaircraft guns, and naval guns. Sand Island is home to a platoon of five M3 Stuart light tanks. Double strands of barbed wire barriers ring both islands.

In addition, mines are strewn across the placid beaches of Sand, some containing a dynamite charge packed with nails. These can be exploded by electric charge, rifle fire, or machine guns.

Anti-tank mines requiring just forty pounds of pressure—fifteen hundred in all—await the arrival of enemy tanks. When all else fails, the marine gunners and infantry have access to three hundred "Victory"—a name used in lieu of the Soviet "Molotov"—cocktails now being distributed.

***

IN EARLY MAY, Admiral Yamamoto outlined his plans for the MI Operation to Admiral Nagumo. It is only in the last week that this new iteration of the *Kidō Butai* came together as a group—carriers *Akagi*, *Kaga*, *Hiryū*, and *Sōryū*; battleships *Haruna* and *Kirishima*; heavy cruisers *Tone* and *Chikuma*; and a dozen cruisers.

They now weigh anchor in Kagoshima and sail east. 0600. May 27. Sixteen submarines serving as advance scouts lead the way. Strict radio silence is observed. *Akagi*, which has just undergone routine repairs, remains Nagumo's flagship.

The Northern Force, three groups who will launch a diversionary attack on the Aleutian Islands near Alaska, gets underway on May 25. They cruise at an average speed of eleven knots toward the Japanese island of Hokkaido, then northeast to Dutch Harbor.

Two days from now, Admiral Yamamoto on battleship *Yamato* will depart for Midway with the main body of the assault. His battleships, light cruisers, and destroyers will escort the light carriers *Hōshō* and *Zuihō*.

But the *Kidō Butai*, as always, is the centerpiece of this enormous undertaking. Her flight crews have undergone rigorous training to rehearse the great aerial battle to come. New pilots have been woven into the mix with seasoned fliers from Pearl Harbor.

Admiral Nagumo's strike group sails through the Inland Sea and the minefields of the Bungo Suidō Channel between Kyushu and Shikoku. *Akagi*, *Kaga*, *Hiryū*, *Sōryū*: two battleships, seven cruisers, fourteen destroyers, and 276 naval aircraft. They proceed on a southeasterly course at fourteen knots. They will rendezvous with supply ships 450 miles south of Tokyo, then proceed through thick fog at an average of 18.3 knots until taking up position off Midway.

The Midway Occupation Force of twelve transports, five thousand men, two battleships, six heavy cruisers, several destroyers, and seventeen patrol seaplanes will sortie from Guam and Saipan.

The 162 warships, plus auxiliary craft and smaller patrol vessels, compose the largest fleet ever to sail the Pacific. Almost the entire Japanese navy is attacking Midway.

Admiral Nimitz has only seventy-six ships to stop this armada.

And Midway.

Every aspect of the atoll's transformation since its discovery in 1859 foreshadows the decisive battle soon to take place. Captain N. C. Brooks raising the flag to stake a claim for the country that defends it still. The first breakwater torn open to let in coal ships, leading to development on both islands. A homicidal Danish carpenter and his relentless building improvements. The nesting birds who have made Midway their home for thousands of years bringing the Japanese predation that is about to reach its peak. Pan Am Clippers bringing flight. That beautiful undersea cable between Midway and Honolulu that allowed Joe Rochefort to pinpoint AF.

Those first United States Marines who stepped off their landing craft onto the fine white sand four decades ago.

Finally, there is Midway's ultimate defense: the coral reef. The invasion must come at high tide. Otherwise, invasion craft will get stuck.

As Midway has shown the world time and again—from the USS *Saginaw* in 1870 to the *Julia E. Whalen* in 1903—heavy seas, sharp coral, and boats of any size just don't get along.

And it all begins with bird poop.

But Nimitz is not done. He adds a new wrinkle to Midway's unlikely history.

The commander in chief of the Pacific Fleet asks a Hollywood director to bring a crew and film the action for posterity.

"Can you guarantee action?" the director asks Ed Layton, who is arranging logistics.

"Near as I can guarantee anything. Where you are going you won't know till you get there, and you won't be able to send any messages," the Hollywood veteran is told. "It's so secret and the United States is right on the line. If you want this assignment we'll put you on an airplane and fly you there this afternoon."

Welcome to the war, John Ford.

***

As THE *Kidō Butai* begins its journey to Midway, USS *Enterprise* and USS *Hornet* and thirty-three other surface ships glide from Pearl Harbor into open water. At sea, the carriers take on planes. The armada forms up and, leaving Diamond Head behind, sets sail for Point Luck, a spot in the ocean 325 miles northeast of Midway. There they will lie in wait, knowing full well Admiral Yamamoto's battle plan, thanks to Joe Rochefort and Hypo.

There is nothing in the newspapers to record the moment that these massive ships and their task forces funnel into the sea. Surely, thousands of Hawaiian residents witnessed such a majestic moment. But to print this amazing news and tip off the Japanese would be treason.

The veil of secrecy is complete.

There is yet another surprise that must be kept from the enemy:

On May 30, three days after entering Dry Dock #1, the USS *Yorktown* also sets sail for Midway.

In Germany, the Royal Air Force bombs the city of Cologne. An astounding thousand British bombers take part.

In Australia, Japanese submarines open fire on Sydney Harbour.

Here at Pearl, exhausted dockyard workers head home, having accomplished the impossible. Welders and fitters and other dockyard crews working nonstop to make the fix. The city of Honolulu has endured power blackouts as electricity needed for the massive overhaul was shunted to the labor force. *Yorktown*'s hull is once again solid steel. Inner portions of the ship are still under repair but that can wait. The most important thing is that Admiral Nimitz now has three carriers at his disposal. Personally paying a visit to the ship's crew at this remarkable moment, the admiral gives a command that is hopeful and succinct:

"Good luck and good hunting."

The stage is set.

EPISODE SEVEN

SIX MINUTES THAT CHANGED
THE WORLD

Commander John Ford   *Public domain*

JOHN FORD

(Part 1)

JUNE 1, 1942
MIDWAY ISLAND
DAWN

The great director is bringing the battle home.

John Ford is a patriot. He loves his country enough to put his Hollywood career on hold to document the war. His new film, *The Battle of Midway*, will bring the fight to Americans in living color.*

Theatergoers across the United States will see exactly what it is like to be on the island as the great turning point in the war unfolds. Ford's dramatic, corny, action-packed documentary begins with a simple opening shot: an olive drab PBY-5A Catalina flying through a bank of thick clouds.

"A navy patrol plane. Routine patrol," intones the voice-over in short, tight phrasing. The drone of an airplane engine. "Only behind every cloud may be an enemy."

The camera cuts to a shot of a tanned, unshaven pilot at the controls. Wire-rimmed sunglasses. Nonchalant. Chewing gum. Cool as a cucumber. Distinctly American.

---

* John Ford's oral history of Midway can be found in the online archives of the Naval History and Heritage Command in Washington, DC. His short film *The Battle of Midway* is on YouTube in its entirety.

Another shot, this from the pilot's point of view as he looks down on Midway. Eastern and Sand Islands set against the emerald green backdrop of the atoll ringed in sand.

"Midway Island. Not much land, right enough. But it's our outpost. Your front yard."

Images of life on Midway: the pier, a navy patrol torpedo boat, the Catalina landing in choppy surf—the dark green coloring of the fuselage a sharp contrast to the dark blue water. Bare-chested marines in standard-issue utility shorts scramble into the sea to assist in docking the aircraft. They drag the PBY back up a concrete ramp onto land.

A patriotic image of a marine color guard in starched khaki uniforms presenting the colors.

No voice-over. Just the sound of a fife and drums, then a male chorus singing "The Marines' Hymn" . . . "we are proud to claim the title of United States Marine."

A quick cut to a white albatross with distinct black markings wheeling in the sky. Close-up of a lone bird waddling in the sand. "These are the natives of Midway," the announcer tells America.

*"Tojo has sworn to liberate them."**

∗∗∗

THE FILM IS intended as an eighteen-minute newsreel. The director has come to Midway in the service of the U.S. Navy. John "Jack" Martin Feeney, as he was born, is forty-eight. In Hollywood, California, where he has worked for a quarter century, he is known as John Ford. The Irishman is on a hot streak right now, with seven enormous box-office successes in a row since 1939: *Stagecoach* with John Wayne; *Young Mr. Lincoln*, *Drums Along the Mohawk*, and *Grapes of Wrath* with Henry

---

* General Hideki Tojo served as prime minister of Japan during World War II. He was executed by hanging in 1948 for war crimes, but not before a U.S. military dentist drilled "Remember Pearl Harbor" in Morse code into Tojo's dentures during his postwar imprisonment.

Fonda; *The Long Voyage Home* with Wayne; *Tobacco Road; How Green Was My Valley.*

Ford's most recent film brings those hits to an end. Early in 1942, he releases *Sex Hygiene,* a thirty-minute training film for the U.S. Army. Now, wearing his trademark sunglasses and broad-brimmed hat, the director awaits the start of the action. Donald Crisp from *How Green Was My Valley* will share voice-over responsibilities with none other than Henry Fonda.*

"Commander" Ford, as his official navy rank suggests, is not a Johnny-come-lately to the war effort. In September 1941, Ford takes a sabbatical from Hollywood, reporting for active duty in the Office of the Chief of Naval Operations in Washington, DC.

In January 1942, Ford receives the summons that eventually brings him to Midway.

"I was called by Admiral Nimitz on the phone, I knew him quite well, [and] he said, 'Throw a bag together and come out here and see me.'"

Ford is taken to Kaneohe air station. Two PBYs are preflighted and ready to go.

"We proceeded then to Midway. I think at the time there was some report of some action impending some place or some movement in the seas, [since] everything and everybody was on KV [a form of alert]."

Operating a handheld 16mm camera, the director now films his observations in gorgeous Technicolor. Though there is every reason to believe the Japanese are planning an attack, the director doesn't think much will come of those rumors.†

---

* Shortly after recording his voice-over for *The Battle of Midway* in 1942, the thirty-seven-year-old actor enlisted in the navy. He served as a quartermaster on the USS *Saterlee* before being commissioned in 1943. Fonda later saw duty in the Pacific Theater aboard the USS *Curtiss.* Henry Fonda will later play the role of Admiral Chester Nimitz in the 1976 film *Midway.*

† Ford's small crew included Jack MacKenzie Jr. and Kenneth Pier, both of whom assisted in filming. *Citizen Kane* cinematographer Gregg Toland later assisted with scenes shot in a studio.

"I proceeded to make a pictorial history of Midway. I photographed the Gooney Birds, I photographed the PT's, and all that sort of thing."

***

JOHN FORD IS yet another Midway visitor charmed by the albatross. A lengthy montage of various seabirds and their simpleminded behavior continues, taking up more screen time than the marching marines.

"The birds seem nervous," intones Donald Crisp in the rich dramatic voice of a Shakespearian thespian. His distinctly British accent is at odds with the Americana Ford shows so deliberately on the screen. "Something in the air. Something behind that sunset."

Two images in silhouette wearing the peaked caps of officers. One man smokes pensively while the other plays a mournful accordion rendition of "Red River Valley." More images of dusk. More sailors wearing concerned looks as the setting sun turns the sky burnt orange.

Thunder, or perhaps artillery, echoes in the distance.

"I didn't believe much in the impending action," Ford admits. "If it did come, I didn't think it was going to touch us."

NIMITZ

Admiral Chester Nimitz is awash in information. Joe Rochefort's codebreakers now provide detailed specifics of the Midway invasion force. The Imperial Japanese Naval code is not completely broken and the new iteration is still a mystery, but the men in the dungeon understand almost entirely what they read. It is as if Nimitz is getting decrypts straight from Admiral Yamamoto himself. First, location. Then date. Which forces are coming and where from. This is the Japanese playbook. The admiral's staff makes careful notation of these details in his own Graybook.

This news is cabled to Midway's defenders. Captain Simard and Colonel Shannon now know precisely what's coming.

Enemy MIDWAY occupation force includes two special pioneer battalions to restore and service airfield for immediate use by Orange [Japanese] planes. Jap carriers and seaplane tenders carrying land planes earmarked MIDWAY Base. Heavy bombers and patrol planes ready to be flown in from WAKE. Ground crew munitions supplies and base equipment embarked with occupation force. Spearhead landing force indicated as Jap Marines plus special Army unit. Principal objective indicated as Eastern Island. They are even bringing guns captured on WAKE to defend our islands. Confident you have the stuff to smear their plays. Watch for razzle-dazzle.

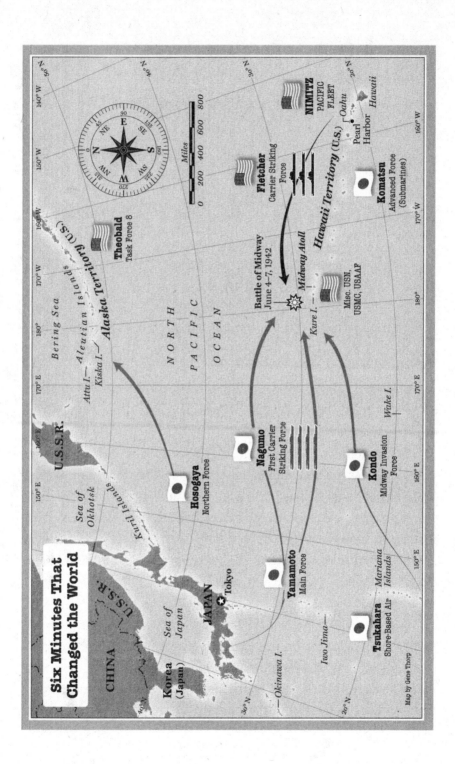

Six Minutes That Changed the World

Battle of Midway
June 4–7, 1942

NORTH PACIFIC OCEAN

NIMITZ
PACIFIC FLEET

Fletcher
Carrier Striking Force

Komatsu
Advanced Force
(Submarines)

Hawaii Territory (U.S.)

Pearl Harbor
Oahu
Hawaii

Theobald
Task Force 8

Alaska Territory (U.S.)
Aleutian Islands
Attu I.
Kiska I.

Bering Sea

Midway Atoll
Kure I.
Misc. USN,
USMC, USAAF

Wake I.

Nagumo
First Carrier Striking Force

Kondo
Midway Invasion Force

Hosogaya
Northern Force

U.S.S.R.

Sea of Okhotsk

Kuril Islands

Yamamoto
Main Force

JAPAN
Tokyo

Korea
(Japan)

Sea of Japan

U.S.S.R.

CHINA

Okinawa I.

Iwo Jima

Mariana Islands

Tsukahara
Shore-Based Air

Map by Gene Thorp

JOHN FORD

(Part 2)

JUNE 3, 1942
MIDWAY ISLAND
MORNING

John Ford sees with his own sunglass-covered eyes that his prediction is wrong.

"The dawn patrol has sighted an enemy fleet!" cries Donald Crisp in *The Battle of Midway*.

The director flies as a passenger in a PBY scout plane. Heavy weather west of Midway has been hiding the *Kidō Butai*. The drone of reconnaissance planes above is heard on decks large and small, but those thick clouds prevent the Americans from seeing the Japanese. This is expected. Historically, storms tend to travel east from Japan's home islands, allowing accurate weather forecasting to the west and north of Midway. Rain, clouds, and areas of low visibility are all factored into Admiral Yamamoto's plan.

Twenty-two PBY-5As launched at dawn to search for the Japanese fleet. Now a single Catalina finds a hole in this ceiling. Completely by accident, the director and the crew of the PBY in which he flies are among the first Americans to lay eyes on the incoming enemy. Ford immediately turns on his camera to film the stunning image of Captain Sadatomo

Miyamoto's minesweeper group trailing long white wakes in the deep blue Pacific.

> *The documentary switches abruptly from pensive faces and orange hues of sunset to an aerial view of the Pacific. John Ford films through the blister window in the rear of a Catalina. He's been invited to fly this morning aerial patrol, northeast triangle segment. Shooting through the clear acrylic, Ford captures a grainy image of distant Japanese ships.*

***

FORD TELLS THE story of how he came to get those images. "On June 3rd, my friend, Massy Hughes, Commander Massy Hughes [*sic*], asked me to take the patrol with him the next day."

The forty-one-year-old Hughes is commander of the Sand Island seaplane base, just recently transferred from Pearl Harbor. Francis Massie Hughes was the first American pilot to get aloft on December 7, taking off in his pajamas during the Japanese attack.

Ford shifts to a Southern accent as he mimics Massie, a Virginian. "He said, 'Well, it looks like there is going to be a little trouble out there . . . you and I are too damned old for this war anyway, so we better take the easy dog leg.'" Ford pauses to clarify that this means the northeast triangle of the seaplane patrol. "So we got aboard, took off, it was very, very cloudy weather, didn't see anything for a long time, finally the radar picked up something, [and] we presumed it was one of our task forces.

"About 60 miles off we saw through a rift in the clouds . . . we suddenly saw a couple of cruiser planes coming for us. Taking a quick look, we realized they were Japanese. We hadn't any idea that we had seen their task force, so Massey [*sic*] did a quick bank, got up in the clouds, stayed there for a while, finally ran out of clouds. We got down to about three feet from the water and really got some speed out of that old PBY."

The slow PBY is lightly armed but no more able to stand a chance against Japanese fighters than Midway's albatross did against poachers.

As the plane finds itself in clear skies, Hughes dives for the ocean, racing for home three feet above the chop, top speed less than 90 miles per hour.

"We managed to get back," says Ford. "It's too bad we just saw the task force for a moment, it was so far away, otherwise I might have gotten a good picture of the disposition and so forth, but we did get a pretty accurate, just in a flash, we got a pretty accurate view, you could tell pretty much what was there."

The defenders at Midway now have visual proof the Japanese are coming. Reconnaissance flights have located a group of minesweepers and the occupation force. No sign of aircraft carriers so far.

"Evidently something was about to pop, great preparations were made," states Ford.

Captain Cyril Simard, commander of NAS Midway, requests the director pay him a visit. The three approaching American carriers are top secret. Instead, for all Ford and the Midway marines know, the crux of this fight is fending off invasion. The defenders believe this coming attack will be much like Wake Island six months ago, another "Alamo of the Pacific."

Simard does not tell Ford otherwise. Army air corps bombers are already in the air looking for Japanese targets.

> I was called into Captain Semard's [sic] office, they were making up plans, and he said "Well, now Ford, you are pretty senior here, and how about you getting up top of the power house, the power station, where the phones are? . . . Do you mind?"
>
> "No, it's a good place to take pictures."
>
> "Well, forget the pictures as much as you can, but I want a good accurate account of the bombing," he said. "We expect to be attacked tomorrow."
>
> And he told me to do the best I can, get out, lay out my phones. I had some wires, two phones with the wires leading to the command dugout, and then I had a sea phone, stationed

those, got everything ready. Tried them out, went to bed that night, upstairs, got a bedroom there, went to sleep.

***

As JOHN FORD slumbers through the night, the Battle of Midway begins far out to sea.

Just after midnight, Admiral Nimitz informs Admiral Spruance, who is commanding Task Force 16 with *Enterprise* and *Hornet*, and Admiral Jack Fletcher of 17 in charge of *Yorktown* that seaplanes have located the main body of the Japanese force. Their distance is 574 miles from Midway. The commanders will soon make their own battle decisions, leaving Nimitz to watch and fret from more than a thousand miles away.

Simultaneously, here on Midway, Captain Simard launches four more PBY-5A Catalinas from Patrol Squadron 24. This is not a reconnaissance mission. Each is armed with a single Bliss-Leavitt 21-inch Mark 9 torpedo. Weighing just over a ton and measuring more than sixteen feet long, the explosive device has a most menacing appearance. But the E. W. Bliss Company stopped making them back in 1921. The weapons have spent the past two decades in storage. As long and heavy as they might be, there is no assurance the Mark 9s will explode upon making contact with enemy hulls.

The moon, bright but not full, reflects off the sea. The flying boats are directed to the Japanese invasion armada by radar. Four hundred miles west of Midway, they locate elements of the Midway Occupation Force. The dark silhouettes cast shadows.

This is not a small gathering of warships, yet it's only a fraction of the Japanese force. Gathered on the sea in tight yet massive formation are *Kiyosumi, Zenyo, Argentina, Brazil, Azuma, Keiyo, Goshu, Kano, Hokuriku, Kirishima, Nankai, Toa, Jintsu, Kuroshio, Oyashio, Yukikaze, Amatsukaze, Tokitsukaze, Hatsukaze, Shiranui, Kasumi,* and *Arare.* Transports, oilers, destroyers, cruisers. These ships took part in Pearl Harbor and the six months of invasion and domination since. Their captains know nothing about defeat, and even less about American airplanes looming out of the darkness to drop torpedoes in their midst. Eight hours ago, B-17s scored two near misses on the same body of ships.

The slow Catalinas come in low, heard but not seen, launching torpedoes, then taking immediate evasive action. Only one Mark 9 detonates, but that is enough. The vintage torpedo slams into the oiler *Akebono Maru*, killing ten crew and wounding thirteen. The ship's bow explodes, lighting up the night. The *"Maru"* designation stands for a merchant ship, so the vessel is filled with men and cargo, not ordnance. She keels over but does not sink. Not tonight. That fateful day will come in 1957 off Okinawa. The American attack is a near miss, a nuisance, pulling men out of their racks in the dead of night to fight the fire—a jarring moment surviving crew will remember through her years of wartime duty.

But this encounter between *Akebono Maru* and an obsolete torpedo dropped by flight leader Lieutenant William L. Richards at 26-34 north latitude, 174-14 west longitude is quite significant.

This is the first successful torpedo attack by either side during the Battle of Midway.

It will not be the last.

As the crew of USS *Yorktown* will attest.

SIX MINUTES

(Part 1)

Mechanics have been up for hours as the ships go to general quarters.

The hangar decks on *Kidō Butai*'s four heavy carriers are well lit, providing the flight crews ample illumination to fuel, arm, and begin the careful process of moving each of the green-and-black aircraft to the elevators and up to the flight deck. Fuel hoses slither across the steel. The vessels sail at a patient twenty knots, with miles of ocean in between. There is little ventilation and the two hangar decks on each ship are completely enclosed. The IJN does not store airplanes on the flight deck, so all operating aircraft are down below. The air in these unventilated spaces reeks of fuel and hydraulic fluid. Smoking is forbidden.

Pilots in brown cotton flight suits arrived an hour ago, having eaten breakfast and listened closely to this morning's briefing at the same time. Zeros will protect the bombers and the weather should be fine. Nothing unusual.

Men push carts laden with bombs to each aircraft. Armorers affix them to the underbellies.

Finally, planes are pushed onto the elevator and lifted to the flight deck. On *Akagi*—*Red Castle*—Admiral Chūichi Nagumo looks down upon the action from the bridge. The air is filled with the thrum of whirring propellers. The sun is already rising. The limited runway length requires wind flowing over the flight deck, so the ships turn into the morning's mild breeze. Each carrier increases cruising speed to enhance flight operations—the faster the better. "Launch the air attack force," orders the admiral. The same command is sent via signal lamp to the other three carriers. Go time. Wheel chocks removed. Planes taxi into launch position. They will race down the flight deck one at a time. The gap between planes is twenty seconds. Pilots must wait for the turbulence created by the previous aircraft to be blown away by prevailing winds. Zeros are the lightest planes and require the shortest runway to get airborne, so they will go first. Half will remain above the ship, circling in defense. The rest will fly straight to the target.

A deck officer blows a whistle and swings a red lantern in a circle. Takeoffs begin.

The time is 0430. Midway is two hours away.

One hundred eight Japanese planes fly into the pale rising sun. Zeros will provide escort and strafe the marines. Agile, with large surface areas on each wing. Fast, climbs better than any plane in the sky, possesses excellent range. Lack of a self-sealing gas tank and pilot armor can make the aircraft fragile, but the Zero is a lethal weapon in the hands of a good pilot.

The Nakajima B5N Kate bombers take off next. They are to attack from the east, the rising sun concealing them from American gunners. Those from *Hiryū* will focus on Sand, Kates from *Sōryū* aiming for Eastern's airfields—though taking care not to damage the runways. Fast for a torpedo bomber, making it perfect for coordinated attack. Like the Zero, the Kate is a light aircraft lacking self-sealing gas tanks and pilot armor, yet so effective they sank five battleships at Pearl Harbor

Then come the Val dive-bombers, thirty-six in all launched from *Akagi* and *Kaga*. Slow and lumbering, with fixed landing gear adding drag that reduces range. Their strength comes in the large wings, which make for amazing maneuverability.

Akagi

These are the planes racing toward Midway.

Ninety minutes later and just thirty miles from the target, the incoming Japanese strike force is spotted by a PBY seaplane that quickly alerts the marine defenders.

Midway already knows. Radar picked up the attackers twenty minutes ago.

JOHN FORD

(Part 3)

JUNE 4, 1942
MIDWAY ISLAND
DAWN

The point of view shifts abruptly to a long row of olive drab B-17 bombers parked wingtip to wingtip. 11th Bombardment Group. Nine-man crew. "Flying Fortresses have landed at Midway," narrator Donald Crisp says with excitement.

The bombers have already flown several missions against the Japanese fleet, each armed with four six-hundred-pound bombs and a bomb-bay fuel tank to increase mission duration.

Close-ups of stacked sandbags and flight crews huddled to discuss the day. Albatross circle the stationary aircraft, their white feathers, the blue sky, and a dark green B-17 in stark contrast to one another.

Strains of "The Army Air Corps," the theme song of military aviation, plays under the images. "Off we go, into the wild blue yonder..."

***

ADMIRAL NIMITZ HAS control of all resources in the Pacific, thus the seventeen B-17s commandeered from the army air corps and four more B-26 Marauders capable of dropping torpedoes. Their arrival is largely symbolic. The bombers' four engines and six-thousand-pound bomb load seem an odd choice as a tactical weapon. The B-17 is not designed for pinpoint bombing, so the wisdom of attacking Japanese carriers from twenty thousand feet is suspect. Left unsaid is that the vaunted Fortresses and Marauders lumber through the skies at 170 miles per hour, an easy target for nimble Zero fighters flying almost twice as fast.

This is a propaganda film. Americans don't want statistics; they want to be inspired.

So John Ford inserts an Americana sequence introducing young B-17 pilot Will Kinney from Springfield, Ohio. Ford will later flesh out the scene with images of Kinney's mother, father, and sister, Patricia, back home—a reminder that the fighting is not being carried out by nameless warriors but by the boy next door.*

The Battle of Midway will soon screen at Springfield's Regent Theatre, thrilling local citizens.

Scenes of a bomb bay being loaded and an airman sitting on a wing, pumping gas. The camera films B-17s taking off one by one, rolling down the long runway fully laden, using the whole length before slowly rising into the air. Time of departure, seven-oh-five a.m.

---

* William E. Kinney will fly seventy combat missions in World War II, including at Midway and Guadalcanal, and he will pilot the first B-29 mission over Japan. He will survive the war but die in the fiery crash of a C-97 cargo plane on May 22, 1947.

JOHN FORD

(Part 4)

Captain Simard orders his flight crews to scramble immediately. Midway's radar station confirms an incoming wave of 108 Japanese aircraft. Ninety-three miles away at eleven thousand feet. Air raid sirens pierce the dawn. Marine and navy pilots race to twenty-seven waiting Buffalo and Wildcat fighters, Dauntless dive-bombers, Avenger torpedo bombers, B-26 bombers, and Vindicator dive-bombers. The sudden drone of dozens of propellers as engines cough to life. One by one, pilots taxi into position for takeoff, then trundle quickly down the runway. The fighter's job is to stop the attack on Midway. The bombers need to find and sink those carriers.

The fighters shoot first. At 0616, American and Japanese pilots find one another, the navy and marine fliers diving into the swarm of Zeros. It's a bloodbath. Thirteen Buffaloes and two Wildcats are shot from the sky. Every American pilot perishes.

Now flying uncontested, the overwhelming Japanese forces hit Midway hard. Kates attack Sand Island. Their focus is fuel supplies, busy antiaircraft batteries, and any aircraft on the ground. Vals attack Eastern, hitting the power plant, hangars, and support facilities. The main hangar erupts in flames. Then Zeros drop their empty spare fuel tanks and strafe the AA batteries.

John Ford films it all.

The Battle of Midway *now shows the silhouettes of small approach-*
ing aircraft. The director's hand is steady as he films, even as the
Japanese fly directly overhead.

"Suddenly, from behind the clouds, the Japs attack!" Crisp thrills.

***

"THERE WERE ABOUT eight Marines in the powerhouse with me. I think
the alarm, of course, I haven't any notes, but the alarm went off, I imagine
around 6:20," Ford recalls in his oral history. "So everybody took their
stations."

The first bomb falls on Midway ten minutes later.

"I imagine the Japs when they attacked thought they had caught us
napping, there was nothing moving, just a lazy sort of a tropical island.
Everything was very quiet and serene . . ." Ford continues. "The first flight
I saw there were about twelve planes. They were coming at about 10,000
feet, so I reported this to the command post, told them that the attack
was about to begin. Everybody was very calm. I was amazed, sort of, at
the lackadaisical air everybody took. You know everybody sort of took to
the line of duty as though they had been living through this sort of thing
all their lives."

That calm does not remain long.

Until this moment in the documentary, John Ford's images of Mid-
way have been contrived. No longer. Now comes a whirr of very real
battle sequences one after another: marines firing 40mm antiaircraft
guns at the approaching fighters from inside a ring of sandbags,
black puffs of smoke from exploding shells, a Zero going down in
flames.

Vindicator dive-bombers launch two at a time. As they take to the sky,
ground observers scan the horizon with powerful binoculars. For the loss
and damage inflicted, the *Akagi*'s striking group is credited with shooting down nine American fighters, strafing a grounded B-17, and setting
fire to three buildings on Eastern Island. Only six Japanese aircraft fail to

return from this mission: three level bombers, two fighters, and one dive-bomber.

The Japanese attack again. Whining of fighters and dive-bombers coming in low. A jarring sequence of destruction as Ford and his camera are knocked down. "I was close to the hangar and I was lined up on it with my camera, figuring it would be one of the first things they got. . . . A Zero flew about fifty feet over it and dropped a bomb and hit it, the whole thing went up. I was knocked unconscious. Just knocked me goofy for a bit, and I pulled myself out of it. I did manage to get the picture. You may have seen it in *The Battle of Midway*. It's where the plane flies over the hangar and everything goes up in smoke and debris, you can see one big chunk coming for the camera."

Images of the lone Zero so very low. The falling bomb. Ford's camera tilting sideways as he is knocked out.

A geyser of sand and lumber, the hangar structure now just random splinters of wood and tangled steel. The first black smoke from burning oil blots out the sky. The hangar in flames, ribs exposed, doors blasted away.

Not all images make it onto the screen.

"I did see one of our kids jump in a parachute, I think it was a Marine flyer," Ford will remember. "It was quite a distance away and I had, that is, I couldn't photograph it—I had to look at it through my glasses. This kid jumped and this Zero went after him and shot him out of his harness. That was observed by about eight people. The kid hit the water and the Jap went up and down strafing the water where he had landed, even sunk the parachute, filled that full of holes, which I thought wasn't very chivalrous at the time. I only prayed to God that I could have gotten a picture out of it."

Chaos. More explosions and flames. Men running for their lives, though such a thing as a safe location is an elusive notion.

"The Star-Spangled Banner" plays under the images, which now resemble a dream sequence. Smoke, flames, explosions, aircraft. Midway appears defenseless. Every image on the screen is one of destruction. An ambulance drives into the fire, bouncing over rubble from the explosions. Weary, concerned looks on the faces of marine defenders. It seems just a matter of time before the Japanese planes will kill them all. Balls of fire climb a hundred feet into the sky, forming the thickest, blackest cloud imaginable—so dark it blots out the sun.

The very opposite of a propaganda film.

"Is this really happening?" asks the narrator.

***

FORD PICKS UP the story.

Suddenly the leading Jap plane peeled off. As he peeled off, evidently the Marines who had left earlier got the rear plane which went down in flames. I photographed that, but my eyes were sort of distracted by the leading plane, the leader of the [Japanese] squadron who dove down to about five thousand feet, did some maneuvers and then dove for the airport. We have all heard stories about this fellow who flew up the ramp on his back, but it was actually true. He dove down to about 100 feet from the ground, turned over on his back and proceeded leisurely flying upside down over the ramp. Everybody was amazed, nobody fired at him, until suddenly some marine said, "What the Hell," . . . then shot him down. [The Japanese aircraft] slid off into the sea.

"But by this time, of course, everybody had been watching this fantastic thing and by that time Hell started to break loose around there, and, of course, the high altitude bombers started to come in." The Zeros evidently—what I took to be Zeros had evidently some sort of small caliber bombs. They started to plaster the ramps or the airfield. They did a very neat job. They went up and down and got the outside area. They didn't touch the field itself—I imagine their idea was to land there later that day themselves. They didn't drop any bombs on the landing mat itself, but did a thoroughly good job of dropping, I would say 200 pounders up and down outside. . . .

The [American] planes had all been pretty well scattered and they didn't get any and as I was saying about this time the high altitude [Japanese] bombs started dropping. This I reported to Captain Semard [*sic*].

Forgot to try to count planes and [do] photography. I got a pretty good estimate, I estimated about, that I saw with my own eyes, I would figure there was from 56 to 62 planes.

By this time the attack had started in earnest . . .

. . . Everybody, of course, nearly everybody except the gun crews were under ground. The Marines did a great job. There was not much shooting but when they did it was evidently the first time these boys had been under fire but they were really well trained. Our bluejackets and our Marine gun crews seemed to me to be excellent. There was no spasmodic firing, there was no firing at nothing. They just waited until they got a shot and it usually counted.

The planes started falling, some of ours, a lot of Jap planes. It seems when you hit a Zero plane, it almost immediately goes into flames. At least that was the impression I got. One [Japanese] fellow dove, I think he was going to [attack] the clubhouse. He dove, dropped a bomb and tried to pull out and crashed into the ground. The place that I was manning, I didn't realize, the powerhouse, but they evidently tried to get that. I think we counted eighteen bombs, some big, some 200 pounders, some 500 pounders, that dropped around that. I would say that the Jap high [altitude] bombing was bad. I don't know whether they hurried or not, but they were not hitting their objective.

All of this takes place in less than twenty minutes. The Japanese raid is done at 0643. Eleven of their planes have been shot down.

Each Imperial Japanese Navy pilot sets a course for their carrier. Lieutenant Joichi Tomonaga of *Hiryū*, commander of the air strike, radios ahead to inform his superiors that the job is not done. The good news is that Midway's runways are still functioning, ready for immediate use when Japan conquers the island. But the marine's defensive fortifications are almost untouched. Until they are destroyed, amphibious troops will be unable to land.

Lieutenant Tomonaga and his fellow pilots need to rearm and refuel. They're not done knocking Midway out of the fight—and they're coming back.

Or so they think.

SIX MINUTES

(Part 2)

Seven-oh-five a.m. Months of waiting, decoding, preparation, and fear compress to a matter of minutes.

Six torpedo dive-bombers launch from Midway. This is the first wave from the squadron known as Torpedo 8.

Japanese flattops are the prime target.

Japanese antiaircraft gunners don't recognize the profile of these navy blue aircraft swooping down to launch torpedoes.

The mysterious plane is the TBF-1, a secret weapon so new that it came straight from the factory with a sweet new coat of paint. These "Avengers" were given their name last October, but some pilots cling to the belief her moniker is a reference to revenge for Pearl Harbor.

So new that these six Avengers attacking *Hiryū* are the only such aircraft seeing action in the entire Pacific Fleet.

So new they arrived in Pearl Harbor only three days ago.

So new Avenger and Pearl Harbor are synonymous. The new torpedo bomber is unveiled to the American public on December 7, 1941, of all dates. Three-man crew of pilot, gunner, radioman/bombardier. The radial engine takes up less space than an in-line power plant like the vaunted Merlin in British Spitfires, making for a long gap between cockpit and propeller, meaning the cockpit is roomy like a small living room. This is the replacement for the loathed and obsolete Devastator torpedo bomber.

When effective, torpedo bombers sink ships by putting holes in the sides of their hulls. Wind, weather, and clouds do not affect their accuracy—although large waves can have an impact. A ship being bombed from above, on the other hand, is often capable of stopping any fires and limping back into port because the integrity of the hull is not affected.

A typical torpedo attack starts at an altitude of several thousand feet. The subsequent dive to wave-top level and approach to the target are done as slowly as possible to increase accuracy. A distance of a thousand yards is optimum for dropping the torpedo and letting it run to the target. The closer the better—though getting too near before releasing ordnance can prove fatal to pilot and plane. Low level and lack of speed make them easy to shoot down.

Torpedo Squadron 8 of the *Hornet* has been chosen as the first airmen to receive shipment of the new Avengers. However, the Doolittle Raid means *Hornet* rushes to the Pacific before planes can be delivered. Eighty officers and men remain in Norfolk to await the first batch, fly twenty one new aircraft cross-country to San Diego, then travel with them by ship to Pearl Harbor—only to find *Hornet* already en route to Point Luck. Six pilots then volunteer to fly to Midway. They are not told of the mission awaiting them, only that their presence is urgently needed.

With the *Kidō Butai* bearing down, the Avenger contingent of Torpedo 8 is stuck. The pilots suspect a major battle is in the offing.

Harry Ferrier, a seventeen-year-old radioman, long remembers the sight of Midway Island being prepared for battle.

As soon as we arrived, we could feel a tension in the air. We were all sure that a meeting with the enemy was not far off. Many planes of all types were in evidence—Brewster F2As, Grumman F4Fs, Douglas SBDs, and Chance Vought SB2Us, all flown by Marines;

and Boeing B-17s, Consolidated B-24s, and Martin B-26s being flown by the Army Air Forces. The B-26s were equipped as torpedo planes, carrying their "fish" externally below the bomb bay. And, of course, the venerable Consolidated PBYs were present. We quickly prepared our planes for combat, which included loading six of the new type of torpedoes, which we had been testing so recently.

On this morning of battle, Avenger crews have been up since four a.m. They launch once radar picks up incoming Japanese aircraft. Leaving Midway's defense to the fighter squadrons, the six dive-bombers form up in two sections of three planes each. Altitude four thousand feet. Pilots are at home in their cockpits after all those long miles to get here.

The startling sight of the *Kidō Butai* comes into view. Fifteen miles in the distance. Four carriers and seventeen support vessels. Almost immediately, Zeros flying combat air patrol pounce on the six brand-new planes. The Avengers are instantly outgunned three to one.

"It was evident at once," Ferrier writes. His aircraft number is TBF-1 BuNo 00380, the very first plane delivered from the factory. "Our pilots immediately pushed over into a dive and applied full throttle to the engines. On the second firing pass by the attacking Zeros, our turret gunner, Manning, was hit and his turret put out of action. I remember looking over my shoulder to see why he had stopped firing. The sight of his slumped and lifeless body startled me."

The radioman adds: "At one point in the battle I glanced out of the small window on my left and saw an airplane streak by on fire and enter a cloud. The glance was so fleeting that I had no chance to identify it. Unfortunately, it later proved to have been one of ours."

The time is 0705. Four B-26 bombers have also found the Japanese carriers and are now focusing their attacks on *Akagi* and *Hiryū*.

A bullet grazes Ferrier's scalp. Blood pours over his machine gun. He passes out.

Twenty-five-year-old Ensign Albert Earnest pilots Ferrier's aircraft.

He hears nothing but silence from the back of the cockpit and believes the other two crew members are dead.

The ensign dives all the way down to two hundred feet. He watches as the five other Avengers explode and crash into the sea, victims of Zeros and antiaircraft fire. All those months training together, the trip across America, sharing quarters on the ship to Hawaii, the boring flight to Midway that made everyone in the cockpit think they'd pee their flight suits—all those memories and good times come to an abrupt and fatal finale.

Believing himself the last living Avenger pilot, Earnest launches his lone torpedo. The young pilot has no combat experience and the odds are stacked against him. Yet he survives. His plane suddenly two thousand pounds lighter, he pulls up, praying to climb away from the relentless gunfire riddling his plane. Bullets chime against the armored back of his seat.

But the cables controlling his flaps have been slashed and his stick doesn't work. Just twenty feet off the water, Earnest thinks to adjust his trim tabs. It works. In the back seat, Radioman Ferrier comes to just as the pilot regains altitude. Both men are wounded and bleeding. The Avenger's radio is broken. There is no compass. The instrument panel doesn't work.

And all those Zeros now focus their attention on Ensign Earnest's battered plane.

***

OTHER MIDWAY AIRCRAFT fare no better. One B-26 bomber is shot down over *Akagi* before dropping its payload. A second B-26 pilot knows his plane is doomed after taking heavy antiaircraft fire from *Hiryū*. Attempting a suicide attack, Major Lofton Henderson dives his plane into *Akagi*.

Admiral Nagumo watches it all from the bridge. He is nearly killed as the American bomber barely misses the superstructure and sends a geyser of water into the air as it crashes into the sea. The final two B-26 hit nothing as they drop their bombs but make it safely back to Midway.

So far, the morning belongs to Japan.

More good news for Admiral Nagumo in the form of an attack on

Akagi by Midway-based Dauntless dive-bombers. Eight are shot down by Zeros. Eight others from Marine Corps squadron VMSB-241 fail to score a hit.

Those B-17 bombers John Ford filmed taking off drop their bombs from twenty thousand feet. Not surprisingly, they all miss.

***

ENSIGN EARNEST AND his Avenger escape. His extremely low altitude prevents antiaircraft gunners from firing at his torpedo bomber, for fear of accidentally hitting the Japanese fighters. As Zeros turn their attention to the other planes from Midway attacking the *Kidō Butai*, the bullet-ridden Avenger tries to find a way home.

Earnest looks for a directional clue, flying east into the sun. Then he sees the smoke on Midway, rising so black and thick and high in the sky. This becomes his guidepost. Earnest aims for the smoke. "Compared to the battle, our landing was fairly smooth even though it was made on only one main wheel, without flaps, the bomb-bay doors open, and limited elevator control available. At least we were able to walk away from it," writes Radioman Ferrier.

Maintenance staff counts sixty-four machine-gun bullet holes and nine other openings where 20mm cannon shells tore through the fuselage. TBF-1 BuNo 00380 will never fly again. Every single brand-new Avenger is either destroyed or sinking seventeen thousand feet to the bottom of the Pacific.

And the worst is still to come for Torpedo Squadron 8.

SIX MINUTES

(Part 3)

Enterprise and *Hornet* enter the action.

Yorktown's planes are held in reserve as the two carriers prepare to launch their air wing.

Hundreds of miles northeast of Midway Island at that random spot in the ocean known as Point Luck. The Japanese still have no idea about the American location. Admiral Raymond Spruance decides to throw every plane in the task force at the *Kido Butai*, launching at 0700. Word is passed to *Hornet*.

Pilots have been awake since 0200. Breakfast was steak and eggs, a meal served only on battle mornings. A single cup of coffee. Food and drink are carefully rationed before the long flight. Accessing the relief tube while flying an aircraft is an awkward procedure, particularly in formation with one hand on the stick. No one wants to return with a "damp"—or worse "smelly"—flight suit, though it happens.

Change into flight suits at 0300. Baggy pockets stuffed with pencils for plotting courses on a plastic chart board, a flashlight, one wool cloth for cleaning the board and another for wiping the windscreen. Then a yellow life preserver draped around the neck, a parachute that will also serve as a lumpy cockpit seat cushion, and a helmet.

The hangar deck is ventilated with openings on the side of the hull. This allows aircraft to be warmed up in this otherwise enclosed space.

Pilots hear the din as they travel the narrow passages from their cramped quarters to the ready room.

Briefing at 0530. The Japanese fleet is 210 miles away—almost too far. Pilots fear running out of gas before making it back. At 0600 an enemy scout plane flies overhead but clouds conceal Task Force 16.

The anxious pilots sit, waiting. The ready room chairs are padded and comfortable. Some men smoke. Jokes. Charts and maps checked and double-checked. Finally, at 0656, the order comes: "Pilots, man your planes."

As the naval aviators rush to their aircraft, the carriers turn into the wind.

Planes ride the elevator from the hangar up to the flight deck. Pushed into position and packed wingtip to wingtip in the open air. *Enterprise* launches first, eight F4F Wildcats taking off for protective combat air patrol. Thirty-seven Dauntless dive-bombers line up next, circling the ship after take-off. A twenty-minute lag as the torpedo bombers are brought up from below. The Japanese carriers are now reported to be 175 miles away.

"As we circled above the task force," one pilot from *Enterprise* will write, "we also expected four squadrons from *Hornet* . . . and three squadrons from *Yorktown* (sailing just over the horizon to the east) to link up with our group . . . we waited and waited but no additional aircraft ever reached the rendezvous. Forty minutes passed and we just continued to circle stupidly above Task Force 16, burning valuable fuel."

At 0745, finally ordered to wait no longer by Admiral Spruance, *Enterprise* dive-bombers race for the last-known position of the *Kidō Butai*.

***

As ALL THIS is happening, Japanese carrier planes that attacked Midway return to their ships. Admiral Nagumo orders them rearmed and refueled, then sent right back out. He is firm in his belief that no American carriers are anywhere nearby. The need for another bombing run on the island is paramount. "Planes in second attack wave stand by to carry out attack today. Reequip yourself with bombs."

But many of the *Kidō Butai*'s aircraft are already outfitted with torpedoes. This change in ordnance is complex, requiring the removal of a special mounting bracket as well as the physical labor of manually wrestling a steel object weighing almost a half ton. This takes time. Follow this with the standard refueling, preflight, and warming of the engine, and this delay could be as much as two hours.

Then the No. 4 scout plane from the *Tone* sends a shocking report: "Sighted what appears to be the enemy composed of ten [ships], bearing ten degrees, distance 240 miles from Midway, on course 150 degrees, speed 20 knots."

A subsequent communiqué confirms the presence of at least one American carrier.

Stunned, Nagumo reverses his order. His planes aren't going back to Midway after all. The great moment of victory is at hand. He will focus on destroying the U.S. carriers. "Leave torpedoes on those attack planes which have not as yet been changed to bombs" comes the new command.

Nagumo also orders a course change. The *Kidō Butai* now sails northeast to find the Americans.

Torpedoes. Course change. Full speed ahead toward the American fleet.

This is razzle-dazzle, *Kido Butai*-style.

***

HORNET BEGINS LAUNCHING aircraft at 0702. The other pilots of Torpedo 8—those still flying antiquated Devastator torpedo bombers instead of the new Avenger—will take off in the second wave. Members of John Ford's crew are on deck filming the squadron cracking jokes and drawing scary chalk faces on their torpedoes in the final moments. First to race down the runway are thirty-five Dauntless dive-bombers. Then the fifteen Devastators of Torpedo 8. Ten F4F Wildcat fighters launch last.

Torpedo Squadron 8 is led by Lieutenant Commander John Waldron, a career naval aviator from South Dakota. He has trained his young pilots relentlessly, leading one to comment that "we could almost look at the back of Waldron's head and know what he was thinking, because he had told us so many times over and over just what we should do under all conditions."

As they take off, many of Waldron's pilots realize they have never flown with a live torpedo.

The Devastator has been in service only five years. They were once revolutionary, with their hydraulically operated landing gear, flaps, and folding wings. Devastators were the first monoplanes to fly off American carriers.

Yet aviation and aircraft design have advanced quickly. The slow, chubby aircraft is already out-of-date, its top speed of 208 miles per hour now pedestrian. Her pilots, the men who should love these planes more than any other, joke that they fly a "suicide coffin."

Perhaps worse, the Devastator carries a single Mark 13 torpedo. This device is singular in its inability to detonate. It is a weapon known for missing targets, sinking to the bottom after being dropped into the sea, or simply banging hard against hulls without causing damage. Unlike dive-bombers, which pounce from on high like hawks swooping down to grab field mice, torpedo bombers approach a target level and low—like savanna lions stalking water buffalo, albeit lions without claws, given the unreliable Mark 13s. The navy knows of these flaws but pretends these weapons will somehow function in combat.

Sometimes they're right. At the Battle of the Coral Sea, seven TBD (Torpedo Bomber Douglas) torpedoes helped sink the light carrier *Shōhō*.

Even so, Devastator pilots know better. As they prepare to take off this morning, many men in Torpedo 8 say goodbye to old friends on the flight deck. Many wrote final letters home last night. The odds of their returning successfully are slim. No one says it out loud, but a bad plane and a lousy torpedo make this a death mission.

Lieutenant Commander Waldron admits that the battle will be dicey. "My greatest hope is that we encounter a favorable tactical situation, but if we don't, and the worst comes to the worst, I want each of us to do his utmost to destroy our enemies. If there is only one plane left to make a final run-in, I want that man to go in and get a hit. May God be with us all. Good luck, happy landings, and give 'em hell."

Waldron has been ordered to fly west to find the Japanese fleet. This is based on their last-known location. Every plane launching from *Hornet* and *Enterprise* will fly in that direction. But the lieutenant commander disagrees. Instead, he disobeys orders, telling Torpedo 8 to follow him on a more southwesterly course, something in his gut telling him the *Kidō Butai* has changed its heading.

Waldron is correct.

Torpedo 8 is the first U.S. carrier squadron to find the enemy fleet. First, with the Avengers and now with the Devastators. The time is 0920. As the other American aircraft fly west and struggle to find the Japanese carriers, Waldron takes advantage of his successful hunch and orders an immediate attack. Torpedo 8 drops down low and flies straight and true toward the *Kidō Butai*. Thirty Zeros swarm the low-flying Devastators, now just above the waves, lining up their shots at a very sluggish 100 mph. Lieutenant Commander Waldron's left fuel tank is hit and bursts into flames. Fire consumes the aircraft. He slides back the canopy and attempts to bail out but cannot. The pilot is killed as his dive-bomber slams into the water.

Every member of Torpedo 8 suffers the same fate. Except one.

Captain Marc Mitscher, commander of *Hornet*, describes his brave Devastator pilots taking a bold swipe at the *Kidō Butai* in the opening round of Midway's carrier battle:

> Beset on all sides by the deadly "Zero" fighters, which were doggedly attacking them in force, and faced with a seemingly impenetrable screen of cruisers and destroyers, the squadron dove in valiantly at short range. Plane after plane was shot down by fighters, anti-aircraft bursts were searing faces and tearing out chunks of fuselage, and still the squadron bored in. Those who were left dropped their torpedoes at short range.

None of them detonate.

Even worse, of the forty-one torpedoes launched by torpedo bombers from all three American carriers throughout the Battle of Midway, not a single one explodes.

Ensign George Gay watches Lieutenant Commander Waldron die, then hears his own gunner breathe his last from the back seat of his Devastator. "They got me, sir," says Aviation Radioman Robert Huntington as he slumps over dead.

Gay ditches in the sea. He steps off his wing into the water but does not inflate his life raft until nightfall, fearing what will become of him if he is taken prisoner. This is a very real fear. *Enterprise* SBD pilot Frank O'Flaherty and gunner Bruno Gaido will be shot down, then rescued from the sea by the Imperial Japanese Navy. After being tortured and interrogated, they will be bound, weighted down, and thrown overboard to drown.

Ensign Gay floats under his seat cushion, eyewitness to the awesome spectacle of four rapacious Japanese aircraft carriers bearing down on Midway. He activates the CO_2 cartridge that inflates his life preserver but does not release the yellow dye marker that tells rescuers where to find him.

Ensign Gay's future is uncertain. The Devastator, however, is finished. From tomorrow onward, the torpedo bomber will never again fly in combat.

***

ADMIRAL NAGUMO'S HEADING alteration is successful. Those aircraft still searching for the *Kidō Butai* based on the old course have no luck finding it. The Wildcats are from *Hornet*; the Dauntless and the Wildcats launch off *Enterprise*.

Unable to find the *Kidō Butai*, the fighters from *Hornet* turn for home, low on gas.

Luck once again favors the Japanese.

Admiral Nagumo watches the rearming of his aircraft with growing impatience. He knows where to find the American carriers; now he just needs to launch planes and sink them.

***

ARRIVING AT THE *Kidō Butai*'s old location at 0920, the Dauntless dive-bombers from *Enterprise* find nothing. Rather than turning back to the ship despite his fuel running low, Lieutenant Commander Clarence Wade

McClusky of Scouting Six orders a box search of the ocean below, each plane flying a grid pattern of forty miles in each direction to find the enemy.

"For the next half hour, I endured a fairly quiet ride," Lieutenant Dusty Kleiss will write. He is the pilot who was so impressed by Nimitz during the medal ceremony last week. The calm is so unexpected that over the intercom he quizzes his gunner about procedures to stay sharp.

"Then, at 9:55, we had a breakthrough. The morning sunlight was passing through a cascade of mist produced by a waterspout far below. It produced a spectrum of beautiful color . . . fifteen miles ahead, and 20,000 feet below us, a white scar was visible on the solid blue expanse of the sea."

The Dauntless formation turns to follow the same heading of the ship below. "Within three short minutes, we found them.

"There it was, the whole Japanese carrier force arrayed across the horizon," the *Enterprise* pilot writes. "Right away, I recognized the two closest to us, *Akaga* [*sic*] and *Kagi* [*sic*] . . . ten miles out I spotted a smaller carrier, *Hiryū*, and finally I observed a large dot on the horizon, which I took to be *Sōryū*."

***

AKAGI'S FLIGHT DECK is bright yellow teak, with a red circle of the rising sun known as a *hinomaru* painted at one end. The American attack begins at 1023 when the first dive-bomber pushes his nose down toward that great big bull's-eye. At first, there is no response from the four carriers. *Kaga* is the first to open fire, antiaircraft rounds racing up to meet the aircraft now pouncing vertically on its position. As the first pilots drop their bombs and miss, which has happened so many times this morning, it becomes clear that this might be their only chance. Sooner or later the Japanese will finish rearming their aircraft and take to the skies.

Time is running out for the Americans to sink a *Kidō Butai* flattop.

Dauntless dive-bombers are extremely accurate. The secret is a steep dive. This allows a low release point—fifteen hundred feet is ideal—and keeps the target in tight focus. A good run starts at twenty thousand feet, making it possible for pilots to avoid Zeros and antiaircraft fire as long as possible. Seventy percent is a good angle once the dive begins. Pilots avoid using rudders because they affect aim, preferring to control the aircraft with stick and ailerons.

Attacks are a single file affair, with the lead pilot selecting the target and going into his descent. The others follow four seconds behind.

Lieutenant Earl Gallaher takes the lead this morning.

"In my humble opinion, Earl Gallaher was the best dive bomber pilot in the fleet," Dusty Kleiss will write. "He saved the day at that moment, bringing our string of plunging craft back on target. Gallaher dived steeply and dropped his bombs as low as our tactics recommended, about 1,500 feet.

"I watched as Gallaher's bombs smashed into the aft section of *Kaga*'s flight deck, just forward of the rear elevator. His 500-pounder landed atop a lone Zero, ripping it to smithereens. The bomb stabbed through the unfortunate plane, pierced the hangar deck, and detonated."

Emboldened, Kleiss noses over next, waiting until just a thousand feet above the Pacific to drop his three bombs—one high-explosive and two incendiary. All three puncture *Kaga*'s flight deck. The explosions are immediate, followed by flames bursting hundreds of feet into the sky.

"I saw the deck rippling and curling back in all directions, exposing that great big hangar deck below," fellow pilot Lieutenant Clarence Dickinson will tell Kleiss later. "I knew the last plane had taken off or landed on that carrier for a long time to come."

Fires beyond extinguishing rage through *Kaga*. The emperor's portrait, a symbol of fealty to the Japanese monarchy, is transferred to the destroyer *Hagikaze*.

"I'd never seen such superb dive bombing," one American fighter pilot will state of what he now witnesses. "I could only see three carriers. I never did see a fourth one. One of them, probably either the *Sōryū* or the *Kaga*, was burning with bright pink and sometimes blue flames. I remember looking at the height of the flames noticing that it was about the height that the ship was long—the length of the ship—just solid flame going up and a lot of smoke on top of that. I saw three carriers burning pretty furiously before I left, picked up one torpedo plane, and flew on back toward the *Yorktown*."

***

BETWEEN 1024 AND 1030 on the morning of June 4, the course of World War II changes dramatically. *Akagi* is hit by two bombs at 1027. *Sōryū* receives three hits. *Kaga* four. Only *Hiryū* is unscathed.

The demise of *Akagi* is typical. At 1029, torpedoes stored belowdecks explode. The ammunition, bomb storage, and forward compartments are immediately flooded to keep her afloat.

At 1042, she shuts down her engines and an order is issued for all hands to assemble at their firefighting stations. But the ship's pumps are damaged, and fires rage out of control. The flames climb higher, almost reaching the bridge. Admiral Nagumo decides to abandon ship, transferring his flag to the light cruiser *Nagara*. There, he radios Admiral Isoroku Yamamoto to tell him what has happened.

Akagi's fires spread. Air personnel and wounded are transferred to the destroyers *Arashi* and *Nowake*. At 1135, more torpedoes and bombs explode belowdecks. *Akagi*'s engines mysteriously roar to life.

At 1138, His Imperial Majesty's portrait is transferred to the *Nowake*. At 1150, the engines shut down for the last time.

Hiryū sends a message: "Please relay the following to *Akagi*: If any of your planes can take off, have them transfer to *Hiryū*."

More than a few angry pilots answer the call.

***

THE *ENTERPRISE*'S DIVE-BOMBERS have done their job but now they are far from the carrier and low on fuel. Each burned precious "av gas" during that long pause after take-off circling the ship and awaiting the command to attack. Their gauges moved closer and closer to "empty" during the long flight to the target. Then came the attack, juking and weaving to escape after dropping their bombs, evasive movements at full throttle burning fuel at a more accelerated rate. The natural inclination is to fly straight back to *Enterprise*. They are not allowed to do so. Each pilot is under strict orders to take a roundabout route to the ship. They actually travel *away* from their flattop home to confuse the enemy about the task force location by flying a forty-mile dogleg route toward Midway. From there, a new course is provided by the YE-ZB homing system. Each carrier has a large antenna transmitting a continuous top secret letter-based signal. This code is changed each day. Pilots simply home in on the letter being broadcast. This line-of-sight technology is good for a distance of thirty-five miles.

Thirty-two Dauntlesses took off from *Enterprise* this morning. They began the flight with 310 gallons of fuel, enough for five hours in the air. The elation of sinking three *Kidō Butai* carriers is now replaced by dread as pilots realize they might not make it to their ship. Throttles are dialed back, speed reduced to conserve gas. High altitude is maintained for the most effective communication with the homing beacon.

Every pilot knows he might not make it. Landing on the Pacific could be the only option. Each plane carries a yellow life raft. Search-and-rescue PBYs will scour the ocean. Downed pilots and gunners can only bob in the water and wait, growing dehydrated and famished in the hot sun. If they're lucky, one of their fellow aviators will see them go down and take note of their position to inform the Catalinas where to find them. Even then, there is no guarantee any man will be located on this vast, unrelenting stretch of blue water. To someone searching from thousands of feet in the air, a little yellow raft isn't much more than a speck.

The dive-bomber pilots press onward, flying and praying and keeping one eye on the gas gauge at all times. One after another soon runs out of gas.

Of the thirty-two SBDs that launched from *Enterprise*, only fourteen return safely.

Of the others, one is shot down, one runs out of fuel before the fight while searching for the *Kidō Butai*, and two land on *Yorktown*.

Fourteen other crews suffer "fuel exhaustion" and crash-land in the sea.

***

HIRYŪ RUNS UNSCATHED, last of the once proud *Kidō Butai*.

And now, the Japanese locate *Yorktown*. *Hiryū* is Japan's final chance to sink an American carrier in this battle.

In a last-gasp attempt to strike back, she launches ten torpedo planes and six Zeros against *Yorktown*. Lieutenant Joichi Tomonaga, commander of the air strike on Midway, is among those hunting CV-5. Once the American carrier is in his sights. the young lieutenant succeeds in his mission, dropping one of the two torpedoes that strike *Yorktown*.

Then Lieutenant Joichi Tomonaga turns back for *Hiryū*, job done.

Commander John Smith "Jimmie" Thach, one of the navy's finest pilots, shoots him down.

The thirty-six-year-old from Arkansas is the officer behind the "Thach Weave," a midair dogfighting tactic employed to make up for the Grumman F4F-4's inferiorities when compared to the Zero. Thach is a man who obsesses about midair combat, often using match sticks to simulate aircraft movement while at dinner. Yet he comes away from the battle less than impressed with his adversaries—and with American aircraft. He believes the Japanese will triumph in future aerial battles unless U.S. planes undergo significant design changes. After landing this afternoon, he will write in his journal, "It is indeed surprising that any of our pilots returned alive. Any success our fighter pilots may have against the Japanese Zero fighter is *not* due to the performance of the airplane we fly but is the result of the comparatively poor marksmanship of the Japanese."

Thach, in a cautionary tone, lashes out at the mediocrity of the planes and torpedoes American pilots were forced to use at Midway: "If we expect to keep our carriers afloat, we must provide a VF airplane superior to the Japanese Zero in at least climb and speed, if not maneuverability."

***

YORKTOWN BEGINS TO sink. Listing hard to port and having lost all power, she is abandoned. The carrier tilts at twenty-six degrees. The ocean seeps into her hangar deck. The men of the ship's complement lower themselves into the water, then bob in their life jackets as cruisers and destroyers from the task force circle, picking them up one by one.

Amazingly, *Yorktown* does not go under. Against all odds, the stricken Jonah, if she can be called that now, remains seaworthy. A working crew returns to the ship, and she is taken under tow to Pearl Harbor. The old girl has survived yet another catastrophe. One week from now, she'll be back in Dry Dock #1, where those Honolulu shipworkers will make her right as rain. Her battle flags snap in the wind as she begins the long, slow journey.

Meanwhile, American pilots launch from *Enterprise* and *Hornet* to find *Hiryū*.

The "SBD" prefix for the Dauntless stands for Scout Bomber Douglas— two functional names plus that of its manufacturer. This is exactly how *Hiryū* is found and killed—a Dauntless scouting mission finds her and a bomber mission sends her to the bottom.

A lone pilot who got away from *Yorktown* before she was hit finds *Hiryū* 110 miles from the American task forces. Admiral Raymond Spruance on *Enterprise* immediately launches a wave of SBD Dauntless dive-bombers. This time, the planes take off and head immediately for the target, not waiting for squadrons from nearby *Hornet*, wasting neither time nor fuel as they fly like a vengeful posse for *Hiryū*'s location. Once

SBD Dauntless dive-bombers   *Public domain*

again, Scouting Six, whose bombs destroyed *Kaga*, is among the three *Enterprise* squadrons on the attack. The SBDs launch at 1545. Seventy minutes later, *Hiryū* is in their sights. Aircrews rush to launch aircraft. Fuel nozzles jammed into wing ports top off gas tanks. Bombs and torpedoes stacked near planes.

Approaching from the south at nineteen thousand feet, Dauntless pilots increase engine rpm, then select "low blower" on the supercharger. Each man tightens his harness straps, anticipating the moment he will pitch forward into the dive, to be followed later by the sudden gravitational force pushing him deep into his seat as he pulls up after releasing his three bombs.

Press the stick forward. Nose drops straight down. For just a moment, each pilot is weightless. Items in pockets float upward. Despite the tightened harness, lack of gravity causes each pilot to hover slightly above his seat.

Dive flaps engage. This keeps airspeed from getting too high and inflicting structural damage to the wings. Pullout altitude is now lowered, allowing for closer proximity to the target when releasing ordnance.

Pull engines back to idle for the descent. Even so, airspeed increases from 130 to more than 250 miles per hour. Gunner in the back seat keeps two hands on the grips of his .30-caliber machine gun, eyes peeled for approaching Zeros.

The target is clearly visible below but the time between starting the dive and dropping bombs is a full minute of controlled seventy-degree free fall.

The rising sun on *Hiryū*'s flight deck makes a perfect target through the bombsight. Some *Enterprise* pilots roll their planes upside down to better track the ship's movement.

Manual bomb release lever is on the left. More accurate than using the electrical release atop the joystick, which sometimes drops too soon.

Pull the lever. Bombs away. Push throttles all the way forward to full military power. Close the flaps. Pull back hard on the stick. Feel the g-force shove the whole body down into the seat. A two-hundred-pound man feels as if he weighs ten times that. Vision narrows to a pinprick. The world turns gray. Sphincters tighten as pilots clench lower body muscles to shunt blood back to the brain and stay conscious.

The bomb takes three seconds to hit the target.

Antiaircraft fire from *Hiryū* and her escorts. Pilots resist the urge to admire their handiwork as bombs strike the carrier. Evasive maneuvers, never flying level or a straight line for more than a few seconds as each dive-bomber makes its escape.

Hiryū's metal flight deck peels back from the hull, flames and explosions so hot that the flat steel curls like a tin can being opened, revealing the hulks of burning Vals and Bettys and Zeros on the hangar deck beneath.

The Zeros harassing the dive-bombers are doomed. There is no place to land. They ditch at sea, hoping for rescue from nearby ships. The Imperial Japanese Navy not only loses four carriers in the Battle of Midway, but also every one of the 248 aircraft that once flew off those decks and 110 of the most highly trained pilots in the world.

Japan does not have the time or the resources to replace any of them.

***

ADMIRAL ISOROKU YAMAMOTO calls it quits. At 0300 on the morning of June 5, after failure to lure the American carriers into a nighttime battle, he orders a simple message radioed to the Combined Fleet: "OPERATION OF AF IS CANCELLED."

It is Joe Rochefort who decrypts this message and passes the news along to Admiral Chester Nimitz.

NIMITZ

Admiral Nimitz reports back to Washington.

It's been more than forty-eight hours. Admiral Ernest King, commander in chief, U.S. fleet—COMINCH—knows nothing of what is happening in the Pacific. Questions about Nimitz's future and the accuracy of Commander Joe Rochefort's Hypo dungeon masters remain unanswered—until now. This message is the closest the admiral comes to boasting.

"From Cincpac to Cominch," begins the transmission.

"June 5 summary to 0600 GCT 6th. MIDWAY attack. No Air Raid on MIDWAY since yesterday morning. Enemy attack forces approached during night and sub fired light bombardment but by daylight all forces sighted were heading westward," Nimitz messages.

"Sinking two aircraft carriers yesterday verified . . .

"No enemy aircraft evident and all his forces believed withdrawing."

***

LATER THAT AFTERNOON, champagne is served in CINCPAC headquarters. Praise is pouring in from Washington about the great victory. Lieutenant Commander Ed Layton suggests to Admiral Nimitz that Joe Rochefort be invited. A car is sent. The codebreaker is his usual rumpled self but cleans up before making his way to Nimitz's office.

Commander Rochefort nervously steps into the party. Nimitz sees him enter. The room is full as the admiral clears his throat to make an announcement. He introduces Rochefort, then adds:

"This officer deserves a major share of the credit for victory at Midway."

Joe Rochefort is stunned and overwhelmed. "I was merely doing what I'm being paid to do," he responds.

YORKTOWN

The Jonah's rotten luck continues.

This is the end. *Yorktown*'s plunge to the bottom begins now.

USS *Vireo* tows CV-5 back to Pearl Harbor. A thousand miles of open ocean between here and there. A crowd of cruisers and destroyers forms a loose circle, the protective force keeping her company.

There is a shark in the water in the form of a Japanese submarine. Eleven years old and 323 feet long, *I-168* took part in the Pearl Harbor attack. Back then she was known as *I-68*. It's only been a month since she was renumbered, like all Japanese submarines, to confuse allied intelligence. U.S. Navy vessels learned of her location fifty miles south of Oahu and tried repeatedly to sink her on December 7, attacking her twenty-one times with high-percussion depth charges. She has been home to Japan for repairs and a change of commanders since then. On May 23, she sails from the Inland Sea. Two days ago, she surfaces off Sand Island and fires six rounds on the Midway marines before they chase her away. Just hours later, the cruiser *Chikuma* spies a listing *Yorktown* and *I-168* receives orders to hunt the wounded beast.

Firing from a little more than a mile away, *I-168* launches torpedoes at one thirty p.m. on June 6. The first shot hits the destroyer USS *Hammann*, sending her to the bottom in just four minutes. Eighty-one members of

USS *Yorktown* (CV-5) listing and abandoned

Public domain / U.S. Naval History and Heritage Command

her crew endure a cruel death after leaping in the water to abandon ship: *Hammann*'s depth charges explode as she sinks. The shock waves turn the men's internal organs to jelly.

I-168's next two torpedoes explode against the thick steel of *Yorktown*'s recently repaired hull. The Japanese submarine becomes prey, with American surface vessels dropping five dozen depth charges on her location and almost sinking her. But she escapes and finds her way home to Japan. *I-168* has one more year to prowl the seas before she is lost with all hands off New Guinea.

Yorktown will be long gone.

I-168's attack ends any attempt to tow *Yorktown* back to Pearl. She is barely afloat. Repair crews depart the ship. Some airplanes remain in the hangar deck, but most have been pushed over the side. She survives from day into night, but once again lists to port. By the following morning, it is clear *Yorktown* is lost. Nearby American ships keep vigil, lowering their flags to half-mast. Her own battle flags continue to flutter in the wind. As the sun rises, *Yorktown* finally rolls completely on one side, revealing her torpedo hole, as if to explain what is about to happen. Two PBYs fly over and dip their wings in salute.

Just after 0700, the USS *Yorktown*, CV-5, is swallowed by the sea. Forever.

JOHN FORD

(Finale)

JUNE 6, 1942
MIDWAY ISLAND
DUSK

Aftermath.

Only now, two days after the *Kidō Butai* sinks in heaps of twisted burning metal, do the marines of Midway learn they were never completely alone. Unlike the defenders of Wake Island waiting in vain for carrier-task-force rescue, Midway has been protected. The collective might of three carriers and their task forces has been out there all along. The euphoria of salvation is complete.

"Back at Midway, Tojo swore he'd liberate the natives," booms Donald Crisp, his voice more dramatic than ever, as if emoting before Shakespeare himself on the London stage.

Abruptly, a surprise: Henry Fonda joins the voice-over narrative, sounding like a giddy Tom Joad. "Yet they're free as they ever were!"

The "natives" onscreen are albatross, plump and indifferent, staring into the camera. Burning hangar girders in the background show the destruction. Billowing black smoke is in contrast to the calm birds. Even in June, when they should be miles out to sea, this is home. Wherever there is an image of destruction, a seabird perches

The birds of Midway   *Public domain*

somewhere in the frame. Battles will be won and lost on these sands, but the birds are as timeless as the coral reef.

Then to scenes of Midway's defenders in uniform, bolt-action M1903 .30-caliber rifles slung over their backs. Eyes scan the horizon for more Japanese planes.

A close shot of a downed enemy fighter, the rising-sun "meatball" plainly visible on a wing shorn from the fuselage. Bent propeller. Burned-out engine. An albatross standing atop a white sand dune, looking down on the wreckage as more smoke fills the overcast blue sky.

"The battle of Midway is over," intones the narrator. "Our front yard is safe.

"But a big job is still to be done."

Cut to an olive drab PBY-5A Catalina flying over open ocean. "Day after day our patrol planes search for survivors. Every tiny coral reef, every distant mile of sea searched for men who fought to the last round of ammunition and flew to the last drop of gas, then crashed into the sea."

An image of a Dauntless dive-bomber floating atop the ocean, its nose tilted downward into the water.

Images of a PBY just landed on Midway. The hatch is being opened by the aircrew.

"Eight days, nine days, ten days, without food or water."

An unshaven pilot emerges from the hatch, smiling but visibly weak. Helping hands reach up to lift him from the plane onto the first dry ground he's felt since the battle.

Another day, another rescued pilot. Ford frames him in close-up, smoking.

Henry Fonda again, a slightly more subdued Tom Joad. "His first cigarette. Boy, that first drag sure tastes good."

Yet another pilot pulled from the ocean. Medics wearing Red Cross armbands escort the flier to an ambulance. He is unshaven and grinning, walking unsteadily, clearly thrilled to be alive.

Back to Donald Crisp. The rescues keep coming. "Eleven days," followed by a close-up of an exhausted, sunburned pilot

Another PBY, hatch open. A stretcher is thrust inside by the ground crew. The next image is a pilot lying flat on his back, the same stretcher being passed hand over hand to waiting medics. The camera focuses on his face, that of an exhausted, disoriented man in uniform too weak to lift his head.

From survivors to heroes. Among the men rescued is George Gay, the lone surviving Devastator pilot of Torpedo 8. He spends thirty hours in the water, where he is an eyewitness to the sinking of Akagi, Kaga, and Sōryū.

The rescues continue for weeks. One lucky crew is plucked from the Pacific after seventeen days adrift.

"Logan Ramsey," the Englishman says suddenly, the video shifting to an image of a heavyset officer rather than rescuers. Ford is playing a trivia game now—Ramsey was on duty at Pearl Harbor the morning of December 7. He sent the legendary flash message to

navy brass telling the world about the bombings: "AIR RAID ON
PEARL HARBOR X THIS IS NOT DRILL."

"Frank Fessler," says Fonda, the image shifting to a beaming PBY
pilot. "Thirteen," adds the narrator, telling how many of his fellow
aviators Fessler rescued after days at sea.

More images of the rescued, some exhausted, some incapacitated,
some grinning in disbelief, thrilled to be back on land. Ford is reas-
suring the viewers back home; the perseverance in these distinctly
American faces is clear for all to see.

Then, as an ambulance drives those lucky pilots to the hospital,
an image of gnarled metal: There is no more hospital. The Japanese
have deliberately bombed and destroyed the building. All that remains are the burned-out remnants of beds and ceiling beams.

Crisp again. "There was a hospital. Clean. Orderly. A hundred
beds. And on its roof a red cross plainly marked, symbol of mercy the
enemy was bound to respect."

A church bell.

Cut to a priest slipping a white surplice over his head before saying Mass. Men sit in chairs next to a gaping hole in the sand caused
by a Japanese bomb. Blue skies scudded with clouds. "The next
morning divine services were held next to a bomb crater that had
once been a chapel."

A row of caskets draped in American flags. Officers in khaki uniforms and enlisted personnel in blue denim and white sailor caps
stand at attention.

"At eventide we buried our heroic dead."

The names are read aloud. Rifles fire in salute. Then the image
shifts from land to sea. Those same caskets now riding the bows
of five patrol boats heading out of the atoll into the dark water offshore.

Ford is too delicate to film the burial at sea, those weighted
wooden coffins tilted overboard and sliding into the depths. The

image instead shifts upward from the water to puffy white clouds,
where the camera lingers.

It is eighty-three years since Captain N. C. Brooks first raised the American flag on the island that would become Midway. So it seems appropriate—through the shipwrecks, coal ships, bird poachers, telegraphy, Pan Am Clipper service, and this world-changing battle—that John Ford's final image is that of a fluttering U.S. flag.

Damage to Midway is not as bad as feared. Four American defenders are dead, ten are wounded, and the islands lost power. But the three runways on Eastern are undamaged. In all, a hundred fifty American planes are lost. Three hundred seventeen American pilots, sailors, and marines die in this battle. Japanese dead exceed three thousand.

Ford cuts to a shot of Midway itself, black smoke from the bombed
and still burning oil supplies filling the tropical skies, framing the
Stars and Stripes fluttering atop a flagpole.

Then a quick cut to a placard stating in bold print the number of
downed Japanese aircraft. A hand reaches in and paints a bold red
"V" for victory across the words.

***

COMMANDER FORD IS given an award for his role in the battle.

"As far as the citation was concerned, I think it was more for being wounded in an exposed position and not leaving my post. Well, hell, you couldn't leave your post. There was no place to go."

EPILOGUE

She's enormously popular.

Here, on the tourist side of San Diego Bay, just south of Little Italy and a few blocks north of where the Padres play, rises CV-41.

Right across the harbor from North Island, where 60s and Hornets take flight, carriers with names like *Carl Vinson*, *Theodore Roosevelt*, and *Abraham Lincoln* dock between deployments. CVN-70, -71, and -72 travel the world, small nuclear-powered cities carrying out the legacy of *Langley*, *Lexington*, *Saratoga*, and the *Yorktown* sisters.

It is worth noting that the current *Queen Elizabeth*–class vessel bearing the name HMS *Prince of Wales*, launched in 2017, is one of the most modern aircraft carriers in the world.

CV-41 was commissioned in 1945, just after World War II ends. Her flight decks make the leap from propellers to jets, allowing the ship to serve until Operation Desert Storm forty-six years later. Once upon a time, she is the biggest aircraft carrier in the world, so large she has to take the long way around from Atlantic to Pacific because she can't squeeze through the Panama Canal.

The first keel block was lowered into place a year after the Battle of Midway. By then the engagement is widely touted as a turning point in World War II. Admiral Nimitz receives widespread acclaim for his planning and leadership in the months leading up to the fight. He will go on to command the Pacific Fleet until the end of the war, personally signing the Japanese Instrument of Surrender in Tokyo Bay.

Despite the stunning losses of four carriers at Midway, and with them Japan's hopes of defeating the United States, Admiral Yamamoto continues to thrive as commander of the Combined Fleet for a year after the battle. Yet Admiral Nimitz once again interferes with Yamamoto's war plans. In April 1943, intelligence reports alert Nimitz to his antagonist's travel itinerary through the Solomon Islands. "Operation Vengeance" is personally approved by the man with blue eyes.

On April 18, while flying from Rabaul to a small island off Bougainville, a Mitsubishi G4M Betty bomber carrying Yamamoto is shot down over the South Pacific. Another Betty carrying the admiral's staff is also lost. The perfectly coordinated attack is carried out by P-38 fighters of the U.S. Army Air Corps' 339th Fighter Squadron.

The fate of Admiral Chūichi Nagumo is just as gruesome. He shoots himself in the head after losing three carriers and six hundred planes at the Battle of the Philippine Sea.

Joe Rochefort is not the man who alerts Nimitz about Admiral Yamamoto's flight. The heroics of Midway are long forgotten by the time Operation Vengeance is launched. Rochefort's enemies in Washington are embarrassed about their intelligence failures. To save face, they block Nimitz's attempt to award Rochefort the U.S. Navy Distinguished Service Medal. Then they relieve Joe Rochefort of command. The officer whose discovery of "AF" changed the course of history serves out the war in San Francisco, commanding a dry dock. Rochefort's breaking of the Japanese code and his role in saving Midway will not become public for decades. There is little Nimitz can do to protect Rochefort—naval intelligence and codebreaking are independent of Nimitz's command. However, Admiral Chester Nimitz never forgets Rochefort. He sees to it that the commander is awarded the Legion of Merit at the end of World War II for "exceptionally meritorious conduct."

Admiral Nimitz dies in 1966 after suffering a stroke. He is buried next to Catherine at the Golden Gate National Cemetery. Two years after his death, the USS *Nimitz* is laid down. She is the first of ten *Nimitz*-class carriers.

Joe Rochefort dies on July 20, 1976, age seventy-six. The commander is buried in Inglewood Park Cemetery outside Los Angeles, alongside Elma, his wife of forty-five years.

Lieutenant Dusty Kleiss lives to be one hundred. Colonel Harold Shannon dies in San Diego from a sudden bout of pneumonia one year after drinking all that coffee on Midway. John Ford goes on to make some of his best films after *The Battle of Midway*. He wins an Academy Award for *The Quiet Man* in 1953.

Fighter pilot John "Jimmie" Thach rises to rear admiral. He dies in Coronado, California, in 1981 and is buried at Fort Rosecrans National Cemetery. Lieutenant George Gay, who survived his torpedo bomber attack on June 4 and spent a day in the Pacific, becomes a Trans World Airlines pilot after the war. Upon his death from a heart attack in 1994, the naval aviator's ashes are spread on the Pacific at the location where he and the members of Torpedo 8 launched their attack on the Japanese carriers.

***

MIDWAY ATOLL IS currently closed to human visitation. Known as the Midway Atoll National Wildlife Refuge, it provides sanctuary to the thousands of seabirds that call it home. Buildings and runways from World War II still exist, though not all are maintained. The U.S. Fish and Wildlife Service manages the atoll. A granite monument to the Battle of Midway can be found along the oceanfront. It reads:

THE UNITED STATES OF AMERICA HONORS THE COURAGE, SACRIFICE, AND ACHIEVEMENTS OF THE AMERICAN ARMED FORCES WHO SUCCESSFULLY DEFENDED THIS ISLAND AND ITS SURROUNDING SEAS AGAINST THE EMPIRE OF JAPAN DURING THE PERIOD OF 4–7 JUNE 1942. OUTNUMBERED AND OUTGUNNED, THEY WITHSTOOD SAVAGE BOMBARDMENT, FOUGHT BACK, AND CARRIED

THE FIGHT TO THE ENEMY. DARING AIR STRIKES IN THE FACE OF FIERCE RESISTANCE SANK FOUR ENEMY AIRCRAFT CARRIERS, TURNING THE TIDE OF WORLD WAR II IN THE PACIFIC. AFTER THE BATTLE OF MIDWAY, THE UNITED STATES AND ITS ALLIES FORGED AHEAD WITH EVER INCREASING STRENGTH AND CONFIDENCE TO FINAL VICTORY, SECURING THE BLESSINGS OF FREEDOM AND LIBERTY FOR GENERATIONS YET UNBORN.

***

Two MONTHS AFTER the Battle of Midway, during the Battle of the Eastern Solomons, USS *Enterprise* endures three direct bomb hits and four near misses. Seventy-four men die and ninety-five are wounded, but she returns to Pearl Harbor under her own power. *Enterprise* is soon back at sea after two months of repairs, then takes two more direct hits at the Battle of the Santa Cruz Islands—though not before damaging the carrier *Zuihō*.

"Big E" survives.

She makes it through the war but is deemed obsolete and sold for scrap in 1958. However, her ship's bell still tolls. It is now located at the United States Naval Academy, directly in front of Bancroft Hall. From their very first day of Plebe Summer, midshipmen are trained to proclaim, "Go Navy, Beat Army," until it becomes a phrase they will reflexively state the rest of their lives. One of the only occasions on which the *Enterprise* bell is rung is that most relished moment when navy beats army in their annual football-rivalry game.

USS *Hornet*, famous for launching the Doolittle Raid, is also present at the Santa Cruz Islands battle, where she seriously damages the carrier *Shōkaku*. But direct hits by Kate torpedo bombers and Val dive-bombers knock her out of commission. One hundred forty of her twenty-two hundred sailors go down with the ship when *Hornet* sinks in the early hours of October 27, 1942.

On May 19, 1998, the wreckage of USS *Yorktown* is discovered and filmed thousands of feet below the Pacific; until now, she has not been seen since her sinking during the Battle of Midway.

In March 2018, the research vessel *Petrel* discovers the remains of USS *Lexington*, CV-2, off Australia, where she sank during the Battle of the Coral Sea. *Petrel* also locates *Akagi* and *Kaga* in seventeen thousand feet of water. Remotely operated underwater vehicles capture photos and video.

USS *Wasp*, ordered to the Pacific in June 1942 to replace the loss of *Yorktown* at Midway, is struck by three torpedoes from a Japanese submarine on September 15, 1942, and sinks. *Petrel* finds her in January 2019, fourteen thousand feet beneath the waves just off the Solomon Islands.

That same month, *Petrel* finds *Hornet.* She sits upright on the bottom of the Pacific at a depth of 17,700 feet. Like the other discovered carriers, she is now designated a war grave and thus a sacred space. The Sunken Military Craft Act of 2004 goes one better, calling these well-preserved locations, untouched by human interaction and not buffeted by strong underwater currents, "Sites of Extraordinary Character."

As is the wreck of the battleship *Prince of Wales*, resting upside down in 223 feet of water in the South China Sea. And *Repulse*, also inverted, 183 feet below. The British prefer the term "Protected Place."

As far underwater as they might be, these vessels remain intact and in good condition. The same cannot be said for the other great ships that fought in World War II. The United States Navy, like other navies around the world, can be callous with how it treats aging vessels. Look no further than USS *Augusta*, one of the most historic ships in American history, a floating museum sold for scrap.

Thus, CV-41 is lucky to have become a major tourist attraction. Pay your money at the dockside kiosk, climb the big steel walkway, and step aboard a real aircraft carrier. Wander the armored flight deck, the cavernous hangar bay, the maze of offices and personal quarters, and even the forecastle. Sightsee on your own or rent the guided tour. Once you look at all the aircraft on static display and pay a visit to the bookstore and coffee shop, wander to the small museum about the pilots and brave men who did something very special on June 4, 1942. There's even a tribute film. So good you'll want to see it twice. Admiral Nimitz and Lieutenant George Gay make a surprise visit every day through the magic of hologram.

CV-41 is the USS *Midway*.

No trip to San Diego is complete without paying homage.

A NOTE ON SOURCES

Writing a book about the Battle of Midway is not to be taken lightly. The sheer volume of data, official reports, biographies of major participants, and the hundreds of books already written—many by major names in naval history like Samuel Eliot Morison—mean not just an enormous number of sources. They also present countless choices on which players to feature, which moments to highlight, and how to weave them all together. I am quite sure *Taking Midway* could have been a thousand pages longer and I would still not tell the complete tale. Halsey, Spruance, and Fletcher could have all had their own chapters. Captain Marc "Pete" Mitscher from *Hornet* could receive more than a paragraph. The Japanese side could be a parallel book unto itself. Perhaps a whole section on the comparisons between pilot training in the United States and Japan. A lengthy segment on the ins and outs of cryptography. All those approaches have been taken by previous generations of authors putting their own spin on Midway, as I soon learned.

I start researching all my works of history by reading an overview of the topic. In this case, it was Ian W. Toll's excellent *Pacific Crucible*. I also enjoyed the high level of detail in Jonathan Parshall and Anthony Tully's *Shattered Sword*. Both are works of such enormous detail and breadth that I was temporarily stopped in my tracks, not knowing how I could tell the story of Midway without duplicating their efforts. Time to get creative. So I dug a little further. Little by little, unique nuggets of information came to light. I began to realize the events that combined to produce this battle are many and spread over millions of years. Each deserved its own explanation. Thus, episodes instead of chapters, each separate and unique, novellas unto themselves. *Taking Midway* is the fourth book in a series, all connected by events and chronography. I ended *Taking London* with HMS *Prince of Wales* and the meeting of FDR and Churchill in August 1941. That scene would prove pivotal to the events leading up to Midway, so I open this book there. The loss of *Wales* in the early days after Pearl Harbor was further evidence that the Imperial Japanese Navy was a major fighting force. That broad detour back to Midway's earliest days gave context to everything that would later occur. I never thought I'd write about bird poop in such great detail, but Midway wouldn't be Midway without it.

The list of books, websites, and official marine corps, navy, and U.S. government documents consulted in *Taking Midway* is ponderous. Listing them all would be a little dull. A short list includes *"And I Was There"* by Admiral Ed Layton (yes, he made admiral), *Joe Rochefort's War* by Elliot Carlson, *Nimitz* by E. B. Potter, *Never Call Me a Hero* by Dusty Kleiss, *Scapegoat* by Martin Stephen, *Enterprise* by Barrett Tillman, and *The Sinking of the Prince of Wales & Repulse* by Martin Middlebrook and Patrick Mahoney. Once I got to nerd-level passion for aircraft carriers, one of the most entertaining and insightful research books was *How Carriers Fought* by Lars Celander. Simply amazing. It's also worth noting that the U.S. Naval Institute's website (www.usni.org) is an amazing repository of naval history. Jimmie Thach's oral history, to name just one of many articles in this voluminous website, helped bring the battle to higher focus.

Once I finish a book, it is my habit to donate my used research books to the Friends of the Library here in Rancho Santa Margarita, California. My office library just isn't big enough to keep them all. If you would like to read some of this research, you know where to find the books.

I live two hours from San Diego. In the hopes of learning what a World War II aircraft carrier looks, feels, and smells like, I got in the habit of driving down to tour the USS *Midway*. There's always something new to see. I'm amazed by the number of foreign languages I hear as I wander the decks. She is bigger and more modern than *Yorktown*, *Enterprise*, and *Hornet*. But they're all gone, so I couldn't very well take a walk around their decks. *Midway* allowed me to see what a hangar deck, a flight deck, sleeping quarters, and a pilots' ready room look like. The museum dedicated to the Battle of Midway has excellent static displays of aircraft, which helped me visualize their appearance before putting descriptions on the page. A docent narrates the opening and closing moments of the film about the six minutes that changed the world, which is shown throughout the day. Once you have written about Ensign George Gay and gotten to know about his life and exploits, it's somewhat startling to see his hologram walk onstage and to hear him, in his own voice, tell what happened to Torpedo 8.

Other travel included the tremendous museums at Pearl Harbor and Ford Island, the Imperial War Museum in London, and the Japanese Imperial War Museum in Tokyo. Standing at Kahuku Point to imagine Japanese planes flying overhead on December 7 was magnified when I saw a sign indicating that I was also in the middle of a Laysan albatross bird sanctuary. I had become a big fan of the seabirds, and learning they were nesting on that spot on Pearl Harbor Day gave me an immediate visual image of that moment. I did not get to the birds of Midway, if only because it is closed to human visitation. However, the next best thing is the virtual tour on the U.S. Fish and Wildlife Service website (https://www.fws.gov/refuge/midway-atoll). The U.S. Naval Academy's excellent museum is a treasure trove of all things navy and has a particularly great section devoted to Admiral Chester Nimitz.

Thanks for reading. Let's do this again soon.

CREDITS

Writing a book is much like the sport of cross-country running: a team event disguised as an individual competition. My office is a small room in the corner of my garage. Carpeting, heating, air-conditioning, bookshelves, a turntable, and a big wooden desk that fills a large chunk of the space. No windows. A map of the world covers the entire wall behind me as I write. I tape up a long sheet of butcher paper from one side of the room to the other, then write the outline and character arcs in black Sharpie. Helps remind me of the big picture when the rabbit hole gets deep.

This is where I spend the months it takes to cobble together a book. My black lab, Sadie, sleeps at my feet. This is the solitary side of writing. I'm an introvert. I love it. Wouldn't change a thing.

But I'm never alone. On those days I get stuck or wonder if my narrative instincts are true, my editor, Jill Schwartzman, is just a phone call away. Her insight and enthusiasm are contagious. It is a joy to work with such a professional.

The same holds true for the entire team at Dutton, led by publisher John Parsley. *Taking Midway* is in very good hands.

My agent and good friend, Eric Simonoff, is a mainstay of my career. His sound advice, discernment, and listening ear in times of concern are indispensable. There's no better agent in the business.

My assistant and social media director, Nikki Nguyen, is a whirlwind. Her reminders to write my weekly blog (www.martindugard.com) and her deft handling of a wide range of matters requiring my attention when I am deep in the creative bunker are those of a wizard.

Mike DiPaola is amazing in his attention to facts and story suggestions. An enormous thanks.

To Dr. Jeremy Harris, Dr. Misako Nagasaka, Dr. Steve Cullen, Cate Cullen, Dr. Mark Burkhardt, and everyone else who has made a difference these past few years, my profound gratitude. Likewise, thank you to the Tough Guys and Diamond Dogs for support, feedback, and friendship.

Thanks to my three wonderful sons—Devin, Connor, and Liam—for enduring my fondness for historical trivia. Much thanks to Devin (USNA '12) and his Navy roommate who went on to serve in the Marine Corps, Jesus Aguilera ('12), for their direction and corrections on all things navy and marines. Any mistakes are mine.

And to Calene. Love of my life. My sunshine. Someday—I don't know when—we're going to get to that place we really want to go to, and we'll walk in the sun.

INDEX

Gallaher, Earl, 316

Gambia, 84, 89, 91, 92

Gay, George, 314, 330, 335

Gellhorn, Martha, 11

General Siegel, 96–102

George VI (king), 63

Ghost Fleet, 161, 170, 219, 241

Gillette, Claude, 272

Glasgow, 62

Goshu, 291

Goshu Maru, 253

Graybook, 267

Grayling, 199, 200

Great White Fleet, 109

Greenbrier, 68

Grew, Joseph, 69, 120

Guam. *See* invasion rehearsal (Guam)

guano, 84–90. *See also* bird poop

Guano Islands Act, 82, 83, 92

Gudgeon, 215

Guz sailors, 43

Hagikaze, 316

Haldis, 154, 155

Halford, William, 94

Halsey, William "Bull," 206, 238, 241,
    267, 268

Hamilton, John, 134–39, 190

    departure of *Philippine Clipper*, 137

    din of aircraft engines heard by, 136

    escape from Wake by, 138, 139

    reconnaissance mission of, 135

    as veteran Pan Am pilot, 134

Hammann, 325–26

Harada, Hakue, 19

Harland, R. F., 156

Haruna, 275

Hastie, Donald H., 273

Hatsukaze, 291

Hawaii, United States' annexation of, 106

Hawaiian Islands, atoll origins of, 89

Hawaii Clipper, 117–20, 138

Hazelwood, Harold R., 142, 143

heavy cruisers (IJN)

    Chōkai, 21

Hell Gate, 116

Hemingway, Ernest, 111–16, 120, 138, 139

Hepburn Report, 120

Hermes, 2, 236

Hirohito, Emperor, 123, 161, 236

Hiryū, 123, 166, 219, 240, 304

    post-Hawaii mission of, 144

    radio silence of, 127

    Thach's shooting down of, 319

Hitler, Adolf, 115

    christening of *Bismarck* attended by, 50

    as Churchill's villain, 54–55

    European battlefront of, 13–14, 37

    Luftwaffe of, 20

    Morton's enthrallment with, 40

    policy of world conquest and
        domination of, 35

    rise of, 58

Hokuriku, 291

Holmes, Wilfred "Jasper," 211, 258, 259

Holtwick, Jack, 211

Honolulu Advertiser, 132, 162

Honolulu Star-Bulletin, 161

Hopkins, Harold Lloyd, 27–28, 29, 39, 66

    aboard *Wales*, 52

    death of, 62

Hornet, 3, 240

    April 18 (1942), 238–43

    B-25 launching off, 242

    damage to *Shōkaku* by, 336

    description of, 208

    Doolittle Raid and, 238–43, 305, 336

    Imperial Japanese Navy's search
        for, 241

    lying in wait, 276–77

    Petrel's finding of, 337

    photograph of, 242

    sinking of, 336

    Torpedo Squadron 8 of, 305, 311, 313

ABOUT THE AUTHOR

Martin Dugard is the *New York Times* bestselling author of several books of history, among them *Taking London*, *Taking Paris*, *Taking Berlin*, the Killing series, and *The Explorers*.